FOOTS

Footsore on the Frontier

Selected Essays and Articles

NIGEL JENKINS

GOMER

First Impression—2001

ISBN 1 85902 982 5

This book is published with the support
of the Arts Council of Wales.

Printed in Wales at
Gomer Press, Llandysul, Ceredigion SA44 4QL

I
Angharad a Branwen
a helpodd fi i wneud y groes 'na

Contents

Acknowledgements

Acknowledgements are due to the following, who first published some of these items: *New Welsh Review, Poetry Wales, Radical Wales, Barn, Golwg, Planet, The Western Mail, Red Kite, Blithe Spirit, The Works, Swagmag*, In Books, University of Wales Press, Gregynog Press, Gomer Press, BBC Radio Four.

To Iwan Bala I owe a debt of gratitude for allowing us to use his painting *Ynys Esgyrn* as a cover illustration.

I would like to thank Francesca Rhydderch, my editor at Gomer, for her eagle-eyed diligence and many constructive recommendations for improvements to the text. Warm thanks (and love) are also due to Margot, who took time to read the proofs and made many valuable suggestions.

The Lie of the Land

The Lie of the Land[1]

The Welsh, as O.M. Edwards famously remarked, are a nation because 'our land is unlike any other land'. Untamed Wales, a peninsula of sea-stormed peninsulas, wind-wracked, rain-lashed mountainous bastion of the tenacious Celt: such is the 'image' that is relentlessly peddled of the smallest and least known of the countries of Britain. But there is more to this land of Wales than meets the casual eye, for it is a realm in which, in the spirit of the legendary tales of *The Mabinogion*, all is by no means what it superficially seems.

To many, visitor and native alike, Wales's rural landscape is wild and unspoilt – and there are three National Parks to prove it. It is, though, neither truly wild nor truly unspoiled: for millennia the inhabitants of these 8,000 square miles have used and sometimes abused, shaped and remoulded the land they have lived on, as the land in turn has shaped them and helped fashion their distinctive culture – a culture in as severe a crisis today as the land, water and air that give it blood and breath.

Wales, edging clear of the shadows of heavy industry, is perhaps too beautiful for her own good. Her poets, many of them 'eco-bards' long before 'green' concerns became commonplace in the 1980s, keep seasoned acquaintance with their country's sometimes fatal attractions. Harri Webb (1920-94), invited to savour the delights of an Area of Outstanding Natural Beauty, dismisses its tweely perceived crags and castles as a 'beauty that is meaningless,/That's bought and sold on every side'. And R.S. Thomas (1913–2000), challenges the consumer of scenery to look beyond the clichéd sheep 'Arranged romantically . . . /On a bleak background of bald stone' and confront 'The fluke and the foot-rot and the fat maggot/Gnawing the skin from the small bones'. His words invite us to engage with the complex reality of an inhabited, worked over, ever-changing landscape, rather than mere 'scenery' that,

---

[1] A slightly longer version of this essay was first published in *Wales: The Lie of the Land*, Jeremy Moore and Nigel Jenkins (Gomer Press, 1996).

innocent of human toil and even the busyness of natural forces, is statically, emptily 'beautiful'.

Undeniably, though, Wales is a beautiful country, and her unpredictable geography ensures frequent ambush, in even the dullest weather, by places and moments that set the spirit soaring. But how is Wales beautiful, when and for whom? Only when we unravel her shape-shifting narratives from the lie of the land do we begin to appreciate a beauty, against a history of harm, that is more than skin deep.

Humankind was not even an itch in the amphibian skull when the mountains of Wales pushed up into their primordial shape; and doubtless, given the speed with which we seem determined to burn ourselves out, they'll weather back down without us too. The mountains of Snowdonia or the louring scarps of the southern beacons might tempt us to concur with the sense of eternal immutability evoked by the poet Ceiriog's (1832-87) observation that 'aros mae'r mynyddoedd mawr' (the great mountains forever abide). They seem to have been there from the beginning of time; but if, as we believe, the Earth was formed 4,600 million years ago, we find no trace in Wales of any rocks older than 702 million years: buried beneath younger deposits, they outcrop on Ynys Môn (Anglesey) and the Llŷn peninsula, in the borderlands and odd pockets of Dyfed. Only about fifteen per cent of the planet's story is recorded in the geology of this patch of earth which, in this current split second of terrestrial time, we Sioni-come-lately death-wise bipeds have shaped to human purposes and labelled with names. What it pleases us, for now, to call 'Cymru' or 'Wales' has been restlessly in the making since the time, 700 million years ago, when it formed part of the long-dispersed continent of Gondwanaland – along with southern Europe, Africa, India, South America, Australia and Antarctica. Originating far south of the Equator, and submerged in shallow, volcano-dotted seas, Wales glided northwards for hundreds of millions of years, a violent passage involving the deaths of oceans and collisions of continents. To see Snowdon from Glyder Fawr, with clouds boiling below the peaks like a frenzied primordial sea, takes the imagination back 450 million years to the mountain-making epoch when the stately heights of Snowdonia were a sulphurous archipelago of lava-belching volcanoes. Upland Wales finally broke clear of the waters a mere sixty-five million years ago – waters programmed by global warming to re-possess, perhaps in our children's lifetime, much of Wales's lowest-lying lands.

Those mountains had many changes of shape and dress still to come. In the glaciations that followed, the Welsh uplands were gouged and sharpened, churned smooth, ramparted, spilled and busted by the colossal but imperceptible violence of ice. Then the meltwaters boiled through narrow gorges, and wind and rain, sun and frost fine-tuned the transformation – a transformation that will go on until the Sun in its death throes, swollen to a red giant and devouring its children, finally gobbles up the Earth. The Welsh mountains, which have stood for many as the very embodiment of unimaginable age and permanence, are in fact mountains on the move, mere youngsters in geological terms which have yet to settle down after the upheavals of the recent ice age. While changes to the landscape by physical processes may seem to occur inconceivably slowly, in contrast with humanity's busy programmes of deforestation, quarrying, building and barraging, the landscape is capable, unassisted, of sudden and radical alteration. Folk stories about the comings and goings of mountains of sand refer to the medieval sandstorms that could obliterate whole villages overnight, such as Cynffig (Kenfig) in Glamorgan or Niwbwrch (Newborough) in Anglesey.

About the only permanent feature of this landscape, mutating over millennia as subtly as Welsh words mutate in different combinations, is its shiftiness. Look at a relief map of Wales and you'll see the familiar boar's head outline of her seaboard 'ghosted', in blurred focus, by two other Waleses: the sparsely populated mountainous core – that central geographical fact of Wales against which all others rest; and, out to sea, a coast-hugging mantle of paler blue, a Wales beneath the waves where no one has lived for thousands of years, but among whose forests of gnarled stumps – at Borth, for instance – you may wander at low tide and hope to pluck from the muddy peat a Mesolithic hunter's flint. Beneath the waters of Bae Ceredigion (Cardigan Bay), according to a legend that has its origins in folk memory from the Stone Age, when Wales and Ireland were joined by a land bridge, there lies the realm of Cantre'r Gwaelod with its sixteen fine cities, all drowned when the drunken dyke-keeper Seithenyn's neglect of the kingdom's sea defences led to a catastrophic inundation.

There is nowhere in Wales today, no matter how remote and

inaccessible, that is untouched by human hand. From the caesium fall-out of Chernobyl, which will linger in the vegetation of the north for decades to come and has rendered hundreds of farms unworkable, to the effects of acid rain on shrinking tree canopies or of man-made drought on lichens wincing into dust on unclimbable cliff faces, human activity has left its mark everywhere. Though guilt about the damage we are doing the planet may seem a new phenomenon, our fall from ecological grace began with the onset of farming six or seven thousand years ago. In a country in which, by now, two thirds of the land have passed under the plough, no virgin or 'prelapsarian' landscapes survive; but we can get close to them in places like the raised peat bogs at Borth and Tregaron, which developed from lakes formed at the end of the last ice age, and on the islanded promontories and sea cliffs which have languished in long isolation from the human mainstream.

The earliest known 'Welsh' people were probably hunters passing through the territory when climatic conditions allowed. In a cave at Paviland in Penrhyn Gŵyr (Gower), which is accessible only at low tide, there were discovered in 1823 the bones of a young man who was ritually buried, with red ochre, shells and ivory rings, at least 26,000 years ago. He and his people, dragging through the tundral cold after herds of mammoth, woolly rhinoceros and bison, were survivors on the very edge of the habitable world. To their north were the great ice-sheets whose melting, about 17,000 years ago, would turn the fertile river plain they beheld from the mouth of their cave into what we know today as the Severn Sea. Paviland man constitutes the first known burial in Britain, and was for many years the earliest hominid bone find. But he has been superseded (in Wales) by some teeth and jaw bones from a limestone cave overlooking the Elwy valley at Pontnewydd in Clwyd, a more recent find that takes us back to an interglacial period some 230,000 years ago.

The haunting corrie lake of Llyn y Fan Fach tucked beneath a frowning scarp of Mynydd Du (the Black Mountain) speaks eloquently of what happened in the ice age and its aftermath. Facing north and short of sun, like all the scarp faces of the Brecon Beacons National Park, this steep sandstone bowl was an early accumulator and late releaser of snow and ice. The lightest of summer winds, shuffling round the almost sheer 500-foot cliff, seems to whisper down the ages of the groaning and grinding of ice as it raked horizontal furrows in the rock face, and ripped away the red rubble with which the lake's edge is strewn.

The first trees to take root when the ice relaxed its grip were the birches. And they are still here – invisible at first, but as you approach the far side of the lake you'll see their silver skins sticking out of the black peat at the water's edge. They could have been felled yesterday, but in fact they have lain here, preserved by the peat's protective juices, for upwards of 5,000 years. Yes, on the barren shores of Llyn y Fan Fach there is a birch forest, and we are padding silently through it, say, 10,000 years ago, stalking reindeer or horse. There are trees as far into the green distance as the eye can see, not only birches but oak, ash, pine, hazel. The lower the slopes, the thicker the forest. Deep, dark, impenetrable. It's only down by the coast, or in the high regions where the trees are fewer, or by lakes such as this that we hunter-gatherers can make a go of things. If only we could thin the forest out a bit. But we don't have the tools, there's no flint in Wales. Then – snap! – I step on a birch twig: the deer vanish and so do the boundless forests of ancient Wales. Almost no primary woodland survives into modern times, but there are isolated fragments here and there – Cwm Gwaun near Abergwaun (Fishguard), for instance, or the Cymerau, Rhygen and Ganllwyd woods in Gwynedd, or those of the Rheidol gorge, inland from Aberystwyth.

The wind-bleached moorland around Llyn y Fan Fach, pocked with sheep and shadowed by ravens, may be considered a 'typical Welsh mountain wilderness', but such wastes, far from being aboriginal wildernesses, are sites of human dereliction on an almost Amazonian scale. About ten thousand years ago, as the climate grew warmer and wetter and the forests thrived, Middle Stone Age food-gatherers, using hand-axes and fire, began tinkering with the trees. Though the changes they wrought in the landscape were small-scale and localised, their removal of forest cover in the damp uplands may occasionally have been a catalyst in the spread of bog mosses and the formation of peat. Then, around 4,000 BC, came the farmers, short dark giants with fields in their hands and history on their backs. These intrepid seafarers sailed in from Spain and western France to settle on the coastal fringes and along river valleys such as the Usk and Dee. They inscribed their story in stone upon the land: their monoliths jut through the heather, their cromlech capstones sail on seas of barley or meadow-grass from Gower and the Vale of Glamorgan to Pembrokeshire, Llŷn and Ynys Môn. The Pentre Ifan cromlech, erected on the lower slopes of the Presely hills within sight of the Irish Sea, presides over the surrounding fields like a stylised milking stool or a farmer's tweed cap, a monument to agriculture. Farming was at the revolutionary centre of Neolithic life. The cromlechs, the oldest surviving 'Welsh' buildings, were houses for the dead: here were deposited the bones of the ancestors, and from here the spirits of the tribe kept tutelary watch over the land and labours of the living. One of the Stone Age farmer's chief labours would have been felling trees to carve out plots for cultivation, and it is at this juncture that the ecological equilibrium of the earlier nomadic Stone Age begins to be lost. With their slash-and-burn clearances these farmer-pastoralists inaugurated an epoch of unprecedented human landscape-making which we are still living through today. The ecological vandalism of opencast coal mining in Glamorgan or the dumping at sea of raw sewage has its genesis in a psychology of environmental mastery that sprang from the blade of a polished stone axe over four thousand years ago.

As populations grew and technologies developed, from stone to socketed bronze and then iron axes, the reduction of virgin forest proceeded at an ever quickening pace. The stories of *The Mabinogion* (translated by Gwyn Jones and Thomas Jones, Everyman's Library, 1949) may have been written down in the eleventh century, but as part of the repertoire of professional storytellers for centuries before, they open many a window on the ways of Iron Age and even earlier customs. In the first task that the giant Ysbaddaden sets for Culhwch, in the tale of Culhwch's wooing of Olwen, we find succinct recall of the ancient deforestations: 'Dost see the great thicket yonder? . . . I must have it uprooted out of the earth and burnt on the face of the ground so that the cinders and ashes thereof be its manure, and that it be ploughed and sown . . .'

It was the open oak and birch woodland of the higher ground that was first to be felled, its terrain much easier to clear than the tangled, swampy forest of the valleys. Having selected a plot of perhaps half a dozen acres, they'd lop the branches off the trees and strip rings of bark from their trunks to kill them; when the sap had dried from the branches they would be burned where they lay, and beneath the dead, still upright trees crops would be sown. After only a few years of farming a particular patch, its fertility would be exhausted and it would be time to attack a fresh group of trees. Under the peat that now blankets the upland plateaux their stumps are still to be found.

As the climate continued to improve in the later Stone Age, these expansionist farmers pushed ever higher into the mountains; by the time Bronze Age culture arrived from central Europe in about 2,000 BC they were able to farm even further sometimes than the present upper tree limit of about 600 metres. The cairn of stones that nipples many a rounded hilltop is the Bronze Age's most prominent signature on the landscape. As communal burials in cromlechs gave way to individual cremations and interments in these mounds of rock, the 'Welsh' farmer seems gradually to have lifted his eyes up from the earth and danced his intelligence through the cosmic halls of the night sky. Locked in our noise-lit streets with a cupola of phosphorescence 'protecting' us from the dark, most of us rarely catch a glimpse of the stars, the Milky Way being nothing more to us than a chocolate bar. You have to travel west, to the Presely hills or the Llŷn peninsula, to find true night and a sense, beneath that ragged ribbon of stars, of our galactic home. To see it, to understand of it what can be understood – the two hundred thousand million suns, the dust, the gas, the matter factories – is both humbling and strangely empowering. 'Tonight,' you might find yourself murmuring in a field in the Preselys, 'tonight I could build Stonehenge.'

And that, in part, is precisely what the Bronze Age folk of the Preselys did. To the Bronze Age people, as to others before and after them, the Preselys were a region of profound spiritual and cultural resonance – so much so that when they built Stonehenge, which came to be recognised as the most important megalithic monument in Europe, they used some blue stones quarried at Carn Meini to form one of the henge's concentric rings. To collect and transport scores of these stones, each weighing four tons, the two hundred miles to the Salisbury Plain was indeed a monumental labour, and testament to the deep spiritual pull exerted down the ages by these numinous hills.

As we attempt to compute the ecological and human turmoil that may ensue from global warming and a likely rise in mean temperatures of three degrees or more, we have only to look back to the end of the Bronze Age to learn of the devastation brought about by a comparable alteration in what was in many ways an ideal climate. The Bronze era, with its economic surpluses, its exquisite artistry and cosmological striving, had something about it, at least from a distance, of a golden age; but early in the first millennium BC, shadows portending great change began to fall across the land.

The first of these, after 1,100 BC, was a relentless deterioration in the climate. Mean temperatures fell by almost two degrees centigrade and increased rainfall led to waterlogging, the acidification of soil and the stifling by peat of the upland acres. These farmers were no doubt coppicers and manurers, but their care for the land could hardly have included an understanding that, had they felled fewer trees, the waterlogging might have been reduced through transpiration. They had to abandon their sodden fields to the curlew, and resettle on lower ground. There too the rains could play murderous havoc with their lives, sending flash floods to wash away their homesteads or silting up their farms, built along the valley bottom. Over the course of three or four centuries they watched water undermine the very basis of their existence – as indeed too little or too much of it is doing in many parts of the world today. Small wonder that the inhabitants of Wales made a god of water, anxiously offering placatory gifts at springs, lakes, rivers, wells, many of which remain sacred into modern times.

Then there was iron, and the wielders of iron – artful, territorial, warrior farmers. The impact on the relatively unbelligerent Bronze Agers of this awesomely hard and versatile metal, which flowed as if by wizardry from molten rock, is remembered in a number of legends associated with lakes, including Llyn Cwm Llwch in the Brecon Beacons, Llyn y Forwyn in Glamorgan, Llyn Du'r Arddu in Snowdonia and, preeminently, Llyn y Fan Fach. The lake-god's daughter who captivates the mooning farm-boy represents an older, pre-Iron Age population driven underground in high, remote places by the warlike newcomers, and re-emerging in myth as the *tylwyth teg*, the fairy folk. The couple's love is doomed when he strikes her inadvertently with iron, the metal that shattered the Bronze Age world.

Along with iron, of course, comes the culture of the Celts. The most vigorous assertion of Celtic presence in the landscape is to be found in the great hillforts whose concentric ramparts crown hundreds of hills in the semi-uplands and scores of coastal promontories. The density of these settlements in southwest Wales reminds us that it was by sea and through her southern and western portals that Wales received much of her prehistoric population.

The highland peoples of Britain, aboriginals in and of the landscape rather than simply movers upon it, seem to have been great absorbers of the new, whereas those of the lowlands have been more susceptible to the cultural clean sweep. The highlanders of Wales were Celts not so much in terms of lineage and 'blood' but in terms of culture, and it was they, in communion with this unique landscape, who laid the foundations for the basic culture of the Welsh people. Though it would be many centuries yet before an identifiable Welsh nation came into being, these forbears of the modern Welsh settled, named, farmed and defended the land in patterns that are discernible and influential today. What is the great chain of hillforts, most of them over fifteen acres, that stretches from the Clwydian range in the northeast to Twm Barlwm in Gwent, if not a border in the making, giving notice to the denizens of the fruity 'English' plain that they mess at their peril with the men and women of the hard Welsh highlands? Not that they were conspicuously united in defence of their land: they may have shared the same language, that early form of Welsh known as Brythonic (which was spoken well after Roman times through most of the island of 'Prydain'), but they rarely spoke with one voice. Though mountains make formidable defences, they are also renowned dividers: the Welsh were, and in some ways still are, a tribal people who, having carved out their territorial patch, are inclined to negotiate unilaterally and in terms dictated by intense local loyalties. When, for instance, the Romans invaded, the Silures of southeast Wales put up a ferocious fight that lasted the best part of thirty years, whereas the Demetae of the southwest seem to have offered no resistance. The tribal divisions of Iron Age Wales, determined to a considerable extent by the lie of the land, echo down the ages: some of the modern counties of Wales, particularly those in place between 1974 and reorganisation in 1996, match uncannily the names and configurations of the ancient kingdoms.

However, while the names of counties may come and go at governmental whim, our internal differences robustly endure, enlivening and sometimes disabling us. They tend most often to be tribally derived, whether we speak Welsh or not, from our attachment to *y filltir sgwâr*, the native square mile, and the less translatable *bro* (locality) within which it lies. Welsh people like to know exactly where other Welsh people are from, and who their parents are and where *they* are from. It is not enough to discover from a fellow's accent merely whether he's a *Gog* (northerner, from *Gogledd*, meaning 'north') or one of that socially incontinent shower from 'down by there', a *Hwntw* (from *tu hwnt*, meaning 'beyond'). There will be the need to establish – if he is a *Hwntw* – whether he's from 'south Wales' or 'South Wales' (and do not doubt that murder, over that S-word, might easily be done); if he's from southwest Wales, whether he's a Turk (from Llanelli) or a Jack (from Swansea); and if he's a cowin' Jack whether he's Swansea East or Swansea West, and if Swansea West whether he's from Townhill or Tycoch, or the Uplands, where it's 'all lace curtains and no knickers', or Sketty, where sex is what they use for delivering the coal. In short, a sense of precisely where in the landscape a person has roots may be expected to reveal a great deal.

You have only to look out from the ramparts of a hillfort such as Tre'r Ceiri in Gwynedd or the sensitively reconstructed Castell Henllys in north Pembrokeshire, to understand the genesis of this *brogarwch,* or 'love of locality'. The Celts devoted themselves to the major task of clearing the dense low-altitude forests, tending to site their hillforts on prominences that gave them a commanding view of the arable acres below. Here, within a sweep of the chieftain's eye, lay his people's more or less self-sufficient world. If you were a young man you might be sent to pass the summer months on the slopes of some higher mountain nearby to watch over your people's sheep, goats and cattle as they fattened on the new grass of the *hafod* (summer place); from these heights, uninhabitable in winter, you might gaze longingly on those little dots of thatch way below, to which there would be no return until summer's end. The custom of transhumance would persist into the nineteenth century, and the ruins of later herdsmen's rough little cabins may still be stumbled upon where the moorland gives way to bog or scree.

The Celtic farmer would have had to be on guard against not only the bear, boar, wolf and lynx, but also raiding parties from neighbouring tribes; complacency could end in ruination. If, to outsiders, the Welsh can sometimes seem defensive or over-protective of their culture, it is because there has never been a time when they could afford the luxury of feeling secure: as a people 'on the edge', they have had to keep their antennae sensitively tuned to the designs of others, some of whom would gladly have pushed them over that edge. The present has invariably had to be fought for; we have never been able to take a future for granted. Or, to put it another way, in the words of Harri Webb, 'What Wales needs, and has always lacked most/Is, instead of an eastern boundary, an East Coast.'

Unlike Scotland's neat little waist of a border, with the great length of the nation stacked up behind it, Wales's sprawling belly of a frontier, which may look from the English plain like an impenetrable bulwark, is effectively no frontier at all. It is both long and riddled with gaping holes: the broad river valleys – of Gwy (Wye), Hafren (Severn), Dyfrdwy (Dee), Fyrnwy – through which invaders have been able to sweep with fatal ease. The Severn could deliver an enemy to the very slopes of Pumlumon, within fifteen or so miles of the Irish Sea, virtually cutting the nation in two.

The borderland hillforts, along with those of tactical importance in the interior, were eventually overrun by the Romans, whose conquest of the Welsh tribes (AD 47-78) proved far trickier than the subjection of the lowland people. If the Celts are by nature a people of the circle and the sinuous, contour-caressing curve, the Romans were by logic and military might a people of the straight line. Wales being a country topographically inimical to straight lines, the Romans had to suffer many an uncharacteristic kink and curve in the rectangular grid of roads which they constructed to link their nodal strongholds of Caerleon, Caer (Chester), Caernarfon and Caerfyrddin (Carmarthen). We drive along many of those roads today; indeed, it was not until the mid-eighteenth century that any significant additions were made to the Roman network. The most famous of their routes, sweeping from north to south, is Sarn Helen (Helen's Causeway), named perhaps not after the legendary Helen, as is often supposed, but from the Welsh for elbow, *elin,* on account of the unusual number of bends the road is forced to take. The natives, getting about on ridgeways, and using mountain crests, forest margins, cairns and stone circles as their landmarks, travelled *with* rather than against the land; the Romans treated the land, like its inhabitants, as an adversary to be overcome and stamped with their rectilinear seal – as, for instance, on Mynydd-bach Trecastell to the west of Pontsenni (Sennybridge), where, if you look down on the moorland from a helicopter, banks outlining two temporary camps look like a pair of overlapping playing cards.

The low swampy badlands of the river valleys, which tended to be no-go areas for the natives, were drained and cleared by the Romans, then roads were laid along them and arable farms established. The Romans played an imporant part in the reclamation of a huge tract of tidally submerged marshland that stretches for twenty miles along the Severn estuary, from Cardiff to the mouth of the Wye. The Gwent Levels, as these willow-fringed polders are known, are a handmade landscape of exceptional fertility and botanical variety, despite their proximity to major conurbations and one of the biggest steelworks in Europe. Drained by a network of ditches or 'reens', some of which date from pre-Roman times, the Levels are threatened today by another bunch of machos addicted to speed and straight lines, the Department of Transport, intent on slapping a new motorway across them.

The Romans, Wales's first big industrialists, were the first serious despoilers of the land. They mined copper at Mynydd Parys near Amlwch, Ynys Môn, a tradition continued on this shattered mountain into our own time; at Dolaucothi, north of the Tywi, native slaves burrowed deep into the hillside to mine gold for their conquerors – the tunnels they worked and died in are now a tourist attraction; spoil heaps from Roman and later lead mines in mid Wales contaminated the soil and polluted rivers. From the Roman era to the present, the biggest changes in the landscape have been wrought by human hand.

Then, quicker than they had come, the Romans, after 350 years, were gone, creating if not exactly 'the Dark Ages', then a vacuum into which new invaders, and new ideas, rushed headlong. The Christianity which a handful of Roman believers had brought into Britain suddenly caught hold of the Celtic imagination, and intrepid missionaries took to muddy tracks and the western seaways to convert not only their own people but those of neighbouring Celtic lands. The hundreds of Welsh places prefixed with 'Llan' are associated invariably with one or more of this army of Celtic missionary 'saints', hardy men (usually) of God whose first base in a locality would be a simple daub-and-wattle hut with a wooden palisade – the *llan* or enclosure that would in due course become the church we see today. Sometimes they would be called to test the spirit against the demands of the flesh, and would 'seek the desert' on barren summits like Carn Ingli in the Preselys or lonely cells of stone, such as St. Govan's chapel, with only the sea and a grumbling belly for companions. The Irish, who settled in large numbers in the south, became collaborators in the Christianisation of Wales: their significant cultural presence is attested by stones inscribed in the Ogam script which are to be found in various churches, north and south. The Ogam words, incised in oblique and horizontal lines down one edge of a monolith, are the earliest written form of a Celtic language; appearing sometimes in tandem with a Latin version, they might be considered our first bilingual signs.

If the Irish were absorbed, in time, by the native population, there was no absorbing the Germanic invaders from the east. What both isolated and created Wales as a distinct entity were two fateful British defeats in the late sixth and seventh centuries, which drove wedges between the 'Welsh' and their fellow Britons in the West Country and Cumbria. Then a civil war in the adjacent kingdom of Mercia thrust Offa (d. 796) to the throne as the most powerful Anglo-Saxon yet, the first to style himself King of the English, and a European power with whom the Pope and Charlemagne were obliged to deal on equal terms. From the time of Penda (623-654) these pushy Anglo-Saxon frontiersmen, grabbing and trying to farm what land they could hold, had thrown up localised defences in the form of short dykes, sixteen of which are still traceable in the central March today: they were to regulate passage along the ridgeways and to block off from Welsh attack the precarious valley settlements. Then, further to the north, came the Wat's Dyke, thirty-eight miles in length, running from Treffynnon (Holywell) to Croesoswallt (Oswestry), believed to be the first effort of the Mercian state to define precisely its limits of conquest – limits which Offa was to push even further west.

The guiding principle of Offa's Dyke, behind which the invaders boxed the *Cymry* (compatriots) away and wrote them off as '*Welisc*' (foreigners) in their own land, was not that it should bristle with soldiers and weaponry throughout but that it should be Mercia's eye on Wales. Accordingly, we find that wherever possible it occupies west-facing slopes and hardly ever risks turning its back on Wales.

Soldiers would have been stationed only at certain points to control trade and traffic between the two peoples, and patrols would have ridden out from garrisons such as Trefyclo (Knighton in English from *Chnichten* – town of the horsemen) to look out for Welsh trouble.

There were laws to govern the Dyke, including a jury system of six Welshmen and six Englishmen to settle disputes, often to do with cattle raiding, a major industry for hundreds of years of this Wild West terrain. But many of these differences continued to be settled in traditional bloody border style, as the famous and anti-Welsh jingle recalls:

> *Taffy was a Welshman, Taffy was a thief;*
> *Taffy came to my house and stole a leg of beef.*
> *I went to Taffy's house, Taffy was in bed;*
> *I picked up a chopper and chopped off his head.*

Poetry, which qualifies Wales as immeasurably more a land of the spoken and written word than it is the fabled 'Land of Song', has always been the handmaiden of this country's history. A journey through the heroic and aristocratic court poetry of the first eight hundred years is likely to draw from the reader a sigh of 'One damn invasion after another', for between the sixth and thirteenth centuries poetry was intimately bound up with the military and political fate of the emerging nation. This was the long and gruelling age of resistance: after the Anglo-Saxons came the Vikings; after the Vikings, the Normans and the Anglo-Normans. The Vikings, in comparison with their Francophone descendants the Normans, seem the least disruptive: they raided, they no doubt pillaged, but they also came to settle on the islands, promontories and river mouths that bear Norse names to this day – Anglesey, Bardsey, Grassholm, Skomer, Worms Head, Swansea – before following the tradition of earlier incomers and eliding smoothly with the natives. There was nothing smooth about the Normans.

Wales has more castles than any other European country, but only a few of them are Welsh castles. Possibly the most important castle in Wales is Dinefwr which stands on a bluff outside Llandeilo, overlooking the eighteenth-century park planned by Capability Brown. Like nearby Dryslwyn and Carreg Cennen, Dinefwr was built by the Welsh princes; it was the hub of power and anti-Norman resistance in Deheubarth, the kingdom of southwest Wales. Of the two other principal courts of medieval Wales, Aberffraw in the kingdom of Gwynedd and Mathrafal in Powys, not a stone remains standing. The smallish, sometimes idiosyncratic castles of the Welsh – Dinas Brân in silhouette high above Llangollen, the solitary tower of Dolbadarn standing sentinel at the foot of Yr Wyddfa (Snowdon) – receive nothing like the visitors who flock to the ramparts of the non-Welsh castles of Wales, the castles of our conquerors.

From the conquistadors' castles, and the towns that grew up around them, the Welsh were banned. If proof be required that the Normans, like the Romans before them, found Wales a much harder nut than England to crack – it took them two hundred years – you have only to consider the size and number of the castles they built, from Caernarfon in the north to Caerffili in the south. They are unambiguous symbols of the brute force that was necessary to crush Welsh independence. The pain of Welsh defeat is embodied to hair-raising effect in the poet Gruffudd Ab Yr Ynad Coch's (fl. 1280) cosmic howl of despair on the killing, in 1282, of Llywelyn ap Gruffudd, the last prince of independent Wales.

Happier relics of the accommodation the Welsh eventually reached with the new order are the monasteries. The Cistercians in particular, who built abbeys such as Ystrad Fflur (Strata Florida), Tintern and Valle Crucis, which even in grassy ruination are hauntingly beautiful ghosts in the landscape, grew to be notable champions of Welsh civilisation; and all the monastic orders were hugely productive farmers, transforming uncultivated ground into good grazing and forests into corn fields.

Between about 1100 and 1800, the Welsh countryside as we recognise it gradually took shape. The Normans, establishing a *Wallia Anglicana* in the March and along the coastal plain, grabbed the best agricultural land for themselves, and left the natives to make what they could of the stony slopes and acid soil of the hills and mountains of *Pura Wallia*. This unequal division is reflected in the place-names and speech of the southern halves of Gower and Pembrokeshire, richly fertile farmland where English has been the dominant language for nine hundred years and from which, in Pembrokeshire's case, the Welsh were excluded by a *cordon sanitaire* of castles known as the Landsker. Gower and south Pembrokeshire, together with the spacious Vale of Glamorgan (which is really a coastal plateau), exemplify the nucleated pattern of feudal settlement that came to characterise the occupied territories: castles built to keep the restless natives at bay, manorial farming villages grown up around churches with tall and strongly embattled towers, and fields divided into landshare strips, a few of which survive in the arable tract at Rhosili known as the Vile.

Above the 200-metre contour line, where life continued with fewer interruptions, the typical Welsh small farm developed. George Owen of Henllys (1552–1613), writing in Elizabethan times, described a landscape of 'several and lone houses' whose main features he would surely recognise today. Villages in the uplands are comparatively few, and distances often considerable between the isolated farmsteads. The farm itself, which might incorporate an old Welsh longhouse, is usually to be found on the lowest slopes of the mountain, in a patchwork of meadows and arable fields. Ranging beyond these fields, to about 300 metres above sea level, are the *ffriddoedd,* the rough sheepwalks where the flocks pasture between spring and autumn, and the lambing, shearing and dipping are done. Beyond the long wall that divides the *ffriddoedd* from the rest of the mountain stretches the barren moorland.

There have been times when social and economic pressures have driven families to settle permanently in the formerly seasonal grazings at altitudes of 400 metres or more. Some of the remotest farms in Wales are to be found high on the eastern bulwarks of Eryri (Snowdonia), where life is a relentless battle against storms and rock, sodden peaty soils and encroaching heather. The hill farmer's age-old struggle with nature is summarised in the well-known triad:

Aur dan yr eithin,
arian dan y rhedyn,
newyn dan y grug.

[Gold under gorse,
silver under fern,
starvation under heather.]

From the early nineteenth century onwards, many of these high altitude farms were abandoned, leaving only a vague geometry of tumble-down walls and the odd windbreak of Scots pines that may have been able to deflect the fury of the northeasterlies, but was useless against harsher, economic gales. Sometimes you'll find an old farmstead buried deep in one of the Forestry Commission's notoriously regimented conifer plantations which, since 1919, have smothered vast acreages of moor and marginal farm land. Some ten per cent of the land of Wales is now the birdless domain of the sitka spruce and lodgepole pine.

With hundreds of hillfarm workers leaving the industry every year, the crisis of rural Wales continues. Not only individual farms but, now, whole farming regions are close to collapse. The blight afflicts the lowland farms too. In Gower, I have watched a farm I love broken up into a cluster of meaningless plots for jaded city types who want a few acres on which to play the farmer. They harrow their fields not to keep the grass in good heart but to give their property the appearance of a neatly striped suburban lawn; no one uses or remembers the resonant, history-laden names of the fields.

Mention 'Wales' and 'industry' together, and most people think of the heavy extractive and manufacturing industries of the south. To many unacquainted with the country, Wales amounts to little more in their imaginings than coal and Tom Jones, the two most famous Welsh exports. But contrary to popular perceptions, the modern industrial era began perhaps with greater vigour in the north than in the south. Copper mining burgeoned anew on Ynys Môn in the 1760s, and Thomas Pennant (1726-98), writing at about that time, described Flintshire as 'black with smoke' from the lead and copper undertakings that, with coal mining, dominated the economy of his home county. Above all, of course, there was slate, north Wales's industry of industries, which has carved enduring monuments to itself in the pyramidal 'benches' of the massive quarries at Dinorwig and Penrhyn, and the colossal tonnages of waste through which peep the houses of Blaenau Ffestiniog and Corris. Slate was mined in north-west Wales from medieval times, but it was not until the mid-eighteenth century that the industry took off, establishing itself by the 1860s as the most important of its kind in the world. No extractive industry has wrought more dramatic alteration upon the Welsh landscape than slate.

It was not until the early nineteenth century that the industrial activity of mid and north Wales began to be overshadowed by the spectacular growth of the coal-based industries in the south, which reached from Llanelli to the eastern valleys of Gwent.

Wales, it has been plausibly argued, is where the world's industrial civilisation began, and it is ultimately to south Wales that we look to find 'South Wales' and the crucible of the Industrial Revolution. In transforming the world, the Industrial Revolution also, of course, radically altered Wales and left seemingly indelible signatures on the landscape. As the novelist Gwyn Thomas (1913-1981) observed of his ravaged Valleys, 'society and nature have come together to achieve some amazing patterns, and they should be told not to do it again.'

Coal was not a significant player in that revolution's precursory rumblings. It was wood that they used for smelting copper and iron in places like Neath and Tintern in the sixteenth and seventeenth centuries. As the timber was exhausted in one area, they would dismantle their furnaces and rebuild them next to a new tract of forest. A famous poem by 'Anon.', translated by Gwyn Williams (1904-90), laments the destruction of Glyn Cynon Wood in Glamorgan:

> *Many a birch tree green of cloak*
> *(I'd like to choke the Saxon!)*
> *is now a flaming heap of fire*
> *where iron workers blacken.*

By 1717 copper was being smelted at Glandŵr (Landore), Swansea. Within less than a hundred years Swansea would become a metallurgical centre of world importance and, effectively, the economic capital of Chile, whence the copper ore was imported. It is perhaps difficult to recall that the Lower Swansea Valley, with its enterprise parks and an ornamental lake, was not so long ago the most polluted landscape in Wales. George Borrow (1803-81), touring 'Wild Wales' in 1854, stood transfixed by the 'accursed pandemonium' of smoke, filth and fire which he observed from the valley side. 'So strange a scene I had never beheld in nature,' he wrote. 'Had it been on canvas, with the addition of a number of diabolical figures . . . it might have stood for Sabbath in Hell . . . and would have formed a picture worthy of the powerful but insane painter Hieronymous Bosch.'

Coal, which had been mined in only a desultory fashion before about 1750, became crucial to this explosion of industrial activity: no coal, no Industrial Revolution. Coal was, and still is, mined in north-east Wales, but it was the great kidney-shaped basin of the south Wales coalfield, stretching from Pontypool in Gwent to St. Bride's Bay in Pembrokeshire, that powered the extraordinary frenzies of

'Copperopolis', the massive iron foundries of Dowlais and Merthyr, and the pioneering developments in steel and tinplate which eventually overtook iron. From 1830 coal was mined for export, to fuel industries and drive ships all over the world. This coal, this extraordinary hoard of fossilised peat, compounded of tropical swamps some 300 million years ago, made poverty-stricken Wales rich overnight. Or rich enough, at any rate, to retain most of her population, and thereby her culture, when other less naturally endowed countries were losing thousands of their people to the chancy sea-paths of emigration. Life in rural Wales could be unremittingly hard; country people, reduced to landless destitution by unofficial enclosures, often saw a better life for themselves among the smoke and noise of the coalmines and foundries, and flocked to the industrial south, 'to seek their freedom', to quote that memorable phrase, from the shackles of near and sometimes actual poverty in their precarious hills. Indeed, it was to south Wales, as well as to America and Australia, that thousands of outsiders – Spanish, Italian, Irish, English – flocked to find a living.

The phenomenal scale and speed of this influx brought a whole new Valleys society and landscape into vibrant being: the terraced housing stretching in long ribbons either side of the narrow valley, the miners' institutes, the pubs and chapels trying to outnumber each other, the pit-head wheels and winding gear, the sprawling black cones of waste, and always, near at hand, that other world, to quote Gwyn Thomas, 'just up the hillside over the ridge [of] a pastoral calm that has never seriously been breached.' King Coal, to be sure, was a hard and unpredictable master, but his coffers were there for the plundering; their depth and width seemed endless. The promised land of socialism appeared to fill the sky beyond the mountain with a blood-red glow.

But it all turned out, in the poet Idris Davies's (1905-1953) words, to be a 'dream and swift disaster'. Coal crashed, the General Strike of 1926 ended in defeat for the miners, and the Depression years that followed brought such hunger and poverty that nearly half a million of the Welsh were driven permanently out of their country.

Wales, since then, has been trying to adjust to the relentless decline and near extinction of her traditional heavy industries. The industrial era concentrated a majority of Wales's population, which for most of her history rarely exceeded a quarter of a million, in the Valleys and coastal towns of the south, and it is here still that you will find three quarters of the population of 2,913,000. The re-greening of the Valleys, which has been under way for nearly thirty years, was set in train by two social calamities: the collapse of that coal tip at Aberfan in October, 1966, which killed 116 children and twenty-eight adults, and stung the Government into action against a degraded and dangerous environment; and the dereliction, after the phoney 'boom years' of the '50s, of south Wales's coal- and steel-based economy. Salmon may swim upstream through Cardiff, against waters that once ran black with slurry, and fresh turf may cover the landscaped tips, but the poverty, ill health and despair that result from chronic unemployment are festering scars on the Valleys landscape that no amount of half-baked and deceitful Government 'initiatives' can grass over.

As we seem to go back in time to a greener Valleys environment, so we return, in places like Cwm Nedd (the Neath Valley), to a pre-modern world of tinpot private mines lost among the trees, operated by three men and a pony. But before we have time to wax sentimental about apparent returns to 'good old small-scale ways', we catch the roar downwind of heavy machinery and see dust drifting up from the other side of the valley: the big deep mine may have all but disappeared, but it is being replaced by opencast mining: this has been described by the House of Commons Select Energy Committee as 'one of the most environmentally destructive processes being carried out in the UK.' Unhindered by any statutory 'ceiling' on opencast activity, the coal companies are forging ahead, while the political climate lasts, with a massive programme of expansion; nowhere between south Pembrokeshire and Blaenafon may be considered safe from their attentions; the Mold-Buckley-Wrexham region in the north-east is also a targeted area. Mid and west Glamorgan currently bear the brunt of opencasting's ruinous assault on the environment, and local opposition is increasingly vigorous and articulate. Wales Against Opencast, one of the fastest growing single-issue campaign groups, is uniting English- and Welsh-speakers alike in a struggle to save a wide range of sensitive woodland and greenfield sites from obliteration in the pursuit of 'cheap' energy. The imaginative direct action tactics of groups such as Earth First! have been welcomed lately by frontline campaigners, ensuring that the rapacious short-termism of a deregulated and privatised coal industry is likely to meet with ever stiffening resistance.

It is on the southern coastal strip that most of what is left of Wales's heavy industry survives, in the steelworks at Newport, Port Talbot and Llanelli, the oil refineries at Milford, the petrochemical works at Baglan and Llandarcy (the only 'Llan' named after an industrialist, one D'Arcy); they have been joined in recent years by the big engineering and microelectronics 'inward investors' from Germany, North America and Japan whose large manufactories hang like garish postmodern jewels from the necklace of the M4 motorway. One expects in rural Wales to be struck by epiphanies, but there's a terrible beauty to be found in industrial Wales too – the luminescent fantasia of Baglan at night, or the sun striking through bundling grey clouds to turn some filth gusting from a smokestack into a wing of silver against the blackly green hills.

The coal-created ribbon settlements of the Valleys have altered less in recent years than towns with more space to expand. Almost every small town with room to manoeuvre has fallen for the fashionable (and uniformly ugly) town's-edge retail sheds and shopping malls which, it has been realised too late in the day, have done lethal damage to the traditional shopping 'ecology' of the High Street. They have also been catalysts in the suburbanisation and itchy-fingered 'improvement' of our towns, a process which has reduced many of them to restlessly transmuting environments bereft of identity and meaning.

The same destructive suburbanising mentality is at work, if less obviously, in rural and coastal Wales, which are the regions most heavily exploited by Wales's major 'replacement' industry, tourism. It is hardly a new industry. The first tourists were no doubt the soldiers of the Roman army, who can scarcely be considered a benign presence. Much later came a gentler, less intrusive visitor, the eighteenth- or nineteenth-century searcher after the 'picturesque' and 'sublime' and quirky Celtic exotica. Dr. Johnson may not have taken to our 'horrid mountains' and 'wretched hovels', but others on their 'Cambrian tours' found much to admire and wrote memorably of their travels in accounts that advertised the delights of this strange land to similarly adventurous (and well-heeled) spirits. They came, and they went, these early tourists, in their hundreds rather than hundreds of thousands, leaving little more to mark their passing than a signature scrawled in sand. Not so, of course, the twentieth-century visitors whose combined impact can have as corrosive an effect on the language and culture of Wales as on her landscape and ecology. Until as recently as the 1940s my native Gower was a virtual agricultural independency, with its own languages (Welsh and the Gower dialect), strong local identity and mutually dependent social relationships. But in the 1950s the Gower which exists now only in the memories of isolated pensioners began to break up and disappear under the joint pressures of suburbanisation and mass tourism. Every fine weekend throughout the summer Britain's first Area of Outstanding Natural Beauty is, like similar honey pots all around the coast, one gigantic traffic jam, so overcrowded that it is impossible for the visitor, no matter how interested they may be in what is left of the culture, to connect with any sense of indigenous life. And when the crowds leave, having experienced little more than crowds, the stigmata of their passing are writ large in the landscape: the sand dunes trampled down, the clifftop paths gouged into broad, earth-beaten highways. Leisure, it is increasingly acknowledged, now threatens to supersede labour as the biggest despoiler of the countryside.

Wales is heavily dependent on tourism. The industry brings £1.3 billion into the economy, nearly 40% of it being spent in the Welsh-language heartland of Gwynedd, and it generates 95,000 full-time jobs. As the poet and environmental critic John Barnie (b. 1941) has noted, 'a nation that depends on tourism as Wales now does must learn to manipulate its culture . . .'

It manipulates its culture by confecting and marketing 'images' of Wales that draw shamelessly on all the flattering old clichés while carefully avoiding the 'downbeat' and troublesome. One awkward fact the 'spin doctors' would rather was kept from troubling the sleep of visitors is the problem of depopulation and immigration. Wales has recently suffered a huge demographic upheaval of which few seem to have taken much notice. It has been calculated that during the 1980s half a million mostly Welsh people, a sixth of the population, moved out of Wales, and half a million mostly non-Welsh people moved in. An equivalent upheaval in England would involve eight million Englishmen leaving dear old Blighty to be replaced by eight million Frenchmen.

The magnet, of course, is the relative tranquillity and apparently 'unspoilt' nature of the land of Wales. As for the Welsh language and culture, many incomers who may not be aware initially of the existence of such things, take pains to discover what country they are in, and make generous and valuable contributions to contemporary life, becoming in due course what the historian Gwyn A. Williams (1925-95) hailed as 'the New Welsh'. Others, alas, do not, electing as mere consumers of lovely scenery to remain indifferent to the people, their languages and ways of being – an ignorance that is shared, it has to be admitted, by not a few natives.

Holidaymakers drawn back to Wales as wealthy retirers or second-home owners tend to settle in 'the most beautiful' parts of Wales which are often in the culturally sensitive *bro Gymraeg* (Welsh-speaking areas). Those displaced by the arrival of this leisured superstratum in the depopulating heartland tend to be former workers of the land with deep family roots; if removed in large numbers their disappearance is as damaging to the 'cultural ecology' as the obliteration of ancient beeches by road-building might be to the ecology of a place like the Clydach gorge.

Violent alteration to the physical environment invariably lays waste to the cultural. Wales has scores of natural lakes: there are sixty in Snowdonia alone. Most of them are small, and even the few big ones, such as Llyn Tegid (Bala), are harmoniously in scale with their surroundings. But there are new lakes in Wales – Claerwen, Clywedog, Celyn – some of which, to the historically attuned sensibility, rather than that of the merry jet-skier, are sharply disharmonious places. Llyn Celyn above all, sometimes known as Llyn Tryweryn, exemplifies the shameful fate of farms and villages that were drowned, in spite of unanimous public opposition, to supply an English city with water. By flooding Cwm Tryweryn and the village of Capel Celyn in the 1960s, the bureaucrats of Liverpool Corporation destroyed unthinkingly, in the words of Bobi Jones's (b. 1929) poem, 'The cynghanedd and the ballads, the close society and the prayer/They could never see at all . . . /. . . the aristocratic spacious thing,/The treasure not hidden at all in any other place – /The warm priceless life . . .' The authorities claimed in hurt dudgeon that Liverpool needed the reservoir to supply drinking water, but later admitted that the water was for 'industrial expansion and re-sale at a profit.'

Water, as Flann O'Brien's fictitious 'authority' De Selby wisely proclaimed, is rarely absent from any wholly satisfactory situation.

And it is water which is increasingly the focus of environmental campaigns, from the struggle against the reckless experiment of barraging river mouths, to Surfers Against Sewage, from the world as a whole against acid rain, to Friends of Cardigan Bay against oil and gas exploration off the west Wales coast, which threatens the habitat of a rare colony of bottle-nose dolphins, and much else besides. Harri Webb, in a beautiful hymn to oceanic variety called 'The Flocks of the Moon', warns careless humanity to heed the silent music of the sea-moving moon:

> *There is no end to her wonders*
> *Yet all are so frail, so frail.*
> *The earth spills poison,*
> *Cities vomit filth,*
> *Soon it may be too late,*
> *The flocks of the moon all die,*
> *Her dancers rot,*
> *Her music vain.*
> *Still she will drag the dead weight of the tides,*
> *No longer an enchantress but a drudge,*
> *An old crazed witch with a blank face*
> *Who will curse to kill*
> *And you too will die.*

We are all, his poem implies, in this mess together, and there are few unilateral solutions to what are invariably global problems.

As we contemplate our long since denuded mountain ridges, bristling here and there with the latest indignity we have inflicted on them in the shape of stark forests of noisy wind turbines, we might call to mind the shrinking rain forests of the Amazon, or the galloping deserts of Africa, or the deluged flatlands of Bangladesh. Cushioned in the overfed and self-indulgent west from the more extreme consequences of human over-expansion, we nevertheless owe responsibilities to such places.

The world is one blue teetering orb, and everyone wants to save the whales; a few of us, living on this particular swathe of it, live in hope also of saving Wales, in all her cultural, topographical and ecological variety. There are signs that we are learning at last the harsh lesson of Tryweryn and other sites of environmental and cultural defeat: that if we don't take responsibility for our own bruised acre of the planet, no one else will; and that abdicating such responsibility hardly equips us for making ourselves useful globally.

Wales has a long tradition of robust popular protest, from Glyndŵr's valiant attempt to restore Welsh independence in the fifteenth century to Cymdeithas yr Iaith's (the Welsh Language Society) daubing of English-only road signs in the 1960s and '70s which eventually persuaded the Government to adopt a bilingual policy. There have been notable successes on the environmental front. In the 1940s, for instance, the people of the Presely hills successfully resisted Ministry of War plans to turn their sacred hills into a tank training range. The people of Hirwaun in the 1970s refused to allow two large gas tanks to be built near their homes. The huge reservoir of Llyn Brianne, to the north of Llanymddyfri (Llandovery), the construction of which involved no dispossessions, is a tribute to the protesters of Cwm Gwendraeth Fach, whose valley to the southeast of Carmarthen was threatened with inundation – until they decided to put a stop to the scheme, as a poem by David Hughes (b. 1948) recounts:

> *When Cwm Gwendraeth Fach was to be put to flood*
> *The people, knowing water is thinner than blood,*
> *Chained gates, drove machinery into gaps.*
> *The civil engineers rolled up their maps.*

A victory as this was for grass-roots resistance, few anticipated at the time the devastation that Llyn Brianne would visit upon the habitat of Rhandir Mwyn, where several unique species have been lost to the world forever.

For every Cwm Gwendraeth Fach there seems to be a Tryweryn; for every Presely mountainside saved from the bombardment of tanks there seem to be huge tracts of Wales – the clifftops at Castlemartin, or Mynydd Epynt in south Powys – lost indefinitely to the war machine.

Our old tribalist tendencies ensure that between our vigorously fought local campaigns and our concern for global issues there is a missing link: a care for the land of Wales as a whole. Perhaps, at last, we are beginning to learn unity, and the time is approaching when we will take responsibility on Welsh terms for the economy, varied habitats and diverse culture of Wales. Then that foggy thing, a Welsh nation, might truly come into connection with the world, and cease to be mistaken for yet another lie of the land.

Garn Goch Iron Age Hillfort[1]

It looks, in plan, like some extinct strain of hammer-headed whale, its wise eye a cairn of stones that has conned the upper Tywi for centuries longer than the grey sandstone ramparts, raised by warrior farmers over two thousand years ago, that raggedly contour the hill's brow.

Nowhere in southern Britain possesses a greater density of Iron Age defended settlements than southwest Wales, the realm of the Demetae who gave their name to modern Dyfed. On a map showing the distribution of hillforts, the Dyfed group are a thick fizz of black dots, the large bubble of Y Garn Goch nudging eastward into a patch of vacant upland that would appear to divide the Demetae from the Silures. Y Gaer Fawr at Garn Goch, two-and-a-half miles southwest of Llangadog, is one of the biggest Iron Age hillforts in south Wales, and among the most impressive in Britain; but few, specialists apart, have heard of it, and fewer still brush through the ferns that throng its rubbled walls to contemplate what possibly was, and to dream of what might be. The warriors today are yowling boozily through Swansea's clubland, or battling with poverty in the dole estates.

And you won't find Garn Goch in the history books, for the good reason that virtually nothing may be reliably supposed about the who, what and when of it. The question marks lie almost as thickly around Garn Goch's sprawling bulwarks as the bracken that waves lime-green in spring and burns red as foxhide in winter. It's the bracken, some say, that names the place – Garn Goch is, in winter at least, a huge red shoulder of land that rears aberrantly from the Tywi's otherwise emerald pastures. Others insist that 'the red cairn' embodies some folk memory of a devastatingly bloody showdown between recalcitrant natives and the legionaries of Vespasian engaged in 'pacifying' the Empire's outlandish extremities. If the still massive walls, in places over twenty feet high, keep dark about their builders' fate, they hint at a story as vivid as the blaze of golden aggregate that lurks inside each weathered lump of sandstone.

[1] First published as *Llangadog* (1996) in the Gregynog Press's 'Places/Y Man a'r Lle' series of essays.

Archaeologists, preoccupied with emergency digs in the constantly transmuting towns, have done little more than map its surface features, although antiquarians, from the mid-nineteenth century onwards, have written of expeditions to the site and conducted small-scale investigations which have yielded the occasional flint chip, the odd shard of Bronze Age pottery. In 1853 Archdeacon John Williams was struck with wonder at this 'immense fortress, which nothing but a strong effort of concentrated power could have constructed . . .'

It has been proposed that Garn Goch, with a population of perhaps two to four thousand, was the 'capital' of the Demetian Welsh before Moridunum (Carmarthen) was made over to them by the Romans as their *civitas*. That Garn Goch was indeed an important regional centre is suggested not only by its 'walls of Cyclopean masonry', to quote a Victorian observer, but by its superb command of Ystrad Tywi. Looking west on a clear day, with the fighter jets screaming imperiously below, as addicted to straight lines as the Roman originators of the A40 that zips by beneath them, you can see past beech-crowned Llandeilo, Dinefwr, Dryslwyn, Grongar and Carmarthen as far as the numinous crests of Presely. At the Garn's foot there's the village of Bethlehem; then, casting your gaze eastward, Llangadog, Mynydd Myddfai and the hills of Powys. Behind you, unseen beyond the cairn-topped hump of Trichrûg, looms the formidable massif of Y Mynydd Du, from which direction no enemy would be so foolish as to mount an attack.

Were the denizens of Garn Goch Demetae, or were they Silures protecting their tribe's western flank? It is possible that they were members of a small buffer tribe controlling the exceptionally rich farmland of the upper Tywi basin, and owing allegiance to neither the Silures nor to the Demetae. Y Gaer Fawr is the largest of a distinct group of hillforts, three of which lie within a mile of its walls; one of these, Y Gaer Fach, nestles on a rounded knoll little more than two hundreds yards away.

From his dry-stone ramparts on this glowering bluff, the 'Celtic' chieftain of this imaginable but long since nameless kingdom might have gazed on a landscape that had changed little, perhaps, in centuries: a patchwork of small, irregular fields, some swaying with corn, some dotted with cattle; smoke twirling from scattered round huts, some of them hidden in the steadily shrinking clumps of forest;

and – maker and sometime taker of his people's wealth – the serpentine, shape-shifting, flood-inflicting Tywi.

The notion that the 'Celticisation' of southern Britain was effected by a huge influx of war-crazed Gauls, Belgae and other Continentals who hammered the Bronzefolk into oblivion and refashioned the island in their own iron image has yielded to the subtler idea that it was the *culture* of the Celts that gradually crept upon the land – their religion, their customs, their language – rather than the Celts themselves in full-scale invasive person. According to this view, there may have been Celts living in Britain as early as 1000 BC, if not earlier. Garn Goch offers persuasive evidence of cultural seepage and continuity rather than violent influx and the wholesale displacement of populations.

The great cairn, for instance, raised in the Bronze Age or even Neolithic times, was not plundered by the 'Celts' for its ready supply of building materials, but conspicuously preserved. Some ancient of pregnant consequence is probably entombed here: when a party of Victorian cairn-busters opened a similar mound a short distance from the southeast end of the fort they found a cist and signs of a cremation. The sacramental significance of Garn Goch, which may have been a hallowed site long before the Celtic era, is augmented by the presence at its heart of an oval pool, silted up these days, but still watery after heavy rain. A hillfort with its own water source is rare. In addition to supplying the inhabitants' daily needs, the pool is likely to have been a focus of ritual and a repository of gifts for the gods.

If Garn Goch was indeed a 'town' like the famous, and much smaller, Tre'r Ceiri on the Llŷn, with its 150 stone-built huts, it might be expected to boast a wealth of roundhouse emplacements, but only one has been identified so far, on a rise a few yards south of the pool. The Iron Age hut, as large in area as many a modern farmer's bungalow, was usually constructed of materials – thatch, daub and wattle – that have long since rotted; in only five per cent of hillforts have traces of huts been found. The circular plan of this and most other British Iron Age huts, in contrast to the rectangular form of mainland Continental dwellings, tends to re-affirm the continuity of native Bronze Age traditions. The 'Celts' who built Garn Goch's fort could well have been descendants of the more peaceable folk who built its cairn.

For generations local farmers have been carting away bits of Y Gaer Fawr to lay steps and build cowsheds. The *murus gallicus* of old, a boxlike grid of timbers filled with rubble and faced with laid masonry, is a blurred approximation of what it was. But still to be seen are the flags that lined the two main gateways and the tumbled uprights that mark the 'postern' or side entrances. One of these, near the hut platform, is wonderfully undamaged: a warrior leading his horse could come panting through it at any moment.

What part might the Romans have played in the spoiling of Garn Goch? The Demetae, it is believed, mounted no opposition to the Romans, and were left, like the Cornish, to themselves. But would the people of Ystrad Tywi, whose Silurian neighbours were renowned for the ferocity of their resistance, have given in without a fight? The 'pacification' of Ystrad Tywi would have been vital to the Romans, both to ensure the successful exploitation of the goldmines at Dolaucothi (with local slaves to work them) and to secure trouble-free passage along the new Carmarthen to Brecon road. East of Moridunum there are ample signs of vigorous military activity on the Romans' part, including forts at Llandeilo, Pumsaint and Llanymddyfri, and two large camps on Mynydd-bach Trecastell . . . all locked like magnets onto the iron core of Ystrad Tywi: ring the barbarians with bowmen and slingmen, *ballistae* and *catapultae*; rub smoke in their eyes; rip at their walls till their walls crumble; then send in the cohorts for such a kill that it will name this monticle the colour of blood for millennia to come. This, or something like it, is perhaps what happened; perhaps not . . .

In time the natives became reconciled to the new dispensation. The magnificent Roman villa unearthed in 1961 at the evocatively named Llys Brychan, just below Garn Goch, may have been the home of a Romano-British nobleman descended from the dynasty that once commanded the hillfort. Tacitus, the great historian of the conquest, was inclined to sneer at the Celtic *nouveaux riches*. 'Gradually,' he wrote, 'the inhabitants of the island succumbed to pleasure and discovered a taste for colonnades, public baths, splendid banquets. In their want of experience, they mistook all of this for civilisation, while in reality it only contributed to their greater subjection.' But Rome's power eventually waned and the natives, advised to look to their own defences, reappropriated what was useful to them from the past, and made a Celtic renewal of themselves.

Llangadog, three generations back, was my family's *bro*. Wearying, like many, of their unproductive acres, they went into business and over the hill. In Swansea, where they discovered a taste for servants, public schools and the English language, the Welsh names of the family gave way to English. One hundred years later, looking back to keep aligned, I return with my daughters, Angharad and Branwen, and my *Cymraeg hanner byw* which they gigglingly correct, as I walk and they scamper, arcane as tomorrow, through the fortifying ruins of Garn Goch.

Welsh White Settlers[1]

'Where do you go on Sundays?' is still, in certain parts of America, a fairly common icebreaker in social situations, and it's not the finer distinctions between the Golden Lion and the Ceffyl Du that your interlocutor is fishing for.

Most Americans still seem to believe in something – with, at times, a Manichaean vengeance. 'To reject God is to embrace Hell,' a lurid roadside billboard warned this fire-singed agnostic on a recent poetry-reading jaunt through the heavily Baptist Carolinas. And when Americans tour Wales they are often aghast at the churches up for sale and the chapels turned into curry houses and bingo clubs. We natives, on the other hand, zonked on a newer trinity of Shopping, Telly and the Holy Lottery, are perhaps less inclined to sorrow at the sight of a corpsed Bethel. Life, we may have concluded, is not a rehearsal; so good riddance to all the mirthless repression and suffocating respectability of a defunct religion. Caradoc – not the smug 'old' buffer in Saturday's *Western Mail*, but the dung-hurling iconoclast from Rhydlewis – said it all, didn't he, when he skewered Nonconformity as a captivity of 'gloom and fraud' to which the Welsh were tethered like cattle? We've been there, done that; we're through with all the infantile paranoia of old-fashioned religion; let's bolt on a brand new satellite dish and see, as night comes on, what the anaesthetising Mr. Murdoch has to offer us.

If we had had a state, Calvinistic Methodism might once have been considered our state religion, but today the formerly mighty *Hen Gorff* can muster fewer than 50,000 souls, a dwindling fraction of the 300,000 boasted by its apparently thriving 'daughter' church in the Khasi Hills of northeast India. The hundreds of thousands that used to flock to chapel two or three times a Sunday are reduced to a barely discernible trickle, a dramatic alteration in Wales's spiritual life which has taken place well within living memory. By waving an unperturbed if not relieved farewell to what Emyr Humphreys has called 'the civilisation of our immediate ancestors', are we not willing ourselves

[1] First published as a review article in *The New Welsh Review* 39, 1998.

into a state of debilitating ignorance about the specifics of that civilisation, and denying that it might possibly have something interesting and useful to say to us?

In constructing what John Tripp used to call 'a benevolent country' for ourselves, there is always the temptation to select the bits that flatter our prejudices and sweep into a corner those that do not. The Adferite will carve out a *bro Gymraeg* that refuses to recognise the English-monoglot southern hordes as Welsh in any shape or form; his 'Valleys nationalist' alter ego will reduce Wales to the size of the coalfield, and pretend that no one ever spoke or thought a word of Welsh 'twixt Pontyberem and Pontypool.

A strident atheist until logic convinced me that atheism was as much a 'belief' as Christianity (and I had *no* belief), I was strongly attracted to the 'vision' of Gwyn Williams, Trefenter, of a pre-Reformation merrie Wales before all that religious scowling wiped the smiles off the fiddlers' and dancers' faces. It suited my narrow-minded atheism to see religion, and Nonconformity in particular, as nothing more than an imposition on people's lives – and to reject it, unexamined.

As I was to discover, you will not understand modern Welsh history, to say nothing of contemporary Wales, if you choose to remain in ignorance of the religious life of the country. Why, for instance, have the Welsh, as a fully enfranchised electorate, never voted for a Conservative government? Part of the answer has to be that in the eighteenth century Griffith Jones, Llanddowror and other dissenting evangelists succeeded, with their circulating schools, in teaching hundreds of thousands of their countrymen and women to read, creating possibly the most literate peasantry in Europe. Their motives, of course, were religious: they wanted their compatriots to be able to read, as individuals, the bible that had been translated into the vernacular by Bishop William Morgan and company in the sixteenth century. Their efforts brought into being a whole Welsh reading and writing world that had never existed before, a new democracy of letters that ushered into social, literary and political life an abiding and combative egalitarianism. From some hedge-school in eighteenth-century Carmarthenshire to the 'Tory-free Wales' of the 1997 general election might seem a somewhat fanciful leap, but the connections are there to be made.

'The Nonconformist tradition' was not a uniformly grey, monolithic abstraction that descended on the land like some prickly horsehair cushion, but a spiritual movement of extraordinary inspirational power. It arose from historical circumstances, and was fashioned by the people, as it in turn helped to fashion them. It was argued over, it had splits and factions, contained liberals and arch conservatives, and had major practical consequences for people's lives. The 'Nonconformist Conscience', with its stress on moral self-discipline and the 'upright' character of the individual, its rewarding of thrift and self-improvement, its condemnation of excess, its innate hostility to the notion of privilege in Church and State, its commitment to democratic systems of organisation, fuelled political radicalism in the nineteenth century and played a vital part in such changes as the widening of electoral suffrage, parliamentary reform, improvements in education and the disestablishment of the Church in Wales. The Methodists may often have been politically quiescent, but the older and more radical dissenting sects – the Baptists, Independents and Unitarians – were far from enthusiastic about the established order. Having struggled long and hard against State-imposed restrictions and disabilities, it was for them a short step from the achievement of religious liberty to the pursuit of political liberty.

It's a movement that is anything but boring, and for those, like me, beyond its spiritual pale, it is probably best understood in concrete situations. Anne Kelly Knowles's book about Welsh immigrants on Ohio's industrial frontier, *Calvinists Incorporated*,[2] is an exemplary description of Calvinistic Methodism in action, and an absorbing study of the relationship between economics and culture. From books like Elwyn Ashton's *The Welsh in the United States* and David Williams's *Cymru ac America/Wales and America*, I knew a little in general terms about Welsh settlements in North America, and was familiar with names like Paddy's Run, Scranton and Wilkes Barre. It wasn't until April of 1997, when I visited southern Ohio with Menna Elfyn and Iwan Llwyd on a poetry reading tour, that I heard of the Welsh settlement in the counties of Jackson and Gallia, an area so strongly associated with maritime mid Wales that it became known among Welsh Americans as 'little Cardiganshire'.

We arrived there after a five-hour drive across and away from the winter-grey flatlands of northern Ohio. 'Like paradise,' said Iwan,

[2] Anne Kelly Knowles, *Calvinists Incorporated* (University of Chicago Press, 1997).

surveying the sunny fields and forested hills of Gallia from the campus of the languid university town of Rio Grande – a paradise, however, without a bar (Rio Grande, to the satisfaction no doubt of the shades of those Cardi pioneers, is a dry town). But things were wet enough in nearby Gallipolis, sitting pretty as a French *ville de province* on the banks of the Ohio river. Here, in the congenial Mogie's bar, we began to learn something of the area's Welsh legacy. The Welsh, we heard, settled here by accident. Intending to join an earlier Welsh settlement at Paddy's Run in southwestern Ohio, a large group landed in Baltimore in 1818 and made their way overland to Pittsburgh, where they purchased boats for the journey downriver. They stopped for the night at Gallipolis, prudently unloaded their goods and awoke the next morning to find their boats stolen. So here in Gallia they stayed, farming, road-building and, later, iron-making. By 1830 there were Welsh churches and Welsh homesteads all over the area. Hardly anyone speaks the language these days, but there is a 'Welsh for beginners' class, and at Oak Hill there is the only Welsh Heritage Museum in the United States. Apparently, much is made in this museum of the Welsh as a sober, chapel-going, tea-drinking, diminutive and terminally solemn breed.

It's a common enough image (not that most North Americans have any image or knowledge of us at all). After a reading at the University of Rio Grande we were approached by a local journalist who said we were not the Triad of Gloom that she had been anticipating. 'We'd always thought of the Welsh as such glum, humourless people,' she said, 'but you guys seem to know what laughing's for.'

Waiting for me on my return, quite by chance, was a review copy of Anne Kelly Knowles's book – all about that very corner of Ohio. Now I began to appreciate the scale of the Welsh influx into Jackson/Gallia. It was, by 1850, one of the five largest rural Welsh settlements in the United States, and, according to Daniel Jenkins Williams, the early twentieth-century historian of Welsh Calvinistic Methodism in America, 'the strongest and best organized Welsh settlement in America in her balmy days, and the best fortified by natural environment against extraneous influences.' What distinguished it from most other Welsh-American settlements was the opportunities it offered the pioneers for work in both agriculture and industry. They became increasingly involved in the region's charcoal iron industry, first as workers and managers, and later, with considerable pricking of the Calvinistic conscience, as reluctant entrepreneurs.

Published by the University of Chicago Press as a 'Geography Research Paper', this substantial volume is, within its academic genre, a *tour de force*. But, being jargon-free and extremely well written, it transcends that genre, and deserves to attract many general readers as well as geographers and historians. Its American author was a lecturer at the Institute of Earth Studies, UCW, Aberystwyth, who learned Welsh and came to an extraordinarily sympathetic understanding of the mentality of the people she writes about, some of whom, in their ferocious, grim-faced fundamentalism, would seem to have been not exactly over-achievers in the charm department. She is able to discern behind such off-putting masks the extraordinary energy and spiritual passion that carried these individuals and their communities through strange and difficult times.

A particular strength of this study is the depth of research undertaken on both sides of the Atlantic, so that a detailed account of what the Welsh got up to in Gallia is complemented and illuminated by a thorough investigation of the Wales they left behind, concentrating on a region of some ten square miles. Mynydd Bach, from which most of the Jackson/Gallia settlers came, was part of what, in the 1760s, Daniel Rowland, Llangeitho had made the very heartland of Welsh Methodism. The emigrants bequeathed no tidy, comprehensive records; the writer has had to piece together her fascinating story from all manner of sources, including obituaries, family biographies, chapel histories, government surveys, the names of farms, and such field research as a chat of over a pint with the owners of the Ship, Cilcennin. The result is a truly 'multiscaled' history whose resourcefulness matches the enterprise of her subjects, and whose attentive regard for the two lands she describes is reflected in her writing – as in this portrait of Mynydd Bach:

> . . . *a curving backbone of rock thinly clad with cotton grass, purple moor grass, gorse and heather. Today, along its exposed upper slopes one can see wind-bent shrubs, remnants of old hedgerows, leaning hard to the east as the prevailing westerlies have pushed them over the years. Bogs and two small lakes fill depressions on the top of the ridge. Down its sides, rough pasture and farmland fall*

away like the folds of a heavy skirt whose hem touches the sea to the west and swings along the arc of the Aeron River.

It was and is hellishly hard land to farm. Both London and the booming industrial settlements of south Wales hatched dreams of leaving in many a Cardi breast, but it was the much more dangerous option of translantic emigration that appealed to the majority of Mynydd Bach's disaffected, most of whom had never before ventured beyond the confines of their native *bro*.

Emigration was, in religious terms, a highly controversial thing to contemplate. Powerful conservatives such as Christmas Evans and John Elias preached vigorously against it, the former dismissing the 'preaching in the wilderness' argument as a flimsy disguise for the real intention, to get rich; anyone who emigrated to America, Evans warned, was lost to religion forever. Emigrants were considered to be guilty of the sin of ambition and the immorality of taking fate into their own hands. They were faced with a severe moral dilemma, and ministers who supported emigration often tied themselves in theological knots trying to justify the popular yearning for a better life than that provided by the crowded farms and acid soil of mid Wales.

Why Ohio rather than London or Merthyr? Anne Kelly Knowles suggests two main reasons: they wanted to own land, and, fearing or scorning 'the unholy atmosphere of rough-and-tumble industrial towns', they were attracted to relatively 'virgin' territory where they could practise their religion 'free from the threats of commercial and industrial ungodliness'.

Although rural Wales as a whole was hard-pressed by crop failures, population growth and the acute distress that followed the end of the Napoleonic Wars, it was not, initially, the poorest who chose to leave. Emigration was an expensive undertaking that could be afforded only by the upper-middle stratum of agricultural society: the cost of transportation alone for a Cardiganshire family of two parents and four children could be at least fifty pounds, the equivalent of a year's profit from a large tenant farm's production. Poorer families, says Anne Kelly Knowles, were unable to leave until their wealthier friends or relatives were established in Ohio and could lend them money for the passage.

The land they acquired was no great improvement on the rough, hilly terrain they'd left behind, as the Americans and wealthier Europeans had already snaffled the best of it; but it was theirs, not some landlord's, and all of them owned at least eighty acres by 1822. They began, indeed, to get rich – in a low-key, Calvinistic kind of way. 'The Welsh may have been less wealthy than their American neighbours,' writes Anne Kelly Knowles, 'but most of them had significantly improved their economic circumstances and fundamentally changed their status in relation to land within a few years of emigrating.'

What didn't change, for quite some time, was the religion they brought with them. They were able to demonstrate to the doubters back home and Welsh settlers elsewhere in the States that religious piety and making good in the New World were not irreconcilable. They'd dotted the Jackson/Gallia landscape with chapels, had forceful and conservative ministers to guide them, and led lives in strict accord with the God-fearing principles and traditions they'd imported from Wales. Old World Puritans may have faced opposition from more liberal elements in other Welsh settlements, but not so the Puritans of southern Ohio who proved 'an exceptionally cohesive, committed, and well-trained religious community.'

The biggest ideological challenge this community had to face, the temptation of capitalism, must have caused soul-searchings similar to those provoked by the debate over the morality of emigration: to invest or not to invest in the burgeoning iron charcoal industry, to become or not to become owners and entrepreneurs? One or two, such as Thomas T. Jones, the richest Welshman in Jackson County, revelled in his capitalist good fortune. But most of those who were drawn into the ways of Mammon allowed themselves to be persuaded of the advantages with considerable unease. The Welsh 'were followers in the development of industrial capitalism in southern Ohio, not leaders,' says Anne Kelly Knowles. Out of the restraints of Calvinistic Methodism grew the cautiousness of the Welsh way of doing business: if the profits weren't huge, neither were the losses.

Eventually the prosperity of the Welsh of Jackson/Gallia began to erode their identity. The wider world found its rumbustious way to their doors, the strong internal control of the deacons broke down, and gradually the Welsh became Americans. What remains today in the minds of some of their descendants is little more than a sour memory. One Harrison Salisbury refers in his memoirs to the intense unhappiness of his mother growing up in the oppressive Welsh Calvinism of Jackson County. 'She hated her Welsh father,' Harrison Salisbury writes, 'the Welshness of him, his hymn-singing, his Sabbath-keeping, prayer meetings, hellfire and damnation.'

All the sad clichés, and, in the way of clichés, they are true no doubt, as far as they go – which isn't very far. There's more to the Nonconformist tradition than this conventional sketch of crabbed misery is inclined to allow. Anne Kelly Knowles's engaged but by no means uncritical account invites us to come to terms with the broader, more detailed picture in all its parti-coloured complexity.

Footsore on the Frontier [1]

A frontier has been described as a line which you can draw where you like as long as you have force enough, the problem being to ensure respect for your line when you have drawn it. The moderns use concrete, guns and barbed wire, the ancients constructed a bank and ditch or a wall . . .

Sir Cyril Fox, *Offa's Dyke: A Field Study of the Western Frontier Works of Mercia in the Seventh and Eighth Centuries AD*

To walk the Dyke, north to south, from sea to sea, in the year of its twelve-hundredth anniversary – that was the plan. But the feet had other ideas, and after tramping only the first third of it, I found myself sent bootless home and blister-beaten back, resigned to the modified project of tackling it in sections as soon as skin and smarting meat had got themselves stuck together again; not that I wasn't tempted, as I stumbled into Oswestry, by the thought of hijacking Gwyn Alf's helicopter for the remaining two thirds . . .

It is of course dodgy history to pin such an anniversary on the year 785: the Dyke was up to twenty years in the making, and we don't know for sure which years of Offa's reign (757–796) they were. A nineteenth-century declaration in stone near Knighton that it was built in 757 is even dodgier history; the Mercian king would have been too preoccupied with his wars against the Welsh to have started work on the Dyke before the more settled 780s. Modern convention has plumped for 785 as 'the year', and this seems to be tolerated by the experts, including the late Sir Cyril Fox who is *the* Dyke authority.

This unnoticed birthday coincides with a lesser one, the thirtieth anniversary of the designation of the Offa's Dyke long-distance footpath, although it wasn't until 1971 that it was formally opened as a walkable proposition throughout its 176 miles. Between eight and nine thousand dykers a year now stump the whole way between Chepstow and Prestatyn, and many more enjoy medium-range excursions along

[1] A slightly longer version of this article appeared in *Planet* 59 (1985–6) and was republished in *Compass Points*, ed. Janet Davies (University of Wales Press, 1993).

popular stretches such as the Wye valley and the Clwydian Hills or the Black Mountains.

'The Marches' are aptly plural, for you keep acquaintance on this walk with three 'marks' that cross and shadow and cross each other the border's length: the modern boundary, the line of the path, and the Dyke itself, the most potent symbol of one of the oldest frontiers in Europe. Conflict has been fundamental to this belt of land from pre-human times, and signs of struggle between the forces that have contended for it are everywhere to be seen, from hills and valleys squeezed, gouged and smoothed into shape by the clash of 'Welsh' and 'English' icefields, to the castles of the Normans who lorded it here a mere eight or nine hundred years ago.

The political frontier has fallen neatly into place along an obvious geological rift between English lowland plain and hard Welsh highland. It was on these hills, formidable enough to scrape by as mountains, that the first Celts in these islands built their 'Iron Age' forts, the huge ramparted refuges of Ffridd Faldwyn, Foel Fenlli, Penycloddiau. On even the hottest day there's a breeze on such heights that chills the sweat – our earliest homes in this land are now the last places that we'd want to settle for more than a few minutes.

These forts were eventually overrun by the Romans whose comparatively brief occupation, with a network of new roads, towns and fortifications, rendered this territory unmistakably a frontier zone, although it would be a good three hundred years after Roman withdrawal (AD 410) before the defining process solidified physically in the great earthwork behind which the latest invaders coralled us away as '*welisc*', foreigners.

Of the dozens of Dyke and border books, Sir Cyril Fox's yard-by-yard study, based on field surveys made between 1926 and 1931, remains the central account. Like a walk of the Dyke, the going is tough and sometimes a chore, but the views, the detailed insights, are worth all the sweat. In some of his conclusions he is understandably tentative, certain questions posed by the Dyke being beyond the archaeological resources of his day. Many exciting re-appraisals can be expected from the Extra-Mural Department of Manchester University which is currently undertaking a complete re-survey of all dykes associated with the West Mercian frontier – using new methods such as the 'land systems' approach which examines the earthwork within the context of geology, relief and drainage, rather than viewing it as an isolated archaeological monument. They hope to solve such problems as why there are only short sections of the Dyke in the Herefordshire plain, and why there was no Dyke built for a thirty-mile stretch north of Redbrook in the Wye Valley.

If, through the *beirdd*, the news from Powys is bad and from Pengwern disastrous, it must not be assumed that imperial Mercia had it all its own way. The presence of English place-names west of the frontier (Buttington, Forden, Evenjobb, Cascob), the unexpected deviations away from its alignment – on Long Mountain, for instance, or Rushock Hill – are evidence that the course of the Dyke was negotiated rather than imposed, Offa accommodating to some extent the territorial claims of Powys in particular, the most powerful of the three border kingdoms with which he had to contend.

You need to follow the Dyke on foot through the sometimes bewildering confusion of broken country over which it travels in order to appreciate the skill of its navigator and the vast ambition of the project. There had been nothing like it in these islands since Hadrian's Wall, and the Mercians were plotting it with none of the precision instruments available to the Romans; laying it out in the field, with the aid of marker posts and hand signals, seems to have been the basic method. If Offa was himself its guiding intelligence, the actual construction work was carried out by a number of gangs under the command of the local magnate through whose land the Dyke in that section passed. Thousands of serfs from a forty-mile radius must have been pulled in to work on each section, and kept at it for years; some may have been Welsh slaves, captives from the wars.

Work began perhaps in the Kerry Hill region where Fox detects signs of experimentation: 'We seem in this zone to be at the birth of a work of genius; to be studying the great earthwork in the limited area where it was evolved, and where by the greatest good luck its condition is sufficiently perfect to permit an exact analysis of its original structure. Here the engineer learned his job: elsewhere he cast off the defects – the mere boundary bank thrown up from a succession of spoil holes – which dim his achievement.'

Local human resources and geological conditions account for many 'inconsistencies' in structure and design. The basic model is a bank, averaging six feet in height, with a ditch on the west side, the whole having a median width of sixty feet. There are humbler stretches appearing as little more than hedgebanks, and these may have been supplemented by timber palisades; but there are many lengths that rear above twenty feet – at Lippet's Grove in the Wye Valley, one of its proudest sections, the Dyke had a scarp of thirty-one feet. Here, perhaps, Offa used the miners of the Forest of Dean whose particular skills were to be in great demand in the Middle Ages for the ditching of castles. Sometimes on this walk there's the excitement of coming across the point where two gangs, working towards each other and using slightly different methods, have at last met, as between Middle Knuck and Hergan where there's a most unusual right-angled join.

Of the 149 miles of Offa's original frontier, eighty-one are traceable on the ground. It is seen at its best in limestone country, such as the lower Wye Valley where erosion and silting have had least effect; where it's made of sandy soils it has often sprawled and lost definition, or been washed away in floods. Human activity has also reduced the earthwork: it has been ransacked for building and road construction, ploughed over and quarried through, built upon and obliterated by conifers; in the grounds of Chirk Castle it disappears beneath the waters of an artificial lake. The most contentious eroder is the human foot: there are archaeologists who want walkers banned from the Dyke, to whom the Offa's Dyke Association reply that little harm is done as long as walkers stick to the parapet of the Dyke rather than scrambling up and down its sides.

Few of those controversial feet seem to be Welsh. I was the only (aspiring) long distance Welshman that I, or any of the other Dykers I met, had seen the hide of, although there were plenty of local evening strollers and joggers. The long-distance majority are English; the Dyke is also quite big with the Dutch who have, plainly, a national interest in such things.

The path itself, which coincides with just a third of the Dyke, is about 180 miles long: most people walk it from south to north – in about a fortnight if it's mainly for the exercise, or three weeks if any investigation of the *meaning* of the area is to be made. There are a fair number of masochistic Chepstow-to-Prestatyn streakers who have little apparent interest in their surroundings: 'Llangollen?' queried one, 'You don't want to go down there, mate, it's off the route.' And there was a young T.A. type who was running it in military gear, his head plugged into a walkman – no skylarks for him. The walking record must go to the Swansea-based sculptor, Philip Chatfield, who does it ritually once a year in four days, Llangollen first stop, walking for as long as it's light and sleeping wherever he drops at nightfall . . . although Phil, to be fair, is one flash o'blue who *does* know his border. A different kind of challenge was being met by an American couple walking the path with their ten-month-old baby.

I chose to walk it from north to south, not because I'd therefore be 'walking down hill', as a sage in the pub had it, but because, being a denizen of south Wales, there'd be the carrot of 'walking home'. Two slight disadvantages are that none of the travel guidebooks covers the path in a north-south direction, and you have to face the toughest stretch of the walk, the Clwydians, in your first couple of days. The path is now well signposted, and there are not likely to be the navigational problems that were common in the early '70s. Good maps are nevertheless a must, both to get a sense of context and to cope with those few places where cantankerous farmers have fiddled with the signs to confuse walkers. It is sufficiently well-trodden these days to be frequently visible, the very grass, in lusher pastures, brushed in a south-north direction; pioneers of the path used to run a high-summer gauntlet of nettles, brambles and thistles in some places, but there are fewer such troubles now.

Borders, frontiers, shadow lines of one kind or another are a familiar and sometimes painful condition of Welsh life. But a walk down the Dyke concentrates the mind on what has made us one, a nation, in spite of our notorious internal dissensions; it invites us to recognise, in Waldo Williams' words, that we have 'un gwraidd dan y canghennau', one root beneath our many branchings. It reminds us too that less than a century after Offa had thrown up his vast earthwork – an engineering project to dwarf all others in eighth-century Europe – his almighty kingdom of Mercia had been annihilated by a combination of West Saxon and Danish invaders; we compatriots, however, are still here, if only just, twelve hundred years later.

'And the Dregs are Mine'

'And the Dregs are Mine . . .'

And they sold the fern and flower
And the groves of pine
For a hovel and a tankard,
And the dregs are mine.

Idris Davies, *Gwalia Deserta*

What's in a name? More than a whisper, sometimes, of cultural history
. . . Meet the family, circa 1900: Meurig, Dilys, Eluned, Eira. Meet the
family again, thirty-odd years later: Ian, Roger, Noel, Rowland. In just
a few decades there has been a convulsive cultural reorientation, not
untypical in the experience of thousands of contemporary Welsh
families, which echoes down, inevitably, to today's Tracys, Darrens,
Lees (and Nigels).

A family myth pinpoints the moment when my people, like many
others at the time, re-oriented themselves away from Cymru and
towards England. The day is remembered when my great-grandfather
William James, who had uprooted himself from a scratch-penny
existence in Llangadog to become a white-bread bourgeois in Abertawe,
came back from the office to his urban *plas* in Ffynone, where a
servant was called if the fire wanted coal, and informed his children
that henceforth he wanted to hear not a word of Welsh on their infant
lips. English, as his entrepreneurial triumphs had so amply demonstrated,
was the language of advancement; Welsh belonged, if it had a place at
all, in those sheep-bitten hills of Carmarthenshire that they were all
well out of – and possibly the chapel, which they had already
abandoned for the church. Their lives would be lived in English alone;
in that instant Abertawe had become Swansea.

Another great-grandfather, John Davies of Waunarlwydd, was also
born to edge his way eastward, on a spectacular trajectory that could
have been designed for him by a Hollywood scriptwriter. From a
working-class home and his start in life as a furnaceman in the works
at Gowerton, he 'rose through the ranks' to become a knighted

magnate of the steel industry. On the day of his funeral, 20,000 Welsh
steelworkers downed tools and stood respectfully in five minutes' cap-
doffed silence. He had been pleased, and surely astonished if he
paused to think about it, to send his four children to English public
schools and to enjoy all the exotic fruits that his resoundingly
successful infiltration of the English establishment had pushed his
way. He and his brood embraced anglicisation and its trappings with
the amnesiac avidity of the *nouveaux riches*. I don't suppose there was
much *bara lawr* consumed in Sir John's country mansion in
Monmouthshire.

In such ways the white dragon worked its magic, so that throughout
the twentieth century the antennae of most of my family were angled
resolutely towards the Mendips; some, indeed, went to live in or
beyond the Mendips, becoming at last entirely English in speech,
habits of mind, identification, 'Welsh' only in the whimsical way that
some American people, as down-home as apple pie, will tell you that
they are 'English' or 'Scottish' or 'German'. But you don't have to set
a foot over Offa's Dyke to be or become English, as many a Cyncoed
or Langland voice attests, and with my parents' generation the family
reached its anglicised apotheosis. So apparently complete was the
clan's alienation from its *cenedl* that I, in all seriousness, could slip to
my English schoolfriends the naughty intelligence that *diolch yn fawr*
was Welsh for 'fuck off'.

And yet, in spite of ourselves, the red dragon was not completely
vanquished. There were glimmerings in all that anglo fog that could
flare into light; tenuous fingerholds that could strengthen into a grasp.
Throughout childhood and well into manhood, to my great good
fortune, my grandmother Dilys, and her sisters, Eluned and Eira, they
who had been forbidden the language by their cultural fugitive father,
were a vibrant part of family life. Being dutiful daughters, they had
obeyed their father's injunction to abstain from the language, but they
had remained on much more than nodding terms with it, and it was
largely thanks to them that there were many Welsh words in the air
about us – *dŵr* and *bara* (the basic necessities), *mochyn* and *taro* (we'd
gone back to the land by then), *twp*, *dinewid*, *bendigedig* and the
magical coupling *nos da* to which the old ones would treat us as they
tucked us in and turned out the light. Welsh cakes, *cawl* and sewin they
fed us, along with groaning platefuls of gossip about the comings and
goings of distant cousins in what I was later to identify as *y fro*

Gymraeg. And being farmers, albeit south Gower farmers, there was no escaping a sense of context. It was during the 1950s that the apparently charmed bucolic Gower of Phil Tanner and Cyril Gwynn slipped quietly out of sight for ever. Its brittle, fading personality was probably less discernible to us kids than the greater pungency – in ploughing matches, agricultural shows, the weekly marts at Gowerton – of the Welsh language. Welsh was inescapably a presence on such occasions, although we understood hardly a word of it, and felt ourselves to be detached from those who spoke it. They were all 'very Welshy', so Welshy, sometimes, that they could hardly speak English. We felt sorry for them, and tittered behind our hands, at the sale dinner, when the farmer's wife, doling out the ham, asked us to pass our *plâts* – what a funny language that had such an hilarious way of saying 'plate'.

It took the English, I now see, to make a Welshman of me. When I was ten my parents, to whom forgiveness but no thanks, sent me away to an English boarding school. There I was informed that Wales was a land of nothing but pits and tips; the Welsh were primitive and lived in caves; the Welsh had no televisions. Any trace of a Welsh accent, in the quite large number of Welsh boys sentenced to what seemed like life in that totalitarian dump, was singled out for pillory and extirpation. On my release in 'the summer of love', 1967, I wanted to return to my Welsh cave but, as usual, there were no jobs going, so I ended up as a junior reporter in Leamington Spa where again, in more sophisticated ways, the English continued to insist on my being Welsh. It was something to do with the timbre of my voice, suggested a colleague, and my (then) prodigious liquid lunches, and my curious tendency to rush off home for the funerals of even quite distant relatives – that, they all felt, was very un-English. I was beginning to be persuaded, and started sending poems to Roland Mathias at *The Anglo-Welsh Review*.

The clincher, probably, was the ten months I spent bumming around Europe and North Africa in the early 1970s, trying to understand other people's cultures and histories, and attempting to define my own national identity. Welsh, by now, I felt myself to be, but what had I done to deserve it? I spoke no Welsh, couldn't sing, hated rugby, and knew next to nothing of the matter of Wales. All I had to go on was a tellurian attraction to a few hills and beaches, and years of family tittle-tattle about long-gone people and remembered places, most of which I had been relieved to let wash way over my head. What *was* Wales? Who were the Welsh? What manner of a Welsh question mark was I? It was time to start paying off a few debts.

As a so-called mature student at the 'University of Excess', as the tabloids used to call my troubled East Anglian *alma mater*, I began to inhabit Wales more purposefully and intensely than I had ever done when I was still living at home, setting myself an unofficial programme of study in Welsh literature, history and contemporary culture, occasionally startling my teachers in the literature department with lengthy disquisitions on the poetry of Dafydd ap Gwilym, of whom no one had ever heard. Tony Conran's translations, Gwyn Williams and *Planet* were my bedside, breakfast table and bar-top reading.

By 1976 I felt I'd earned a return, so I came back, to a Nissen hut in a corner of what had been the family farm, and got down to work on the language itself. A ten-week Wlpan course, under the congenial direction of two heroes of the language, Robat Powel and Heini Gruffudd, opened the door to the wonderful world of *Cymraeg byw*, or *hanner byw* in my case, for I continue to be, years later, a fumbling learner, my conversation crude, grotesquely ungrammatical and mismutated. If I am lodged still on the anglo side of the linguistic divide, I have enough of a latchhold to keep the door at least ajar – and life, for both man and writer, has been transformed. While I resist the finger-wagging admonition of R.S. Thomas and others that without the language you are not Welsh at all (even the Americans, according to him, are 'really English'), there is no doubt in my mind that to be able to speak it, even as mumblingly as I do, makes one an immeasurably more fulfilled Welsh person; it also helps strengthen the culture as a whole, particularly if I can encourage my two bilingual daughters in their use of Welsh, for it seems to me clear that if the language dies away from us, we will fizzle as ineluctably into England as Cornwall has.

Attempting to square my debt to Wales enabled me to find my feet as a writer on my patch of home ground, my *milltir sgwâr*, my *bro*; it enabled me, indeed, to *read* my *bro*, and potentially to read the whole of Wales, in a way which had not been possible before. Take, for instance, the name of a field on a neighbouring farm, *Pwll-y-bloggi*, one of the few Welsh place-names in the parish. It means, I was able to discover, 'resort of the wolf dog', and would seem to record a battle against the Normans on April 15, 1136 after which packs of wolves descended from the mountains to devour the bodies of the 516 men killed in the conflict. Then there was the name of our own farm, Kilvrough. My parents used to joke that it meant 'the abode of swine', which I took to be a groundless fancy until my smattering of Welsh enabled me to take the etymology a step further: if, as Harri Webb once told me, 'Kilvrough' was an anglicisation, might not the original Welsh have been *cil-yr-hwch* (retreat of the sow)? And had I not read somewhere that Llywelyn Fawr had been known hereabouts as *'yr hwch'* for the swinish ferocity with which he and his warriors would rout up everything that stood in their path? Imagine my excitement at discovering that the strange name 'Kilvrough' could possibly embody a momentous, 800-year-old visitation. Thanks to the sensitising influence of Welsh, I began to open up, absurdly late in life, to all kinds of 'Welsh matter' that should be as fundamental a part of every Welsh citizen's hoard of knowledge as the understanding that fire is hot and ice is cold. The illuminating meanings of 'Welsh' and *'Cymry'*, for instance, which Welsh speakers absorb with their mothers' milk, were unknown to me until *yr hen iaith* broke the news.

Any language, of course, presents its own set both of advantages and hindrances to its users. English, or our particular versions of it, can still be pressed singingly into Welsh service, but it is in several obvious respects, particularly in its official, 'received pronunciation' guise, an oppressor language: as an imperialist coloniser (of which Wales was an early victim); as a money-made language instinct with the practices and values of mercantile capitalism (as Welsh may be considered a language founded on agriculture); as the language used most actively to pursue the proliferation of weapons of mass destruction. When the Scottish poet Hugh MacDiarmid was asked to explain why he chose to write in Lallans rather than 'straight' English, he gave as a reason his belief that all the important words in English – 'honour', 'integrity', 'valour', 'love' – had been shot to pieces in the First World War. The 'MacDiarmid consideration' continues to be poignantly applicable, when we have had recently a government which can describe as simply 'disagreeable' or 'regrettable' the deaths, through a possible nuclear war, of millions of people. In such circumstances 'Anglo-Welsh' writers might look with envy to their Welsh-speaking brothers and sisters or their Goidelic cousins: when named in Lallans or Gaelic or Welsh, significant values and powerful

emotions seem much less inclined to raise a snigger and do a quick
bunk. Fortunate indeed is the *bardd* who has at his or her disposal a
language *apparently* uncompromised by the jingoistic sloganising and
huge public deceit to which English, in common with French, German,
Russian and certain other 'big' languages, has been forced in recent
times.

Now, although the words that constitute a poem are to a large extent
'found' or 'given', yet always subtly shifting and mutating, the
language itself – English, Welsh, Spanish, Japanese words in
relationship with each other – has to be re-made with each new poem;
it's here, in the creation of this relationship, that the transformative
possibilities of the poet's craft reside, and the tired old words are
re-invested with power. If those words, for many of us, are bound to be
English, that does not mean that we have to turn our backs on Welsh
and the heritage that goes with it. Hurrah for Tony Conran when he
writes in the preface to *Welsh Verse*:

> *Our attitude to the Welsh language should be predatory. We should
> take from it everything we can get, and two things in particular: a
> knowledge of the chosen ways that have led to what we call our
> Welshness; and a weapon, the jawbone of an ass, against our
> Englishness.*

The Welsh poet's age-old social contract; praise and dispraise; a
relishing in language, in words as music; the poet as maker, the
fascination with form, the imaginative *transformation* of 'reality';
triads, gnomes, *tribannau*, *englynion*; a sense of audience,
responsibility to community, liberation from the tiny intensities of the
little world of one . . . Such is the wealth which is ours to plunder; the
strange thing is that so far we have been little tempted by it, most of us
preferring to slot our Welsh being into English literary shapes and
tones.

Each new generation of Welsh writers in English has to find its own
starting point for a journey which seems to get longer and harder each
time round. Roland Mathias, commenting in 1984 on the offerings of a
younger generation, seemed to doubt that many of them even had their
boots on, and saw little hope for the future of writing in English that
may deserve to be called Welsh. My own prodding along the way was
occasioned, no doubt, by the glimpses I had had in my family's

experience of the absolute nullification of Wales. I had enough of Wales under my skin, fortunately, to want to say 'no' to that chilling possibility. The alienation from Wales in my own upbringing, which ultimately I came to reject, is to be witnessed, of course, across all classes and in most parts of the country. There are the rugby fetishists for whom Wales exists only on the rugby field; the cooers over royalty; those who see Wales only in terms of her beautiful 'scenery'; Valleys sentimentalists who never visit the Valleys; crack-voiced choristers in Labour clubs who get pissed enough now and then to croak out a garbled version of 'Calon Lân' (no, I don't know the words either); stirling socialists of the Kinnock kind who'll support any national liberation cause as long as it's thousands of miles away; and yes, indeed, those who think Wales is *only* its language, who would divorce the language from the country's history, and scramble to get their kids educated in it for no reason other than monetary or social advancement.

I do not subscribe to the view propagated by Emyr Humphreys that the sole function of the English-language writer in Wales it to protect and succour the Welsh language. If a writer's talents exist *solely* to support the language, or CND or Friends of the Earth or Calvinistic Methodism or whatever, then too much, which is to say the rest of life on this planet, is excluded, and the writing is born hopelessly misshapen, thinly shrieking slogans. I do believe, though, that writers in this country should discover all they can about the specifically Welsh context in which they operate: for if they ignore it they will, at best, position themselves on the national periphery, and their writings will remain of marginal interest; at worst, they will be actively conniving in the death of a culture.

Getting Old for Two[1]

He died on December 11, 1971, just six months after his forty-eighth birthday. I, the eldest of his three children, was twenty-two. It's been a date to remember, but a short while ago another date crept up on me out of time's ticking shadows, the moment at which, turning forty-eight and a half, I found myself overtaking my father. If my luck holds for ten or twenty years more, I could be the grey and balding paterfamilias that my youthful old man never lived to become.

The ancient Celts believed that no one truly died; you simply shuffled off into the Celtic underworld, and could return from time to time to mingle with the living. And that's how it seems in our dreams sometimes, when the dead come back and wander round inside our heads, insisting by sheer force of presence, and the persuasiveness of a conman, that surely there's been some absurd mistake, they never died, how could anyone have imagined such a thing? For years after his death my dad would pay nocturnal visits, urging on me all manner of resurrectionist scams, until, seeing through his resourceful yarns, I'd have to take him regretfully by the arm and say 'Dad, mun, you're dead, now lie back down, and leave me alone'. Then I'd wake up, and, yes, Dad would be dead.

But with an afterlife in the memories of the living, the dead rarely leave us alone for long, and as far as most of mine are concerned, they've got a key to the house and can wander back in whenever they want. These encounters can take place in various forms – dreams, recollections, family chats or, in Dad's case, a poem. He was a great horseman, so what better, I thought, than to couch the moment of my overtaking him in terms of a horse race, with him on my mother's black-maned mare and me astride a certain grand if mildly delinquent bay. We were never great talkers, my Dad and me, but we managed to communicate least dysfunctionally, I suppose, when we were out together on horseback. And there were some things now, approaching forty-eight and a half, that I wanted to talk to him about – not least my

---

[1] Broadcast on John Peel's *Home Truths*, BBC Radio 4, October 28, 2000.

fears that somehow I'd fail to overtake him, and my horse would take a fatal stumble at the off.

I wanted this race to be not so much a reckoning as a reconciliation, a working through and settling of differences – a celebration, finally, in spite of all that had divided us as I floundered towards manhood through my adolescent, and what would be his last, years. There had indeed been furlongs between us. What about, Dad, the anglicising public school so-called education that brought a happy childhood to such a ragged end, and did its best to turn a boyish Taff into an English toff? What about the foxhunting? What about that penchant for the Tory-voting hang-'n'-flog-em shires? Against his Brylcreemed mohawk I had raised a revenge of tresses sufficient to thatch an army of Guevaras. Against the alleged music of Sir Harry Lauder I had turned, full-volume, the orgasmitudes of Hendrix. I didn't want to be a farmer, Dad.

Then, neck and neck, through the months of his heart's perplexed liberation after the release – for them both – of my parents' divorce, we found mutual forgiveness for perceived shortcomings, found in each other the boy and the man. Able at last to see our matters of division from the other's point of view, we could raise our glasses – his a Scotch, mine a Guinness – to the future.

Death, though, had another plan. To the black wart on his wrist that was not a wart, my father took an agricultural knife, sporing cancer before long through the whole of his body. He was dead within months. 'So young,' said mourner after head-shaking mourner. It was, I remember feeling, daylight, scorched-earth robbery.

But back to the race, and after twenty-seven years of catching up, the plashy nostrils of my lathered mount are panting down my father's skeletal neck, and he'll be lost any second in flying hoof-scoops of earth and grass – unless, unless, yes, c'mon, Dad, gimme your hand, I gotcha: leap! Leap up behind me! And we're riding on together in galloping tandem, my Dad forever aged forty-eight and a half, and me, perhaps – we'll see – getting old for the pair of us.

Hymns and Bloody Arias[1]

'You call yourself a Welshman – and you're not interested in rugby?' The Englishman on the Swansea-bound Intercity couldn't believe his ears: 'Can you sing?' I had to admit shortcomings in that department too. 'But,' I ventured, 'I drank a Britvic with Gwynfor Evans once, and I've a friend who plays the harp.'

He was not impressed. 'A Welshman who doesn't like rugby,' he mused, tutting at the damp fields of Wiltshire. 'Isn't that a contradiction in terms?'

Such also is the view of certain compatriots. More common, however, is a sense of sheer disbelief that any supposed Taff, no matter how inadequate in other respects, could be so fumblingly bereft of knowledge of, or care for, a sport which fills the gap left vacant by religion in many a Welshman's life. My declared indifference has been labelled a pose, a cunning affectation designed to hide some deep wound to the spirit occasioned by too many seasons of lost international games.

That my ignorance is the genuine article, found only in women and teepee dwellers, was proved some years ago in all its shocking blatancy at a literary wine-tippling in Cardiff. Glass to glass with a bloke I didn't know, in a huddle of otherwise familiar faces, I chirpily asked the stranger what his name was. Chattering jaws dropped and eyebrows departed for the ceiling: you could have heard a dustmite fart. 'Well,' said the stranger, doing his best to warm to what he doubtless construed as a weak stab at drollery on my part, 'I haven't been *feeling* quite myself today, and evidently I'm not *looking* myself either.' The company leapt at this invitation to laughter as if they'd been starved of merriment for most of their adult lives. Then, with a forgiving grin, the stranger introduced himself and we shook hands. His name, though, meant as little to me as mine to him, and when, by way of a conversational ice-breaker, I asked him where he was from and what he did, the aghast intake of breath from everyone else was of a violence that threatened to bring the ceiling and walls down on top of us. Now, spectacularly, I

[1] First published in *Radical Wales* 28, Winter 1990.

had demonstrated beyond doubt the extent of my ignorance – for this, hissed a friend, this was none other than Dai Jones, the great inside-out or upside-down or some such thing. That I, in all wide-eyed honesty, had never heard of this hero of the fields of praise rendered me, truly, a phenomenon. If Wales had had a national zoo, I'd have been in it.

How to explain this bizarre antipathy? Some have suggested a defect in the genes, and other predictable jokers, favouring nurture over nature, have put it down to a defect in the jeans.

My school, I'm sure, has much to answer for. As a tubby eight or nine year old I enjoyed a lollop on the soccer field: sport seemed to be fun, and I remember looking forward to the muddy rough'n'tumble of rugby in the 'big' school to come. But at that big school, which provided me with a handy education in totalitarianism if little else, I was disabused of my funster illusions. Gazing dreamily across the greensward during a midfield lecture on my first afternoon of rugby, I felt a sudden pain commensurate with the top of my head caving in: a ball had been fired at me from point blank range by an instructor frothing with rage at my inattention. I would never be any good at rugby or anything else if I didn't concentrate – slap! – concentrate – slap! – CONCENTRATE! But it wasn't wise, I soon learned, to be too good at rugby because you might risk ending up in the first fifteen whose lot it was, if they persisted in losing, to be beaten by the Head until they started to win. Nor, on the other hand, was it sensible to be hopeless at the game: teachers would make a spectacle of you by rubbing your face in the midfield mire before sending you on your way with a boot up the arse; sometimes they'd make you play a whole game without shorts. Spectating too was not without its dangers: beatings and punitive long-distance runs would be doled out by the dozen to those whose cheering lacked conviction. Rugby soared to the top of my list of pet hates nurtured within the school walls, closely followed by cabbage, poetry and music.

But that, people would later argue, that was school rugby. Real rugby's not like that at all. They would regale me with images of epic beer-swilling, Niagaras of urine tumbling majestically down the terraces, hymns and arias, streakers and tries. But always I had something better to do, like defrosting the fridge or exercising the goldfish. I grew indeed to savour my lonely notoriety as the only living Welshman never to have witnessed an International.

'But how,' said a kinsman in exasperation, as he dangled once again a Ticket before me, 'how can you know it's all so banal if you've never even been to a decent match?' He had a philosophical point. So, to prove my prejudices correct and to silence the nagging for good, I took the wretched Ticket and negotiated the loan of a red and white bobble hat for my first International – which I assured them all would be my last.

So we boarded a train one Saturday morning for Cardiff – a banker, a Nonconformist minister, a policeman and their hairy sidekick, the Reluctant Fan. The train was crowded but subdued, mostly, I'd guess, because of hangovers; then we pulled into Bridgend and hundreds more bobble hats sardined aboard, the beer started to flow and – 'Oggy! Oggy! Oggy!' – the aforementioned fun began. I wasn't, it seemed, the only Welshman who couldn't sing.

There was only one destination for the tags and empty cans – out the window and onto the line. Rugby fans, it appeared, were not environmentalists. I wondered too, from the lyrics of some of the songs, if they were altogether sound in their attitude towards women. But one remark – 'Watch your fuckin' language, boys, there's cunt about!' – seemed to suggest that even here, in a clumsy kind of way, New Man, freshly concerned for the tender sensibilities of the second sex, was struggling to be born. As it happened, he need not have alarmed himself: the suspected female presence turned out to be a kilted Scotsman.

There was only one thing on Cardiff's mind that Saturday lunchtime: 'WA-les! WA-les! WA-les!' The streets were a swirling mass of chanting fans, sellers of scarves, hawkers of saltires and dragons; there were jazz bands and silver bands and impromptu choirs of men in trilbies and caps. The city had atmosphere, no doubt of that. It also had far more drinkers than the pubs could handle, but I knew of a gay pub where Macho Rugby Man was less likely to venture; after not too long a wait at the bar we were able to struggle back out, with two pints apiece, to the noisily confident, good-humoured street.

'Where were this lot on March the First, 1979?' I asked my companions; I seemed to have said something faintly embarrassing. 'If we could drum up this kind of *hwyl* for Cymru on the other 364 days of the year we'd be getting somewhere.' It was an idea that had little evident appeal to our policeman whose truncheon hand rushed a nervous gulp of Brains to his lips.

We got to the ground with half an hour to spare, and wormed our way through grey tunnels and, for all I knew, Niagaras of wee, to take our place among the lurching, swaying thousands on the terraces. All, so far, had been much as I had anticipated. But then things turned interestingly strange. My first glimpse, over the massed heads, of that famous rectangle of brilliant green, was a heady delight. The next surprise was how the hair stood to attention on the back of my neck, and all the rivers of Wales coursed in one electric moment down the length of my spine as the boys in red ran out onto the pitch. The concentration of emotion, as 'Hen Wlad Fy Nhadau' rose up from the stands, was surely enough in itself to defeat the poor boys in blue shirts, without so much as a boot being raised to kick a ball. They, the unfortunates, lacking an anthem of their own, had to put up with 'God Save the Queen' – which was suitably hissed and booed by nearly everyone, the Scots included.

I was hooked. Mine too was the horror as Scotland scored within the first minute of the game. Things went on looking bad for us until well into the second half when, quite unexpectedly, the score began to tilt in our favour. When the points were scored that lifted Wales into the lead, hundreds of spectators rushed onto the pitch. I liked this, it was exciting – but it was generally disapproved of by the rest of the crowd who yelled for the invaders to get off. Whenever Wales looked close to scoring, the crowd set up an expectant sort of booming sound, deep and rhythmic, like a Welsh interpretation of the earthy and bloody Spanish *duende*.

Then the whistle blew and the game was Cymru's. Thousands, including our Nonconformist minister, closer to ecstasy now than ever he would be in heaven, poured onto the pitch. When we caught up with him later he was clutching a stolen fistful of the hallowed turf which, he explained, he was taking back to the manse to plant in his lawn. The policeman turned a sympathetic blind eye.

Back in a Swansea pub there was much discussion of the match, which most of those present had watched on mere television. The technicalities of the debate were beyond me, but occasionally I'd feel qualified to risk correcting an erroneous second-hand impression – because, as I said, 'I was there.' Now where had I heard those words before?

'I think we've made some progress,' said the policeman, stuffing another pint into my fist. 'We'll make a normal Welshman of you yet. D'you want a ticket for the next one?'

I told him not to rush me; I'd have to think about it. It would depend on whether or not the fridge needed defrosting.

The Scars of Imagination

The Scars of Imagination:
A Profile of John Cale[1]

'I didn't start singing or playing till I was fifteen and heard the Velvet Underground,' said Jonathan Richman. 'They made an atmosphere and I knew then that I could make one too!' He got sanction: Richman signed with Warner Bros., which had hired John Cale, late of the Velvet Underground, as a staff producer, and it was Cale who was assigned to produce Jonathan Richman – Adam went into the studio with God.

Greil Marcus, *Lipstick Traces: A Secret History of the Twentieth Century* (1989)

When, if ever, the stardust settles and the obscuring static of Radio Gaga subsides sufficiently for us to win a clear view of who rock music's genuine innovators have been, John Cale, the son of a miner and a schoolteacher from Garnant near Swansea, will deserve a high place in the top twenty of pop's frontier busters – along with people such as Elvis Presley, Phil Spector, Brian Wilson, Bob Dylan, Captain Beefheart and the Sex Pistols.

In a field where success is measured largely in terms of megabuck sales and adulation's decibels, John Cale, who has never struck chart gold, is normally accounted an honourable failure, forever banished, therefore, from the popular airwaves. As one critic has observed of Cale's long and erratic solo career, 'he has not simply avoided success but tried to throttle it with both hands.' 'Someone is always telling me "You're just a loser",' sings the man himself, 'But I don't pay them too much attention.' He simply gets on with making music whose range and unpredictability is perhaps too awkwardly individual for contentedly provincial home tastes – the country's premier rock venues are rarely full when he does a concert in Wales. John Cale is indisputably, and enduringly, Wales's one world-class rock innovator

---

[1] The title of this essay is taken from 'Thoughtless Kind' on John Cale's album *Music for a New Society*. A shorter version of this essay appeared in *Planet* 79 (1991).

and probably the greatest Welsh musician, across all genres, of the twentieth century, yet he's anything but a familiar name in households more comfortable with the offerings of Tom Jones or Bonnie 'Total Eclipse of the Heart' Tyler. The 'children' of Cale, internationally renowned bands such as the Stereophonics, the Manic Street Preachers and Catatonia, with whom Cale has made a film, *Beautiful Mistake* (2000), abound and multiply, but Cale's own products are hard to find outside the big record shops of Cardiff.

True, Cale has had only a visitor's relationship with Wales since leaving for London in 1960 as a prelude to his long-desired escape to the States, where he has lived most of the time ever since. But unlike certain blown-aways who scurry to drown their identities as soon as they cross the border, Cale has disdained the cultural cleansing which afflicts many an ambitious Taff. Wales has been a natural, vital ingredient in both his life and art. He may have absented himself physically from the small-town constraints of his youth, which drove him to a nervous breakdown and threatened to stifle his creativity, but in the imagination *Cymru* is a country he can never leave.

For newcomers to Cale country, the best introductions to the work and the life are, respectively, his anthology *Fragments of a Rainy Season* (1992) and his autobiography *What's Welsh for Zen* (1999). This, the most exuberantly unconventional book I have seen for years, is a generous, weighty fistful of a volume with a slightly spongy, brown cardboard cover, and 272 individually designed pages, employing photographs, drawings, cartoons, superimpositions, collages, and all manner of typographical dramas to conjure additional atmosphere and meaning.

The honest, psychologically perceptive and sometimes harshly self-critical tenor of this absorbing self-portrait is signalled by an unflattering cover photograph of the middle-aged rock-legend clutching his crumple-nosed face in what might be grief or dismay, an anticipation perhaps of one of the moods he articulates within: 'There was always this competition to see how low you could go and how fast you could rise. I was competing with myself. I'm getting sadder and sadder thinking about my lack of self-knowledge as I write this book. I'm distraught about my lack of any sense of my own worth, and about my visions of myself.'

Discipline and chaos have been the energising and sometimes dementing poles of his life. They have both informed the creative tensions of his art, and have threatened at times – as the prohibitive influences of his background have collided with the anarchy of those tricksy 'liberators' alcohol, cocaine and heroin – to run his life off the rails. His sense of discipline was instilled in a home which he admits could have been lifted straight from the pages of Richard Llewellyn's *How Green Was My Valley* – not so much by school and church as by his mother, a teacher known for her progressive approach to education who nevertheless ruled the roost with a sharp tongue and regular beatings administered, on her instruction, by the boy's collier father. William Arthur George Cale is portrayed as a somewhat browbeaten, taciturn figure who was so painfully 'absent' from Cale's upbringing that 'in adolescence . . . I had to be my own father'.

An only child, he was born on 5 December, 1942 into what used to be thought of a stereotypically Welsh world – coal-mining, socialist, Welsh-speaking and musical. The Cales' detached stone-built house in Cwmamman Road marked them out as a comparatively prosperous family, with the church, rather than the chapel, as their place of worship. Both father and son were members of Christchurch choir, and John performed impressively at an early age on the church organ.

Mam wanted her boy to go in for medicine or the law, and had toyed with sending him to a public school. She insisted, no matter what he pursued, on the highest standards, signing him up for classical piano lessons when he was seven, the age at which, coincidentally, he began to learn English (although his father was monoglot English, Welsh was the language of his upbringing). A reluctant pupil initially, Cale quickly found that music solved certain problems of identity and purpose. 'I realised that playing music gave me a stronger sense of who I was . . . I was so inspired and comfortable when [my mother] was there that I began to see her presence as crucial. Thus was born a lifelong reliance upon a collaborator to complete not only the work but *me*.' His mother was his first and, with the possible exceptions of Lou Reed and Andy Warhol, most significant collaborator.

He had two musically distinguished collier uncles on his mother's side – Wili Davies who played with the BBC Welsh Orchestra and toured the Valleys with the Swansea-based Morgan Lloyd Orchestra, and Davey Davies, whose compositions include well-known hymn tunes. Davey Davies was married to Mai Jones, a radio producer and the composer of the nostalgic tear-jerker 'We'll Keep a Welcome in the Hillsides', whose lachrymose jollities are a continent away from the high-tension paranoia of most of her nephew's musical offerings. It was through Davey and Mai that John, considered a prodigy, found himself playing piano pieces on BBC radio at the age of eight. The autobiography offers a pathetic vignette of this couple in alcoholic shock after being thrown ruthlessly on the scrapheap by the BBC. Mai soon died, but Davey lingered on, 'a perpetually sozzled, whining old man' who drove Cale's house-proud mother to such infuriated despair that the boy found himself, in her defence but to his immediate regret, boxing his uncle's ears: 'My favourite person in the whole world! The one I could discuss any and all music with. The one who "understood" me. A lush with a giant Welsh heart and an even bigger denial problem. He scrambled up the stairs, whimpering like a persecuted dog.' Cale felt like running away or committing suicide. Falling out with key collaborators was a tendency which would repeat itself.

Although rock music and the Velvet Underground made Cale famous, he started out as a classicist. The musical trajectory on which Margaret Cale set her son led him to the position of violist, aged thirteen, with the Welsh Youth Orchestra. He progressed, aged seventeen, to Goldsmiths College, London, from which it was expected that he would graduate as a teacher. But, determined to pursue a career in music, he neglected his academic studies. For a youngster making his way in classical music, and oblivious to the fact that the Rolling Stones were belting out the blues in a nearby club, the avant-garde exerted a powerful magnetism. One of Cale's teachers was Cornelius Cardew, who was a champion of John Cage, La Monte Young and other American avant-gardists; Cale was soon taking part in electronic music performances with the English composer Humphrey Searle.

He was not a model student. 'They threw me out because I hadn't fulfilled my intellectual obligations,' he told me when I interviewed him in the 1980s. So, intent on crossing the Atlantic, he contacted John Cage. 'Come rain or come shine I was bent on going to New York,' he said. 'So I wrote to John Cage and asked him if he was interested in having anyone collaborate with him on some music in the summer of 1963, and he wrote and said "Yeah, I'll be at home, if you do get to New York then call me".'

Aaron Copland, who had seen Cale perform in London, secured him a Leonard Bernstein scholarship to study modern composition with the Franco-Greek composer Iannis Xenakis in the Eastman Conservatory at Tanglewood, Massachusetts. The fruits of Cale's attendance at that summer school were 'too destructive' for him to be allowed to perform them. 'Eventually they did let me,' he said. I didn't tell them what I was going to do. There was a table and another pianist. I was working away inside the piano and I just took an axe and – ! – right in the middle of the table. People were running out of there, but I also had the acolytes who came backstage afterwards in tears. I got all the reactions. It was the element of surprise, and I hope I've kept that. It's very important for me to keep leading people up the garden path, and then turn around, BOING!'

By September he was playing with John Cage, in an historic performance of Erik Satie's eighteen-hour piece *Vexations*. He also joined forces with La Monte Young who was at that time writing pieces in which the musician talked to the piano or screamed a potted plant to death. In La Monte Young's minimalist outfits, Dream Syndicate and the Theatre of Eternal Music, Cale needed to be able to play his viola loud, so he filed down its bridge, strung it with guitar strings and amplified it, lending the instrument that unique engine-like drone that distinguished his playing with the Velvet Underground.

At heart a melodist, Cale's interest in the austere, regimented programmes of the avant-garde began to lose ground to a growing curiosity about rock music. In New York he met up with Lou Reed who was churning out bubblegum songs for a 'hit factory' called Pickwick Records. With guitarist Sterling Morrison, Cale and Reed became Pickwick's instantly invented band The Primitives – also known as The Warlocks and The Falling Spikes – and they went out on a wave of hype to play at weekends before screaming kids.

Reed was attracted to Cale because he embodied the European avant-garde, and Cale to Reed because the American was a professional pop musician with the kind of garage-band rock training that the Welsh classicist lacked. But he was dubious about Reed's working with an acoustic guitar, suspecting an inclination towards folk music, 'that Dylan stuff and so on – I was not interested in people writing songs that had nothing but questions in them.' A dose of 'Heroin' and 'Waiting for the Man' changed his mind, and they began a seemingly inseparable creative partnership. Adding drummer Maureen Tucker to their line-up in 1965, they formed the Velvet Underground and became part of Andy Warhol's multi-media arts circus.

This was the era of clean, bright American pop – Joey Dee, Jay and the Americans – and the Velvets wanted no part of it. Their colour was black; they were a counter-culture, looking ten years ahead to the *fleurs du mal* of punk and 'New Wave', although they could not have predicted the extent to which they were destined to be idolised as the cult heroes of that mid '70s anarchic explosion. Whatever had been established as good, hit-making rock'n'roll behaviour, the Velvets, the first alliance between pop music and the avant-garde, did the reverse. Preferring the feedback and fizz of a cheap p.a. to 'professional' sound production, they would often turn their backs on the audience throughout their relentlessly loud and experimental shows. 'Always leave the audience wanting less,' was the band's policy.

Rock had never rolled like this before, nor indeed had it ever attended to the feelings and experiences to which the Velvets gave voice. There were love songs – deceptively pretty at times; but there was much, also, about drugs, paranoia, urban ennui, transvestism and sado-masochism, delivered, without moralising, in a deadpan, witty and demotic spirit. Their East Coast cynicism and speedy amphetamine 'uptightness' were at glaring odds with the 'love everybody' naiveties of the West Coast flower children, for whom 'down' – on dope – was out and away. Californian rock impresario Bill Graham dismissed the Velvets as 'you disgusting germs from New York', and the *Chicago Daily News* described them as 'an assemblage that actually vibrates with menace . . . Let's hope it's killed before it spreads.'

Cale, on keyboards, viola and frenetically inventive bass, appeared on the Velvet's first two milestone albums, *The Velvet Underground and Nico* (1967) and *White Light/White Heat* (1968). Then, difficulties in the always volatile and competitive Cale-Reed relationship resulted in the American edging Cale out of the band, in order to occupy centre stage himself.

Cale was ready, anyway, for a change. 'I got a lot out of the Velvet Underground, but it took me a long time to regain my vitality,' he said in 1989 when he and Reed started working together again for the first time in two decades, on *Songs for Drella*, a requiem for Andy Warhol. 'I was glad to begin something new. It gave me a chance to breathe and exercise some new ideas. My attitude to the Velvet Underground has changed this last year. After working again with Louis, I know how much we can do. After the first day with him, I thought, 'Holy shit! If we only had our heads together in 1969. We'd have covered so much more ground.'

His first new job on leaving the Velvets was producing Nico's

Marble Index and the Stooges' first album. He went on to produce Iggy Pop, Patti Smith, Jonathan Richman, Sham '69, Squeeze and others; but it is chiefly as originator of some of the most varied and arresting music of our time that he deserves attention.

Cale has often seen himself as primarily a European composer, in the tradition of Brahms, Sibelius, Mahler and Vaughan Williams, and said in the 1980s he'd like nothing better than to settle down to write symphonies for the rest of his life, and have nothing further to do with rock'n'roll audiences. However, a remark by the photographer Nat Finkelstein – 'I could never figure out whether John Cale wanted to be Elvis Presley, the Frankenstein monster or young Chopin' – points to the central creative tension, between the rock and 'classical' or art music impulses, which drives the best of his work.

The man's range is remarkable, attesting to a musical grammar and vocabulary which dwarf those of most others in the field. The original melodies and distinctive words of his first album, the country-inflected *Vintage Violence* (1969) contrast strikingly with the minimalist improvisations of *Church of Anthrax* (1971), a largely instrumental sequence which he recorded with Terry Riley. Then, in 1972, came his boldly experimental *The Academy in Peril*, a record of predominantly 'classical' compositions made with the Royal Philharmonic Orchestra. His best work of the 1970s, on *Paris 1919* (1973), *Fear* (1974) and *Slow Dazzle* (1975), is generated from a struggle between powerful lyrical impulses (perilously close to slush on *Helen of Troy* (1975)) and forces within the music which function to subvert and undermine the melody – forces which are dominant in *Sabotage/Live* (1979) and *Honi Soit* (1981). Cale's usual articulacy partly breaks down on these two albums, where he invokes the big guns of thumping bass, sizzling guitar and screamed direct statement to assault his targets. His earnest and sometimes incomprehensible socio-political hectoring may have won him the punk vote, but he is harder and more effectively cutting when he is prettier. The violence that is always present in Cale's work, contained and directed, can spill forth in anarchistic abandon: 'Me and nigger marched, yes,/Me and nigger blasted our way outa here . . . Burn down the buildings, leave just shells.' But what wins through in *Honi Soit* is the lyrical strain. The banal observations of 'Fighter Pilot' – 'You're a hero now/But you're a terrible man' – are surpassed by the subtler demolition of the more melodic 'Dead or Alive':

I was happy to see her in the back of the limousine,
Laughing and crying at everything she'd seen.
Well, enough of that, she should have known better anyway,
When I told her what I'd seen she was so ashamed.

The album's most successful track, 'Riverbank', harks back to Cale's masterpiece of the '70s, the tunefully romantic *Paris 1919*: 'They heard nothing, saw even less/Of the hunger in their souls . . .' This mood of sad, tired, quietly desperate yearning anticipates 1982's bleak and icily beautiful *Music for a New Society*, which represents Cale in the depths of desolation while at the peak of his creative powers. Recorded under intense emotional and artistic pressure, with few interventions from guest musicians, it is a solo album in the fullest sense, yet the experience of listening to these songs about a world on the verge of collapse is not finally a depressing one; we are rescued from despair by the compassion that rings through it, and a defiant, restorative rage.

New Society has proved a near impossible act to surpass, but subsequent albums of new work, including *Caribbean Sunset* (1984), *Artificial Intelligence* (1985) and *Walking on Locusts* (1996), do more than hold their own. The political interest resurfaces, with a somewhat right-wing shading, but it is mediated obliquely, with few bludgeoning statements from the pulpit of rock.

Cale's lyrics, when you can hear them, betoken an engaged literary sensibility, particularly in his numerous sharp character vignettes and the love songs. Orthodox 'moon/June' whimsicalities are absent here; so too is the self-contained narrative. His method is to string together words and images, fragments of a life, and allow them to suggest their own context. From deft throwaway lines such as 'You know more than I know' or 'She makes me so unsure of myself/Standing there and never ever talking sense', to the hissing, deranged jealousy of 'The bugger in the short sleeves fucked my wife/Did it quick and split', we are in a world of wholly plausible human emotions, and implicated as participants, rather than observers, because he denies us the comfortable objectivity of being able to examine the whole picture from a safe distance. His tableaux of pain, isolation and broken promise come at us in bits and pieces, as in life, and he leaves us to battle our own way out of the confusion. Cale's fascination with masks as stage props – helmets, visors, dark glasses – carries through into his songs; his 'I' is seldom straightforwardly autobiographical; he adopts various personae and then 'method acts' them in song, so that the songs develop as experiences in themselves, rather than standing as neat encapsulations of easily isolated events.

His world, at its bleakest, has much in common with the corpsed universe of Samuel Beckett: 'We're already dead but not yet in the ground,' he suggests in 'Fear', an emotion which he cites as 'man's best friend'. Where there's fear, however, there must be life – although that life, according to Cale, is a paranoid, risky affair: 'We can all feel safe like Sharon Tate.' Within this frightened and frightening world, Cale values children, friends and steadfast love, while lamenting the fickleness of affections and the human capacity for self-destruction; carelessness emerges as a major sin.

Murdered children, blown talent, wasted opportunities, powerlessness, broken hearts and damaged minds: the experience of loss, in many forms, is Cale's main theme. Another depredation that is keenly felt is the loss of heritage and a profound sense of homelessness in a world close to apocalypse:

> *And I was thinking about my mother,*
> *I was thinking about what's mine.*
> *I was living like a Hollywood*
> *But I was dying on the vine.*

There's probably no 'going back' by now, no mansion such as that bought by Tom Jones in the Vale of Glamorgan. New York has held him for longer than Wales, and he seems as settled there as it is possible for a man of his restless imagination to feel 'settled'. Another difficult collaborative field has been that of sex, love and his three failed marriages. Much of the trouble, he suggests in *What's Welsh for Zen*, goes back to childhood. That he was touched up as a boy by two men in the village, including the church organist, seems much less disturbing than the lack of a relationship with his father, and his mother's 'taking away' of his 'inner life'. Near the end of the book there's a moving passage in which he describes watching a broadcast from the White House of three distinguished poets performing their work. He phones his daughter, Eden Myfanwy (b. 1985), whose absence from his daily life brings him 'the sharpest pain I have experienced in many years'. He wants her to share his sense of wonder at the language of these poets:

*When I hung up and turned to the screen the tears erupted. It was
the closest I had got to enjoying the beauty of the language I had
learned at my mother's side again. It was a realisation of how much
beauty I had been made aware of by her presence in the learning
process. I still hear the darkness echo in our house in Garnant. It
comes to visit when I see my future darkly. The sounds have a
longing in their worry.*

Wales, in spite of Cale's desperate flight from its constrictions in his
youth, has always been important to him, and there is no doubt that
Americans who have known him, surveying his Welsh background
with baffled awe, see Cale's Welshness as the foundation of his
creativity. Lou Reed has been quoted as saying that: 'I only hope that
one day John will be recognised as the Beethoven or something of his
day. He knows so much about music, he's such a great musician. He's
completely mad – but that's because he's Welsh.' And Cale's first wife,
Betsey Johnson, seems to identify, a little bizarrely, Cymric strangeness
(in tandem with cough mixture!) as the force behind his talent:

*John used to tell me about Wales and growing up. His parents kept
him on that Dr Brown's mixture. It was heavily laced with codeine,
and he had some kind of bronchial problem – you can imagine in
that climate – till he was like eight or ten, so he was on really heavy
doses. It's just really codeined out. So he was high the whole time as
a kid. And then being high in Wales, which is just weirdness in the
air. The outhouse was way in the backyard, icy, icy cold. You had to
go out to go to the bathroom. His father chopped coal. He had no
refrigeration. It wasn't like they were a poor family isolated from
middle-class people. The whole situation there was poor. Very close
but very weird.*

These rather droll variations on the Celtic twilight theme nevertheless
point towards the kind of expatriate who, far from immersing his
identity in the new culture, has kept his Welshness alive and active.
From the beginning of his solo career Wales has featured naturally in
his songs. His speaking and singing voice could not be other than
Welsh; a journey begun in Memphis can terminate, unfashionably, in
sight of Mumbles; Bangor, Swansea, Ammanford, Garnant are there,
and he has voiced a desire to record in Welsh at some time in the

future. 'I have strong feelings about the survival of the Welsh language,' he told me. 'It was the language of my home in Garnant, and I didn't learn English until I went to school. It's a beautiful language, and I hope that there's enough resistance in the people to maintain it. I think there is.'

Another Welsh input has been the influence of Dylan Thomas. Echoes of Dylan flicker through Cale's songs: 'the long-legged bait' glides by in one, and 'Come on honey, shipwreck in my heart' turns up elsewhere. Then there's his major lyrical statement, 'A Child's Christmas in Wales' on *Paris 1919* in which the piling on of images seems to owe much to the early French Surrealists as tinkered with by Dylan. But Cale abandoned plans for the opera on Dylan's life that he was once considering: 'The man was a prick'.

One Dylan project that came to fruition in 1989 was the sequence of settings of four Dylan Thomas poems on *Words for the Dying*, which he recorded with the Orchestra of Symphonic and Popular Music of Gosteleradio (USSR) and the choir of Llandaff Cathedral Choir School, Cardiff. It had been in gestation since 1982. 'The reason it took so long,' he explained at the time, 'is that I had to find music which was unobtrusive to the words. I wasn't thinking of writing anything epic. I wanted the music to be understated.' Cale the romantic European composer comes to the fore here, with a set of appealingly melodic treatments which pack a considerable emotional punch at times. His rendition of 'Do Not Go Gentle', the villanelle about Dylan's dying father, seems at first bizarrely jaunty, but its gaiety is tempered at last by a crescendo of chords and an angry great clash of percussion. One's only complaint is that Cale, working on these settings at the time of Mrs Thatcher's bloody electioneering in the South Atlantic, chose to entitle them 'The Falklands Suite', and clumsily invested some of the poetry with Falklands reverberations, a trespass thankfully not reiterated in his reprise of the poems on *Fragments of a Rainy Season*: to sign up Dylan Thomas's normally unpublic poetry for some kind of comment on the Falklands War – whether 'for' or 'against' – seemed crassly impertinent, and destructively limiting of Dylan's intentions.

Cale may not, so far, have fulfilled his symphonic aspirations, but his 'classical' output, flourishing alongside his rock activities, includes his *Four Sketches for String Quartet*, the ballet music *Sanctus* and *Carnival*, and soundtracks for numerous films, notably *La Naissance de l'Amour* (1992) whose piano *études* are among the most plangently lyrical of anything he has written. He has continued to enjoy creative partnerships with a wide range of artists, including Brian Eno and Bob Neuwirth, with whom he made the quirky but enjoyable *Last Day on Earth* (1994). But difficulties in his relationship with Lou Reed, caustically itemised in the autobiography, are likely to preclude any more joint projects. The Velvet Underground toured again in 1995, but the reunion was not a success; by 1998 two of the band had died, and Cale's relationship with Reed seemed to have deteriorated beyond repair.

Of all the generative dualisms that provide the foundation of Cale's art, one of the most fundamental is that between Wales and America. A double-page spread near the beginning of *What's Welsh for Zen* sweeps the eye, in an unbroken line, across the tidal marshes of the Llwchwr estuary to the waterfront not of the steel town of Llanelli, which you would expect, but of New York. The traffic between those two poles is constant throughout the book – and the life.

Wales, today, seems to hold fewer spooks for Cale than at any time in the Calvinistically-straitened past. His final paragraph is an appreciative reconstruction of a visit home in 1997, when BBC Wales made a film about his life:

> *Embraced once again by the warmth of the hills, the setting sun that shines on the church spire and flicks the tips of the gravestones, and by the warmth of the people, I felt a sense of wonder. Going home always gives me another lease of life; I am still fascinated by the emotional curve of my journey from Wales to New York and back again. When I return to the Amman Valley it is as if to the bosom of a friend. That friend floats in the language and seduces me with each translation. I am also blessed by having a lot of work to do, a lot of art to make, a lot of voices to translate into songs or music.*

Expect – BOING! – more surprises as Cale leads us a merry dance up that garden path.

Singing for Wales:
The Poetry of Harri Webb[1]

The cultured classes
Like the poems of all *the Thomases*
But the works of Webb
Are considered rather pleb.
'Discrimination', *Harri Webb: Collected Poems*

One December night a few years ago, in a pub in Aberdare, I caught a glimpse of the revolution. Taking Harri Webb's poetry as their raw material, a team of students from Ysgol Gyfun Rhydfelen delivered the most energetic, inventive, witty, generous and passionate explosion of poetry-in-performance that I have ever witnessed. These kids, I thought, should spend no more time in school: give them their honorary A-levels, provide them with a bus and send them out on the roads to raise flagging morale throughout the land.

In an Oxbridge-oriented critical climate which deems it distinctly uncool to get heated about politics, Harri Webb (1920-94) has been anything but 'fashionable' among the 'cultured classes'. The *gwerin*, however, tell a different tale, for Harri Webb was arguably Wales's most popular poet, in either Welsh or English, during the last decades of the twentieth century. Why was he popular? Because he had important, disturbing, necessary and entertaining things to say to and about the people of Wales. The people of Wales needed, and still need, Harri Webb's poems – in ways that they do not need the poetry of Flossie Timkins who came here from Hemel Hempstead to pen exquisite immortelles about nature, cats and her stepfather's Welsh great-grandmother. He appealed not only to those with a taste for the literary sophistications of more internationally famous poets such as Dylan Thomas, R.S. Thomas and Dannie Abse, but to that far larger constituency of readers and listeners with little or no apparent interest

---

[1] Material in this essay is drawn from various publications, including *Planet* 83 (October/November 1990), *The New Welsh Review* 24 (Spring, 1994), *Swagmag* 3 and 5, and *Golwg*.

in poetry. His work belongs to the unbroken, 1500-years-old Welsh tradition of the poet as social activist, with a significant role to play in the lives of his people. His only rival among the English-writing dead, reaching out to a similar republican, socialist and nationalist constituency, has been Idris Davies. But for the last twenty years the arbiters of literary taste have presided over the suppression of that socially engaged tradition, and have promoted instead an invasion of our culture by the poetry of demure ego, whimsical anecdote, genteel suburban regret and detail-obsessed imagism.

The usual critical line taken against Harri Webb is that his poetry is outmoded in both form and content; it is unacceptably forthright – 'Sing for Wales or shut your trap/All the rest's a load of crap' – violently affronting those for whom poetry is the art of graceful circumlocution; and, in its 'narrow' and 'parochial' obsession with Wales, it fails the test of 'universality'. The man himself did little to advance his cause when he issued mischievous statements to *The Western Mail* writing off 'Anglo-Welsh literature', including his own, as 'more or less a load of old rubbish'.

The poet, in good health, was a forceful performer, kicking off, perhaps, with a classic of wry comedy, 'Synopsis of the Great Welsh Novel', then sliding in some satire, such as 'Epitaph on a Public Man':

> *Where now he lies his old routine*
> *Will suffer scant disruption*
> *For none could say he'd ever been*
> *A stranger to corruption.*

He'd skilfully mix the mood. His slam-in-the-guts poem about Gwenallt, for example, might give way to the Hopkinsian music of 'Carmarthen Coast':

> *Sea-hung cages of singing, hymn-barns*
> *In villages of lace and brass and limewash*
> *Look over the grey water. Held*
> *In the lapse of a landscape's liquid outline*
> *The islands float in air . . .*

He might then break that spell with a blast against smokers:

> *Puffpig was a smoker*
> *Puffpig was a lout,*
> *Puffpig came to my house*
> *And stank the whole place out.*
> *I went to Puffpig's house*
> *Filled with rightful ire,*
> *Took things one stage further*
> *And set the swine on fire.*

Followed perhaps, while we're about such incendiary business, by a dig at compatriots who profit from the second homes market:

> *Tai haf, mae'n warthus, ac mae rhai*
> *Yn brwydro ac yn aberthu.*
> *Ie, Saeson, wir, sy'n prynu'n tai—*
> *Ond pwy sydd yn eu gwerthu?*
>
> *(Second homes—it's disgraceful—and some*
> *are opposing them, making sacrifices.*
> *Yes, it's true it's the English who're buying our houses,*
> *but who is it that's selling them?)*

He could work the silences, and hold with a word fifty or sixty people, many of whom might not previously have attended a poetry reading. Sometimes in his eagerness to 'speak the same language' as his audience, he drifted towards doggerel – he was never shy of the word 'entertainment' – but he was no Max Boyce of 'Anglo-Welsh' letters. 'To defend and be useful to his friends or to offend his enemies is that which all mortals most aspire to' was the motto of another politician poet, John Milton, that Harri Webb used to keep pinned at eyelevel above his work table as a declaration of literary intent. He exulted in putting the boot in where necessary, scandalising the genteel, and upsetting political opponents; he relished flying in the face of that 'ghastly good taste' which, he said, was 'one of the pervading weaknesses of the Anglo-Welsh generally'. Unlike the poems of R.S. Thomas, his are not afraid of the future tense, his defiant (and sometimes excessive) optimism positively willing alteration, and, in the process, doing violence to established codes of literary decorum – it being so much easier, as Ioan Bowen Rees once remarked, to reconcile pessimism with good taste. 'My job is to communicate with as wide an audience as possible,' he would declare. 'The poetry that "makes nothing happen" is something we cannot afford.'

Born to a working-class family in Swansea, he found it impossible to ignore the poverty of the '30s: classmates went without shoes, and in the nearby Swansea Valley there were children whose rotten teeth and dribbling mouths were signs of lead poisoning. Such things, he said, 'kindled a spark of anger, this was not what we were born for.'

He read for a degree in Modern Languages at Oxford University, then volunteered to serve in the Royal Navy. At the end of World War II, some of which he spent escorting convoys in the Mediterranean, he decided to return to Wales and 'slog it out with her enemies, using whatever weapons had been given me.'

For most of his life Harri Webb was an intensely busy political being. After the war he drifted in and out of various short-term jobs until, in 1954, he became a librarian, which would remain his profession until his retirement. Profoundly influenced by the Scottish poet Hugh MacDiarmid, he was a Welsh Republican in the 1950s, and later joined Plaid Cymru as a left-wing activist. He pursued an unrepentantly nationalistic campaign on all fronts: as politician, public speaker and Union Jack burner; as pamphleteer and essayist; as dramatist and documentary film-maker. But it is as a poet that he made his most distinctive mark, contributing to the nation's wealth at least a dozen 'classics', some of which, such as 'Colli Iaith', have merged so naturally with the cultural landscape that they are often thought of as simply 'Trad.' rather than Webb-authored.

Although he learned Welsh as an adult, and could write memorably in the language, Harri Webb wrote mainly in English. He consciously imposed limitations on the formal development of his poetry, resorting unashamedly to accessible and traditional modes, and seeking platforms with the broadest possible appeal. As Gwyn Alf Williams observed, Harri Webb was at once a *clerwr* and a *prydydd*, a sophisticate who was both an adept manipulator of appealing folk forms, such as the ballad, and one who was profoundly influenced by a wide range of writers and writing, from thirteenth-century Provençal intricacies such as the sestina, through the *cywydd* (in the language of Caradoc Evans!), to the outer reaches of twentieth-century Modernism. The formal breakthrough, he acknowledged, was necessary, but its pursuit, given the urgency of the political situation, was not for him.

His imposition of checks on literary aspirations could issue, paradoxically, in poetry of the highest order (in 'A Crown for Branwen', for example).

As a political activist, Harri Webb was conscious of the importance of seeing Wales whole, historically and physically, rather than clutching like an Adferite or Valleys parochialist only at those bits of Wales which flatter one's prejudices. He lowers a respectful brow before the great national shrines and icons – Abaty Cwmhir, Tŷ Ddewi, Llywelyn Fawr, Glyndŵr – while at the same time according detailed attention and respect to the working-class Welsh of the south. Drawn to 'the more extrovert and active side of our national history and character' such as sport, pubs, industrial inventions, class solidarity, he operated in undisguised opposition to the nationalists of thinly-populated ruralism for whom the monoglot southern hordes are beneath contempt and beyond consideration.

He is equally impatient, however, with those who place the Industrial Revolution and the working class at centre stage, being as critical as Idris Davies of the damage done to mind, body and environment by industrial and technological processes. The welcome prosperity which those processes brought to many promoted in its train a consumerist fetishism which has done little to advance the national culture.

Rural Wales, with a 'green desert' at its heart, also bears the scars of Webb's century: abandoned farms, valleys drowned for reservoirs, the hills suffocated by sitka pines. Harri Webb makes of these, and old thoroughfares that nowadays lead nowhere, forceful symbols of broken connections and present inaction. For all his urban conviviality, Harri Webb's identification with rural Wales is profound; his sinewy lyricism is intensely evocative of country places, raising up the buried meanings of Abaty Cwmhir or the wilderness above Tregaron. He is concerned about such places not only as a nationalist deploring his people's amnesia, but, often, as an observer keenly aware of ecological harm. Poems of the '60s and '70s which lament the pollution of rivers and sea, and the 'plunder[ing] to exhaustion' of the Earth mark out Harri Webb as an 'eco-bard' long before such positions became fashionable.

The past in this poetry is constantly breaking in on the present. Ponies invading the streets of Merthyr are:

> *The foals of Epona that have brought the Cymry*
> *From out of legend and the lands of summer*
> *To the last stand . . .*

And Aneurin Bevan addressing a crowd

> *. . . could have been a scene*
> *Anytime in our history, the chieftain aloft*
> *And the host mustered to follow.*

Most of Harri Webb's best poetry will not fully connect with the reader unless he or she is attuned to cultural and historical resonances, some of which – 'Irfon, guilty water' – are fleeting. A first exposure to the poetry of Harri Webb may be for some a disconcerting confrontation with their own ignorance, but his intention is to beguile rather than repel, persuading such readers to engage more profoundly with 'matter' which, in a culturally healthy situation, should be common affective property.

When his *Collected Poems*, edited by Meic Stephens, appeared posthumously in 1995, readers were able to appreciate for the first time the extraordinary variety of his poetic *oeuvre*. There emerges from the pages of this book a poet more complex and diverse than even many of his admirers had anticipated. The poems are arranged in chronological order, from his earliest published poem, a hymn of praise to 'The Stars' written in Arabian waters in 1942 and printed in *The Western Mail*, to 1989's song of praise to Dowlais, the place which, more than any other, anchored the poet in the culture of Wales.

Only half of the book's 350 poems appeared in his four earlier collections, and there are at least a hundred which had never before seen the light of print. In addition to Harri Webb's original poems, there are ten translations from the Welsh, the Chilean poet Pablo Neruda's magnificent *Alturas de Macchu Picchu* translated *into* Welsh, and over a dozen original poems in Welsh; there are two dozen translations from French, Spanish and several minority languages (favourite poets include Fredrico García Lorca and Jacques Prévert); and there are the many verse commentaries that Harri, a poet of facts as he always insisted, wrote for television documentaries.

In these days of whimsical anecdote, hermetic clever-dickery and media-hyped 'poetry stars' who come and go like the latest fashionable drink, Harri Webb offers a timely reminder, by force of example and odd lines of manifesto, that 'Always in Europe/The true poet has sung for the people,/ . . . Always in Wales/The poet has been a craftsman, *saer cerdd,*/The carpenter of song . . .'. His passionate commitment to the people of Wales, no matter what their language, and his command of an extraordinary array of literary modes and techniques are flourished here in all their breathtaking variety, barbed wit and beery camaraderie.

It has been the received critical wisdom of recent years that nationalistic poetry (Welsh, that is, rather than, say, African) is third-league, parochialist stuff, of interest maybe to a few people in Gwynedd, but otherwise of small account in the mainstream of our times. Birth, suffering and death, we are advised, are the big themes, the 'universal' subjects. Such critics, whose literary 'arguments' are often poorly disguised political grouses, of course, will find in Harri Webb's poetry, if they care to look, plenty of birth, suffering and death, although they refer in this case more to a people and their varieties of life than to the isolated individual. And Harri Webb's abiding theme, the desire for national self-determination and freedom, is surely as 'universal' in Wales as it is in South Africa or Chechenia.

While close to R.S. Thomas in his fierce defence of the Welsh language (which he learned in Dowlais) and denunciations of tinsel-town anglicised Wales, Harri Webb operated in other respects as a counterweight to the defeatist priest of Llŷn, who must sometimes have looked down his long nose of a northern peninsula and despaired at the decadent conviviality and Webbian optimism of the crowded urban south. Some of his positions have dated, such as his enthusiasm for opencast coaling and 'sunshine miners', but there are many lines in gloriously bad taste, such the 'Anglomaniac Anthem' of 1973, which continue to bristle with contemporary relevance:

> *. . . we're looking up England's arsehole*
> *It's the loveliest scene of all,*
> *Yes, we're looking up England's arsehole,*
> *Waiting for the manna to fall . . .*

His notorious advice to a young poet in the early '70s to 'Sing for Wales or shut your trap' was not a recommendation he followed too rigidly himself. As a self-confessed Parnassian (the Parnassians believed in *l'art pour l'art* – art for art's sake – and a personality-denying objectivism), he experienced a creative tension between the aesthetic satisfactions of constructing poems and the day-to-day hurly-burly of various political imperatives. In his early, wartime poems it's not so much Wales but the perils of war and the exotic sights of unfamiliar climes that engage his imagination. A verbally exuberant poem, 'Flying Fish' (1944), is surely an ancestor of 'The Flocks of the Moon', which he wrote for the environmental magazine *Resurgence* in 1975.

He may not have chosen to publish them, but he wrote poems of a more personal nature throughout his career, from lines addressed to a shipmate in 1944 acknowledging a shared sense of black-doggish despair, to various love poems which hint, sometimes, at considerable torment. 'My love, my lost and only love,' he writes in the double sestina 'Henryd' (1973), 'I go/Without you and alone, the gnawing ache/That those who never loved will not believe . . .' And in the 'Sonnets for Mali' he cries to the omni-absent she, in acrostic code, *'Tyrd yn ôl gariad'* ('Come back my love') and *'Dere lan eto Mali'* ('Come up again Mali'). These sonnets had a job to do: to get his woman back. But I doubt that they succeeded. His characteristic 'folk anonymity' combines with the formalism of his verse patterns and the language of an outmoded kind of 'love poetry' to keep us at arms' length from the real players and their real feelings. Though his emotional range is narrow, he is certainly capable of an affecting tenderness, as is demonstrated by his poem 'The Old Men':

> *I have seen the old men die, have watched them*
> *Every winter edge a step nearer to death,*
> *Until the last winter toppled them into the grave.*
> . . .
> *I have seen them at street corners, washed,*
> *Tidied and put out in the sun, or leaning*
> *Against familiar walls, seeing less and less with every day.*

The 'I' of his poems seems to me a carefully constructed 'persona' that invites us no further than is absolutely necessary into its creator's inner world. Harri Webb is at his best when he is praising, satirising, lamenting, exhorting on his people's behalf. His *Collected Poems* conveys a stronger impression than ever of a thoroughly professional scion of the Welsh bardic tradition, responding as promptly and efficiently as possible to the many demands made on him by a wide variety of patrons, from the BBC and other broadcasters who were constantly commissioning poems from him, to the organisers of political rallies and – why not? – a local children's pony club. He had little need of the self-preening and largely irrelevant literary magazines that, from the early '70s onwards, routinely turned down some of the best of his work: the people of Wales were buying his books by the thousand.

Like Waldo Williams, Harri Webb functioned both as an artist of high literary sophistication and an entertaining folk poet, drawn to the latter role, initially, by the example of Cyril Gwynn who was active in Harri's youth as 'the bard of Gower', and with whose family Harri Webb's Gower relatives enjoyed close family ties. The youngster, who was a keen diarist from the age of eleven, possibly even earlier, would have seen Cyril Gwynn in action as a fully-fledged *bardd gwlad* (country or folk poet), albeit in the English language, who'd go out two or three nights a week to fulfil his obligations as his people's poet, celebrating their achievements, chronicling their conflicts and raising high hilarity with his Gower 'yarns' (only the most 'printable' of which, unfortunately, have survived in book form).

Harri was aware, along with George Bernard Shaw, that if you want to tell people the truth you had better make them laugh or they'll kill you. All sorts of writers came to influence the development of his comic muse, but the example of Cyril Gwynn was seminal. In his narrative folk ballads, Cyril was a kind of Gower 'nationalist' defending his patch against the urban blight of Swansea, and celebrating the triumph of local wit and wisdom over the pretensions and pomposities of the interloper. Cyril's yarns use strong rhymes to underpin their gentle humour, and they invariably climax in a gleeful 'twist' which, uniting the audience in laughter, joins them in solidarity with their poet's view of a situation.

The humour of Harri Webb is similarly collaborative: the poet is 'one of us' rather than a prophet standing on some mountain in Gwynedd dishing out the thunderbolts. But it is on the whole much less gentle; beneath his 'cheery and beery' conviviality – his promotion, as Brian Morris remarked in his essay on Webb produced for the Writers of Wales series (published by the University of Wales Press), of The Revolution as fun – there is sometimes a barbed and acid violence born of the desperation he could feel about the fecklessness of the nation, and his frustration with Plaid Cymru's pacifism.

Morris quotes extensively from a letter written to Gwilym Prys-Davies in the early 1970s in which Harri Webb gives voice to the increasing violence of his political passions. Faced with the apparent collapse of the *gwerin* as the last social bulwark, and fired apparently by Padraic Pearse's belief in the necessity for a redemptive 'blood sacrifice', Harri Webb concludes that the burden of defending Wales has fallen on the shoulders of a select few. 'The [Welsh] Republicans said that they would not shrink from shedding blood if necessary,' he writes. 'They said that bloodshed would probably be necessary. I say now, that such sacrifice is not only probably necessary, a predictable statistical likelihood, but ABSOLUTELY NECESSARY. Without it there will be no wholeness or health in any of the other actions that lead us forward. It is necessary, first to redeem the Welsh from shame . . . Today . . . I am quite psychologically prepared for anything – jail, disruption of personal life, hardship, the lot. I am on active service. I have been called up.'

The notion of Wales being redeemed 'by a few individuals of an unparalleled responsibility' winds us back logically to the most primitive and profoundly non-Republican of social bulwarks, the tribal prince. For a poet of professed democratic convictions, a problem he runs into as he analyses the present and anticipates the future in terms of Wales's past, which he does frequently, is that that past is bound up in strictly hierarchical social structures. Webb's new Wales is willed into existence through endless reference to princes, princesses, and other royal and aristocratic leaders of the past. It may well be, as he suggests in 'The Nightingales', that we cannot call again '[the birds] of Safaddan that sing only for princes', but he cannot rid himself, in his poetry, of more than a sneaking admiration for the arisocratic superstrata:

> The hall is not yet built, the church not hallowed
> That dares to house the royalty of Wales.
>
> 'By a Mountain Pool'

And in 1983, he astonished fellow republicans by writing the words for the gala opening *by the Queen Mother* of St. David's Hall, Cardiff – an eventuality as stunningly implausible, many had thought, as, say, Dafydd Elis Thomas taking the ermine . . .

The steely solemmnity of the commitment expressed in the letter to

Gwilym Prys-Davies rarely surfaces in the poetry, nor does the extent of his political frustration. Indeed, in his determination to live a national freedom that does not yet exist, he tends to gloss over certain awkward complexities, and to insist uncritically that 'west is best'. His routine sugaring of the nationalist pill can lead to black-and-white simplifications in which truth is invariably a casualty.

'The Stars of Mexico', for instance, makes a hero of an exiled Welsh Chartist for escaping 'the cruel laws of England' and shouldering his rifle ''neath the flag of Uncle Sam': but the poem omits to mention what Uncle Sam was up to beneath his flag, namely annexing huge swathes of Mexico – a venture of questionable virtue, surely, for a Welsh freedom-fighter to get himself involved in? Similarly, in 'The Red Dragon' we are invited to join the poet in remembering with due national pride the voyage of a ship called *The Red Dragon*, flagship of the East India Company, on a mission of the most blatant imperialism.

This uncritical view of Wales and Welsh deeds is of a piece with Harri Webb's sometimes blinkered optimism, when the glorious dawn of our liberated future is envisioned with all the clattering insincerity of a greetings card jingle:

> *When I was young and serious*
> *About the land I went*
> *And heard no song to cheer me*
> *In Gower or in Gwent.*
>
> *Now I'm too old for weeping*
> *And happier every hour*
> *To hear the song that's sweeping*
> *The land from Gwent to Gower.*
>   'Generation Gap'

This kind of thing, where his useful 'folk anonymity' runs badly to seed, was the price that Harri sometimes paid for his popularity. But then, as MacDiarmid would have said, a volcano belches mud as well as flame, and a certain 'tosh-content' is no doubt inevitable where ambitions beyond the norm are concerned.

Harri Webb as a republican, socialist and nationalist had much in common with John Tripp: they often read their poetry from the same platforms in the 1960s and early 1970s. But they differ in at least one important respect. Tripp was unashamedly an individualist who built his poetry around the goings-on and gettings-up-to – laughter, tears, farts'n'all – of a persona more or less identifiable with the poet himself; Harri Webb, for all his frolicsome sociability, remained an intensely private person, temperamentally disinclined to make art out of the griefs and foibles of selfhood.

A librarian at Dowlais and subsequently Mountain Ash until his retirement in 1974, he was housebound by illness from the early '80s. Old age came cruelly early to Harri Webb. By the time his fourth volume of poetry was published in 1983, he had more or less closed down as a writer, having embarked on a series of illnesses, including a stroke in 1985, which rendered him housebound in his ground-floor, mountain-top flat in Cwmbach, Aberdare for the rest of his days.

In the summer of 1994 he suffered a strange and highly contagious virus that necessitated a long stay in a quarantine unit. He lost his beard and even the zimmer-assisted mobility that was his before the virus struck; he survived, just. But he had to abandon any idea of a return to the semi-independent life he led in Cwmbach. In November of that year the old sailor sought a last haven in a rest home in his native Swansea, and it was there, on New Year's Eve, that he died.

'Wales,' the determined optimist would insist, 'is marching backwards into independence, everybody desperately pretending that we are going somewhere else.' If he's right, and national liberation is indeed a glimmer on the horizon, his life and work will have played a not insignificant part in the achievement of that freedom. In the meantime, there is work for his poetry still to do before 'the coulter drives/A fertile furrow over our old wars/For the strong corn, our children's bread.'

Sprocket and Ball Cock Tripp:
John Tripp's prose[1]

John Tripp left school at the age of sixteen, and trained as a writer – unlike most of his university-educated contemporaries – in the world of radio, advertising and public relations. When he began to write poetry in his mid thirties he was already an accomplished writer of journalistic rather than academic prose, the practice of which was to remain his primary source of income for most of his life. In spite of the shadow of R.S. Thomas, which dogs the poetry of his first three books, he was in possession from the beginning of a uniquely 'Trippian' voice that owes more to his grounding in journalism than to any other influence.

Both his prose and poetry benefit from the fundamental journalistic skills: to sum up a situation, no matter how unfamiliar, by interrogating it with the reporter's six prime questions, 'Who?', 'What?', 'When?', 'Where?', 'Why?', 'How?'; to develop an eye for detail and an ear for the telling phrase; to write accurately, briefly, clearly; to pitch the tone of your copy differently for different readerships; to 'hook' your readers with a striking first paragraph, and then hold their interest with a well-structured argument entertainingly presented, before reaching a conclusion as arresting as your opening sentence.

He also picked up some of the less desirable habits of the newsroom such as skimpy research, superficial generalisation and the lifting of other people's copy. When his energy flags, as in some of his *Arcade* television columns of the early 1980s (which had more to say on the subject of Tripp than television), the formulaic application of stylistic features can deteriorate into mannerism: the blanket use of 'corkscrews' for scheming people, especially politicians; the reiteration from article to article of favourite phrases ('as sincere as an Italian waiter in a crowded restaurant at two o'clock in the morning'); the insistent attempts to revivify stock phrases and clichés ('Women's Release',

---

[1] This article was published as 'John Tripp's Prose' in *The Works* 1 (Welsh Union of Writers, ed. Tôpher Mills), 1988.

'mouse race', 'detergent operetta'; or, more inventively, 'dull talking skulls', 'Crime Minister'). He had a magpie's fascination for the dazzling phrases of others which he would often then hijack himself. For instance, Gramsci's famous dictum about the lack of a sense of history being like walking without a shadow is repeated in items of both poetry and prose. And one of his most treasured sayings – 'None of us is going to get out of this alive' – which was quoted by John Ormond in his obituary in *The Times*, was culled, probably, from an interview with Tennessee Williams published in 1963; it was used even earlier, in the 1950s, as a Lettrist International slogan, and Jim Morrison of The Doors and Bob Marley also used the line.

His prose at its best – ironically humorous, adjectivally idiosyncratic – moves with what Glyn Jones has called 'a sort of thrusting incisiveness'; it might appear effortless, but it is the fruit of years of wide reading and long apprenticeship. He took its practice no less seriously than the writing of poetry, even at the level of letters to friends which he would sometimes work through several drafts before arriving at a definitive version; he enjoyed quoting Scott Fitzgerald's remark, 'I'm writing a letter with margins for my editor's footnotes'.

He had an excellent ear for speaking and writing styles other than his own, having been from childhood an unusually gifted mimic. Dilys Roderick, a contemporary of John's at the BBC in Cardiff in the early 1940s, used to watch the sixteen year old at work:

> *Being a very keen cinema-goer, he used to imitate people like Charles Boyer – you just couldn't tell the difference, it was remarkable. He could do a complete orchestra, and you could see the movement in his neck and throat. I've rarely seen mimicry like it, he really was a first-class mimic.*

Peter Owen, a friend through school and into early manhood, also remembers his genius for mimicry:

> *There used to be a programme every night during the war for Allied forces, and he could imitate them brilliantly in all their languages – French, Hindustani, you name it, he could do it. We would go on a train journey, and suddenly, to the alarm of fellow passengers, you'd hear the whine of an attacking plane – and it would be John, doing a dive-bomber.*

Later, he would delight in 'inventing' different literary personae for himself or imitating the modes of others. To Fay Williams, his *cariad* of the early seventies, he sent numerous letters and cards from his bungalow in Whitchurch readdressed as 'Pendarves Manor', perhaps, or the 'Royal Pendarves Hotel', and written in the literary manner of Dr Zhivago, Henry Thynne 6th Marquis of Bath, or, to give an example, John Keats:

> *My dearest girl,*
> *I have been a walk this morning with a book in my hand, but as usual I have been occupied with nothing but you . . . They talk of my going to Patagonia. 'Tis certain I shall never recover if I am to be so long separate from you . . . I saw the poet Ormond on Monday and he is much occupied with his own things; he is a very trumpet about his own work. But he is a good friend, as is wise Mr Stephens, a good sort of fellow, I know his love and friendship for us, and at this moment I should be without pence but for his patronage . . .*

This juggling with alternative identities would sometimes spill over into the wider world. In one of his running feuds with the novelist Alexander Cordell in the letters column of *The Western Mail*, one 'Lloyd Llewelyn' eventually comes to the poet's defence – Mr Llewelyn being none other than Mr Tripp himself under one of several pseudonyms he used in *The London Welshman*.

Such pleasure in mimicry and role-play feeds naturally into the craft of fiction, at which he first tried his hand as a schoolboy under the mesmerising influence of Ernest Hemingway. His job as a press assistant at the Indonesian Embassy (1958–1967), also, it seems, gave him scope to develop his skills as a fiction writer:

> *They would pass me reams of rubbish typed in pidgin-English from their European news agency in Amsterdam and I would have to condense and re-write it for British and Continental consumption. If there wasn't enough news for the six sheets* [of the cyclostyled bulletin Indonesian Embassy], *I used to make it up . . . Really, in many ways it was the worst sort of hack-work, except for those more creative paragraphs when one could use the imagination to invent news items.*

'Indonesian Interlude', *Planet* 22, March 1974

At about this time he was attending University of London summer schools held annually at Westonbirt, the girls' public school in Gloucestershire, where his contributions to the regular 'pantomime' written and presented by staff and students were a high point of the week. The musical director at the summer school was the composer Geoffrey Bush, who much admired Tripp's routines:

He wrote and delivered a satirical review, in prose, of the week's events, a format almost like that of Priestley's wartime broadcast epilogues (though in every respect different as regards contents!) Fun was poked at everyone (not least the staff) without malice, and was accompanied by an almost continuous ripple of laughter from the listeners – in the best sense, a most polished performance (and a professional one).

Although there is little of Tripp's work in *The London Welshman* (his main platform in the later 1960s) that is particularly effective as a short story, we can observe him here starting to take prose beyond the bounds of literary journalism or the critical essay. In a number of sketches he is interested mainly in ideas, character mediated through convincing dialogue, and situation (particularly the tensions of the moment prior to a resolution of conflict). He shows virtually no interest in plot in any of the stories, apart from a couple which are little more than 'definitive versions' of hoary old chestnuts. The narrator, as in most of Tripp's stories, is normally an observer on the sidelines, rarely a participant in the action or debate.

In 1971 the Welsh Arts Council advertised a competition for 'creative prose', and three years later the results, twenty-two stories by fourteen 'new' writers, were published in *The Old Man of the Mist*, edited by Lynn Hughes for the London publishing house, Martin Brian & O'Keefe. John Tripp's three short items were generally among the best received in a book that had mixed reviews. In *The Anglo-Welsh Review*, for example, Tony Curtis looked forward to Tripp developing formally along the lines of B.S. Johnson. 'Small Boat Distress Signals', written in three brief sections that chronicle the decline into suicide of a champion boxer, is a familiar Welsh theme with obvious appeal to a writer intrigued by the great or famous brought low by time and misfortune. The copious details of Tripp's description of food are excessive in much of his writing, but here the description of three distinct meals is vitally a part of the story's structure, as it is in the second, 'Apricot Sponge with a Sage'. In 'Matt Prytherch', the final story, the narrator is absent; it is told as a monologue, in the words of a working-class Valleys drop-out who lives alone in the woods. Reminiscent of Alan Bennett's monologues, it is a sharply observed, acutely *heard* little speech, the desolation and sadness registering *between* the lines of the speaker rather than in what he actually says.

Like Gwyn Thomas, from whom he learned a few tricks, John Tripp is fascinated by quirky people living on the margins of society – the alienated, the outcast, the mildly criminal, those who, like Tripp, himself a borderer, do not quite fit. He enjoyed the conversation of prostitutes in the clubs and bars of Cardiff's docklands, and the company of winos on the Hayes Island benches. They articulate, in extreme form, fundamental aspects of the twentieth-century condition, pitting against hardship and injury a robust wit that locks in with his own:

> *Humour shouldn't be stowed away in the attic with yesterday's sepia album, but flourished in the face of most that life can throw our way. The trend of the modern temper may be towards gloom, despair, morbidity and resignation, but morose periods have come and gone before, through 20 centuries, along with ruinous decadence. When we moan, we should do well to recall happier phases in history such as the Black Death.*
>
> 'The Way the Biscuit Crumbles', *Planet* 26/27

These three stories are among his most successful, but, like those to come, they are thin on action. The narrator's advice to the philosopher in 'Apricot Sponge with a Sage' – 'This is one of those intellectual Westerns where they just talk' – could apply to much of John Tripp's fiction.

Most of the eight short pieces published in *Planet* during the '70s are 'factions', set in the antechambers of history, in which one idea predominates: the conflict between revolutionary action and humane doubt. They are short Platonic dialogues rather than stories, energetically and plausibly argued, and refreshingly uncluttered with political cliché, for it is the psychology *behind* the slogan that intrigues Tripp; the historical background is convincingly recreated, many of the pieces testifying to their author's long-standing interest in military tactics. Characterisation, however, is slight, with little in the way of linguistic variation to distinguish one speaker from another; both often sound like Tripp himself, although he rarely lets himself be seen voting for any particular side. In literature as in later life, Tripp could grow quickly impatient with hard-and-fast commitments – 'His certainty was frightening and disgusting; there was no room in his head for doubt' ('Connection at Ust', *Planet* 36). These 'stories' argue persuasively that doubt, far from being a prevaricating weakness, is a humanising strength. But doubt is also, in this anti-collectivist form (the classic position of liberal individualism), a notable incapacitator, urging us to settle into the self-indulgent comforts of despair and inaction; there is nothing more to do because nothing more *can* be done, except talk – or write – about it. The immobilisation of John Tripp's prose characters is conditioned by a suspicion that in the somewhat fatalistic universe to which he condemns them they are not free to make choices: they lack the conviction that choice, any choice, could free them. The potential torment of this situation is defused by both humour, Tripp's weary irony, and, indeed, by a qualified heroising of the doubter, he who incapacitates revolutionary change, either by mocking its pretentions, believing nothing will change, or by finding the cost in suffering prohibitively high.

The four stories of his first (and heavily misprinted) collection, *The Thinskin Award* (Edge Press, 1978), display a deeper concern with character, which tends to a greater development of actual *story*. These comedies of mainly middle-class manners, focusing on seedy characters and doings in the literary world, are racily and wittily told to an extent that a rushed reading might miss an important minor-key underpinning of the often cynical laughter, namely Tripp's insistent awareness, with Thoreau, of 'the quiet desperation' of most people's lives, and how the obsession with fame, money, food, sex, is a futile distraction from the onset of crow's feet and the inevitability of death.

Most of the *Thinskin* characters are 'messy products of their appalling time', greedy, predatory, rapacious, so self-absorbed that relationships have little potential to be anything other than exploitative. Isolation and loneliness form the basic condition here, but few of Tripp's characters are entirely incapable of finer feelings or lacking in the means to survive the world's harshness.

There is a certain ostentation of language about *The Thinskin Award*, to match the 'shock effect' of the distended condom on the cover; this pretence to a daring in matters sexual cannot disguise a fundamentally conventional sexual morality that feels itself undermined by 'queers' and shocked by lesbians. Women as a whole are generally, in Tripp's stories, shallow and heartless users and discarders of men.

The somewhat frenzied pace and style of these stories gives way in his next collection, *Last Day in England* (Alun Books, 1979), to a more restrained tone and a more gradual unfolding of events and characters. The title-story is a rather Chekhovian piece, resonant with impending change, about a young Englishman named York who is about to sail to Spain to fight for the Republicans in the civil war. In spite of his over-playing of the period detail, Tripp gives us an affecting and delicate portrait of a lonely young socialist without much sociality, poignantly aware of the incongruities of what could turn out to be his last day in England

> . . . *spent drinking two pints of ale and eating a pork pie, looking at an old boat that would take him to war, booking into a luxury hotel, and talking to a posh girl over a pot of tea.*

York is buoyed up by 'the happiness that comes from a commitment to something' – as is the very different protagonist of the following story, 'Go Home, Davy Tuck', whose 'cause' is a five-wheeler Briggs and Stratton Flyer. He is another of life's sideliners, inadequate, inarticulate, rejected by his peers because he is not 'hard', and by his girlfriend because she finds his car ridiculous. The sadness of this story is all the more heartrending due to its oblique articulation, as Davy tries to explain to his equally taciturn father why he is upset. The old man can offer little comfort, wishing only that Davy's mother was 'still here to say something', and proffering the twin consolations of home – and the Flyer. The reader is only too aware of how fugitive is the first consolation and how pathetic the second, being based on no social relations at all but simply a machine – which the rest of the world laughs at.

The final story, 'No Peace for Dando', offers a surer sense of social relationship, although it is severely limited. The only lifeline of the hopelessly alcoholic Dando is the community solidarity of the Valleys people; it protects him for a while, but it is ultimately no match against wider 'market forces'. Dando ends up dead in a ditch:

At the inquest the coroner said it was death by misadventure, which could have meant anything, though it was no accident. Perhaps he thought it was impossible for anyone to starve to death in a welfare state.

Ultimate power lies well beyond the community's sphere of influence; people are clients (and victims) of it rather than partakers, fatalistically incapable of exerting control over the forces that shape and misshape their lives.

Most of John Tripp's stories remain scattered through magazines and anthologies. A selection of the best of them brought together with those from his two collections would make a sizeable and impressive volume.

An underestimated element of Tripp's prose output is his work as a reviewer and critic. Aware of what he had learned himself from poet-critics such as Jeremy Hooker and Roland Mathias, he was conscious of his own responsibilities to fellow writers when commenting on their work:

Good, constructive critics are worth their weight in silver. They can soon detect talent if it is there, and help a poet to eliminate his own 'wildness' and to remind him of the importance of tone.
'One Poet's Track', *Book News from Wales*, Winter 1978

His own critical creed is summarised in a response to a *Poetry Wales* questionnaire on the subject:

Criticism should be intelligent, perceptive, humorous – a sense of humour usually means a sense of proportion – and even 'domestic' if the poets being examined do not look far beyond their back doors (they should be approached with understanding, on their own terms, to see what they have to offer). But not necessarily 'affirmatory of Wales' if a critic thinks that the poetry is bad or uneven; he should not let his patriotism get in the way of his objectivity . . . So much of modern criticism seems to have been butchery disguised as criticism, unhelpful to say the least – and poets, on the whole, are not butchers. They do not relish opportunities for the cavalier dismissal of others. Sometimes they have to review in order to earn bread, and this can be a mistake because they know how difficult it

*is to write good poetry, and so they tend to soften the blows when
faced by inferior stuff. But this is better than being responsible for a
massacre.*

Poetry Wales 15, ii, Autumn 1979

It was in 1965, in the short-lived *Welsh Outlook* and *The London
Welshman*, that John Tripp published his first literary criticism,
perceptive from the outset of other writers' techniques and able to
express his admiration in succinct terms, as in this judgment on Emyr
Humphreys' *Outside the House of Baal*:

*We are back once more in the country of clarified hopelessness.
Nobody appears to win here, but in the attempt is dignity, and, in the
inevitable acceptance of defeat, a resignation not wholly stippled
with despair.*

'Old Man in the Ruins', *Welsh Outlook*, June 1965

In addition to his regular commendations in *The London Welshman* of
R.S. Thomas, we find John Tripp warmly hospitable to writers of less
obvious appeal to his tastes, such as Vernon Watkins and Gerard Manley
Hopkins. At a time when the nationalist press were reviling Gwyn
Thomas, Tripp is happy to acknowledge him as 'one of the best authors
to come out of Wales' (while adding, somewhat disingenuously, that
Thomas 'also, mysteriously, dislikes Welsh nationalism'). Conversely,
when the Western media were fawning over Solzhenitsyn, Tripp could
blithely mount an unfashionable attack on the Russian writer in
'Aimez-vous Solzhenitsyn?' (*Planet* 23, 1974). Just as he will normally
temper a positive review with a note of qualification, so too will he go
out of his way to find something of value in work about which he feels
generally negative. But he does not hesitate to condemn laziness,
sloppiness and pseudo-sophisticated cleverness. In a review of three
American poets he declares himself hostile to

*. . . another reputation being made within a closed circle of university
droolers and their acolytes. Not a pretty sight. The wit may be
immaculate, the accomplishment thrilling in a purely linguistic
sense where the choice of language is often quite piercing. But why
all this sophisticated show and glitter, and to what end . . . Sheer
facility may indeed work wonders and succeed in covering a*

hollowness at the core. They have not yet forgiven Lowell, Berryman and Roethke for exposing their guts, and pay homage only to Wallace Stevens and his brilliant conundrums. Everything is more or less respectably safe here. I couldn't help thinking of old Matthew Arnold when he looked out over Dover Beach and thought of faith's decline, and heard a melancholy, long, withdrawing roar. The tide having continued to go out for another century, there is not much left except a distant whisper and the smell of seaweed.

Poetry Wales 16, iii, Winter 1981

John Tripp's criticism creates the unmistakable impression among readers that poetry matters to this man, it is too important an art to be left to the self-communing academics. His approach to the writing of criticism is deliberately ungenteel and unrespectable.

. . . Amis, after doing his habitual smarty-pants bit and taking the customary unsubtle English piss out of the Welsh . . .

Planet 18

or

Jeremy Hooker leaves most of his fellow Englishmen in the metropolis looking like spitters of microscopic cherrystones and stunted purveyors of scurrilous crap.

Planet 16

His criticism is direct, entertaining and by no means unsophisticated, while deliberately eschewing the 'bilge-words of lit crit' of the 'smart-arsed' 'mandarin critics' and 'university scissormen', as he used to desribe them. Innocent of the flamboyant over-compensation some might anticipate in an autodidact, evidence of his wide reading comes unaffectedly through; he places a high value on humility, offering his views with none of the superiority that reads so offensively in certain academic sermonising: he is the intelligent citizen addressing himself to other intelligent citizens. His great *journalistic* gift to 'Anglo-Welsh literary criticism' is to treat poetry as a matter of vital concern to the world in which most of us live. Few 'scissormen' with a BA behind them would risk commending Dannie Abse's poem, 'A night out', in these dangerously personal terms:

*Soon after that reading in London, I heard an insensitive pig in a
bar in Richmond say that he agreed with the Final Solution of the
Jewish problem and I had a violent argument with him. Most of the
customers – decent Englishmen – were on my side and they told the
pig to shut up or get out. I doubt whether I would have bothered
with the dreadful, misguided human being if Abse's poem had not
been still fresh in my memory.*

'Dannie Abse revisited', *Poetry Wales* 13, ii

'Sprocket and Ball Cock Tripp', as they called him at the Central
Office of Information for his ability to write effectively about even the
most ordinary of industrial artefacts, was a witty and lucid writer of
prose with a skilled journalist's ability to turn his pen to almost
anything and still succeed in engaging his reader. It is regrettable that
The Western Mail at that time was not more intelligently and
imaginatively edited, like *The Scotsman* or *The Irish Times*: had he
been given a regular column, the nation – and the needy columnist –
would have been the richer for it.

'It was what he would have wanted':
John Tripp's finale

16.ii.86
Jean Henderson phones to say that John Tripp is dead. They'd been out
yesterday on a jaunt, to Caerleon first, where they had talked over a
few drinks by an open fire, and then across to Usk where they'd taken
a walk in the bitter cold. John had bought a half bottle of whisky, and
Jean had dropped him off at the bungalow in Whitchurch at the end of
their day. His father had gone to bed, and he had planned to watch the
boxing and drink the whisky. It seems he was just going to bed, having
prepared a hot water bottle, when he must have had a heart attack as he
sat, fully dressed, on the sofa. Paul found him there in the morning,
and phoned Jean. She had not been long at the bungalow, and, waiting
for an ambulance to come and take him away, she had phoned me. I
offer to phone round friends and Union comrades, which I spend the
rest of the day doing. Also try to gather a few ideas about how to
handle the funeral. Jean, understandably, not keen on a hardline,
silent, atheist's ceremony. We decide it might be a good idea to ask
Glyn Jones to say a few words at the crematorium, and, possibly, find
someone to play some Tallis, and maybe sing a couple of hymns,
although neither of us knows what John thought about hymns. Above
all, though, we should celebrate his life and work by holding a wake
reading in a Cardiff pub, preferably a Brains house. Robin Reeves
working on this. Feel strangely numb as I go about these practicalities;
not enough time to think about John himself. Feel guilty too that I
hadn't seen him for months, indeed that I had probably chosen to
avoid him lately: a surfeit of 'tragic cabarets'.

17.ii.86
Start the morning with a few phone calls, and continue in this way
until gone midnight, trying to sort out the funeral, the reading and
associated complications. Robin finds a pub, the Gower in Gwennyth
Street, Cathays. Jean fixes the funeral for 3.30 on Friday, the last

funeral of the week; we can get into the pub straight afterwards, with tea and sandwiches until opening time at 5.30. Am getting oblique signals, though no one actually says anything, that certain 'senior' *littérateurs* are resentful of the Union's role in these arrangements, believing we have hijacked John's corpse. The main problem is what form this secular funeral should take. Tony Bianchi suggests involving Côr Cochion Caerdydd (Cardiff Red Choir), which would be ideal, and there's general agreement that Glyn Jones should make a comprehensive address at the crem, and that we should all sing something together, such as 'Cwm Rhondda', rather than simply sit there as funereal 'consumers'. Seems like a fair idea to me – Hywel Francis says it worked well when he organised Will Paynter's secular funeral; but Jean less keen on 'Cwm Rhondda', suggesting 'Onward Christian Soldiers'. Last entry in John's pocket diary, Jean tells me, reads 'Usk with J. ICY. Very cold. Pissed.', which he must have written shortly before he died.

18.ii.86

The Red Choir plan falls through – Bianchi can't get enough of them together to do a daytime session, but he has managed to bring them together for the reading in the evening. The biggest of our many problems is that there doesn't seem to be any money to pay for this funeral, the very cheapest being £523. The funeral, Jean has been told, can't go ahead until (a) she identifies John in the mortuary, which she doesn't mind doing, and (b) she signs on the dotted line that she'll be responsible for meeting the funeral costs. John used to say he thought his father may have had some compensation for the demolition of his forge, but had never asked him. Paul himself says he hasn't got the money to pay for the funeral; could chip in a few pounds, and as for the rest, 'Why don't they all have a bit of a whip-round?' Someone's suggestion that we raffle his last whisky bottle with 'Usk' written across the label, and his baccy tin, with his last rolled fag inside, is not generally well received. Meic Stephens suggests the Academy and the Union meeting the expenses; I suggest the Academy, the Union and the *Arts Council* (fat chance: they'd probably have to reach a decision at a committee meeting in about six months' time). Another problem is we don't yet have an MC, if that is the term for a non-clerical officiator. Ormond has declined. Rhydwen Williams, who would be ideal, might not be up to it, having suffered a stroke recently. In the evening Pete Finch comes over to do a workshop on sound poetry for my extra-mural class. Over the road for a few beers afterwards, and spend most of the time talking about arrangements for the funeral. Who should be the bearers? Who should be the 'bouncers' to stand at the door and hand out a leaflet explaining how to get to the pub afterwards? Pete brings over a copy of M.S.'s Big Book, the *Companion*. Exciting to have it between my hands at last, after all these years of preparation – about which John had been habitually scathing. But he's in there, with the best part of a column devoted to him: 'A laconic eye is often turned on himself as poet-observer, grizzled by suburban living but still capable of humour, anger and compassion.' After the headword 'TRIPP, JOHN' is the year of his birth and an expectant dash, after which I pencil in '86'.

19.2.86
Brilliant sunny day, the hills across the bay bright with snow. Spend most of the morning on the phone. Meic says Rhydwen would not be up to MC-ing, so I phone Roland Mathias who, to my relief, says he will gladly officiate. He has some good ideas, and, being a lay-preacher, will know what *not* to say. Am anticipating trouble with the undertaker, a Mr Payne, who is clearly ill at ease with our unorthodox plans. He has told Jean she can't use the word 'pub' in the death notice, and that it must be changed to the more decorous 'hotel'.

20.2.86
Jean asks a friend called Phil to play the organ at the crem. Although a light entertainer whose first instrument is the piano, he says he can play Handel's 'Largo', 'Cwm Rhondda' and some filing out music. Phone the unctuous Payne who informs me there is a perfectly adequate council organist at the crem. Phil may play the 'Largo', if he must, but it must not be used as filing-in music, it must be a 'feature' number as the coffin disappears from sight. He has unsurprising views on the whip-round: it should not go to help out John's father but to pay the funeral costs. He gets all the names muddled up: the deceased is 'Mr Trick', and our chosen hymn gets confused with our main speaker, to become 'Glyn Rhondda'. Payne tries again to persuade me to drop our plan and revert to a 'normal' service. He knows a perfectly adequate 'Church of England' vicar who'll do a professional, Christian

committal, irrespective of the beliefs, or lack of, of the deceased. Have a chat with Glyn, who asks me to read a couple of poems during the service. He suggests 'Headmaster', but on re-reading it I'm not that keen, because John's characteristic self-disparagement ends on too negative a note, minimising his contribution. Phone Paul early evening. Poor old fellow. Says he feels terribly low, the house seeming so empty without John. I tell him of the many occasions that John asked me, should anything happen to his father to keep an eye on the old boy, and ask him to remember that. 'Alright, boy, yes, I'll remember that. Alright, boy, thanks.' The tone of his voice, so like his son's, reminding me of many of John's mannerisms: the way he'd pinch his thin nose between two fingers and a thumb, rubbing it up and down two or three times while making a remark; his nasal way of saying 'Jones' or 'sponge', as in 'apricot sponge'; his insistence on 'intelligence, perception, sensitivity and compassion' . . . Jean told me that John's father knows reams of poetry, and often recites it aloud, his favourite being 'Patience Strong' – although John had told her not to mention that to anyone. John Osmond remembers the time he called to collect John's telly review for *Arcade*, and found the Union Jack, the butcher's apron, flying high outside the bungalow. His father had run it up for some 'patriotic' occasion, and John was very embarrassed: 'Don't tell anyone!'

21.2.86
Crisp and sunny, although still freezing cold. This 'scimitar winter', as John had told Glyn. Train to Cardiff, picking up Terry at Neath, still trying to decide what poems to read at the crem. Jean picks me up at the Westgate and we drive to the 'funeral home' (ah, the Trippian ironies). Huge Victorian house, like a posh hotel with very silent guests. We are shown into the 'Family Meeting Room' (this is added to the bill too), a vast room with oil paintings, a lake of pink carpet, and chairs and sofas around the walls. Enter, then, the glozing Payne, whose appearance does not disappoint: waxy, pale, podgy head, and smiles 'as sincere as those of an Italian waiter in a crowded restaurant at two o'clock in the morning', which cannot conceal his impatience with the whole eccentric caper. Phil, he says, will not be allowed to take over from the council organist to play the 'Largo', and we had better be sure that our service takes no more than the allotted twenty minutes. I choose not to disturb him with the certain knowledge that,

being the last funeral of the week, and therefore inconveniencing no
subsequent funeral parties, the service is likely to last double that time.
At Thornhill, there's a phalanx of younger poets ready to bear John
shoulder high into the crematorium, rather than trundle him in Tesco-
style – Mr Payne's prefererence – on the silver trolley. The crem is
full, with standing room only at the back. Roland leads the service
with great dignity and sensitivity, and Glyn gives a warmly
affectionate address on John the man, and a brief appraisal of his work
as a poet. He quotes John's 'Notes on the way to the block':

> *There's a good crowd here today*
> *to see me off.*
> *I never knew I had so many friends*
> *or enemies.*
> *. . .*
> *I don't see anyone crying.*

– and describes him as 'a lyric poet of great skill and unfailing
fecundity . . . [who moved] rapidly from farce to compassion, from
indignation to fun-making, from conviction to scepticism'. I read 'Stop
on a Journey', we sit to listen to the council version of 'Largo', then,
after some parting words from Roland, we file out to stare at seven or
eight packets of flowers on the grass, and to chat in the sun. The venue
for the wake is a scruffy upstairs room with a couple of peeling silver
'stars' at the performance end – the kind of seedy place John would
have relished. We have tea and vegetarian sandwiches to start with,
and, at about 5.15, launch into the reminiscences and readings from
John's poems, with ten contributors in each of three sets, and the BBC
and our own man on hand to record the proceedings.[1] It's a warm-
hearted, genuinely celebratory occasion, although I can't get John's
father out of my mind, sitting in that empty bungalow about as alone
as it's possible for a nonagenerian to be. Some drunks from downstairs
come up and hover noisily at the back, but they are generally
containable. There is, however, one 'incident' of an aptly Trippian
kind. Sitting near the front as Côr Cochion Caerdydd rip into 'The
Internationale', I imagine I see a sandwich flying over my head and
into the fisted raised arms of the choir; and then another sandwich; and

[1] The recording of these songs, poems and reminiscences is available as *A Wake for
John Tripp* (Welsh Union of Writers, 1986).

then – I am not imagining it – a full pint of lager; next, the sandwich donor in person comes lurching to the front, clearly unhappy with the political bias of the musical programme, yelling 'No, you bastards, no, John was my friend, you can't do this!', and hurling more sandwiches at the choir. Robert Minhinnick and I 'surround' the sandwich man and shuffle him away, while the choir breaks immediately into 'Hen Wlad fy Nhadau', and everyone leaps to their feet to join in the singing, which brings to a conclusion the magnificent, if troubled, contribution of Côr Cochion Caerdydd. A whip-round towards the end of the evening raises nearly £200 for John's father.

4.xi.88

Drive over to Pentyrch, nearly three years after John's death, to help Jean scatter his ashes. She has been keeping him, with Paul who died soon afterwards, in the airing cupboard, waiting for an opportunity to scatter his ashes in an appropriate manner. In the back garden, before we set out for the Garth, she takes the £60 oak casket out of the cardboard box in which it had come from the undertaker, to discover that it is impossible to get into it without a screwdriver. She fetches one from the house, and I undo the four screws that secure the bottom of the expensive but shoddily presented casket: 'John Howell Tripp' is crudely inscribed on a metal plaque that has been stuck askew on the lid of the casket, whose wood is only perfunctorily varnished. The bottom comes away to reveal the ashes themselves, loosely wrapped in a plastic bag which is so gossamer thin that in lifting it out of the casket my fingers rupture the bag and plunge straight into the ashes. We need something stronger, so Jean goes into the house for a shopping bag – a bright purple one with 'Liberty' emblazoned in gold letters. We decant John into the Liberty bag, and set out across the fields. We climb up an old burial mound to the triangulation point, Jean talking about belting across these heights on horseback, with her daughter, before a fall and hairline fracture of the spine put her off riding. We drop down, and make for the eastern and slightly lower hump of the Garth, where she has decided she wants the ashes spread. Below us is Taff's Well, site of the long-demolished Oak Tree Forge where John's father 'shod horses in the sun/while I threw old shoes at an iron pin.' Jean takes the purple bag and empties a zaggy stream of ashes onto the sheep-nibbled grass; then, having emptied about half, she hands me the bag and I empty the rest. Off-white ashes, here and there of a yellowish tinge, some of a darker grey; much of the more powdery content takes to the wind, but doesn't, thankfully, blow on us. What are we afraid of? They are only ashes, and who's to say even, in fact, that they are John's? There's no escaping echoes of John's poem, 'Ashes on the Cotswolds', where he describes accompanying a friend on a mission to scatter his sister-in-law's ashes; the friend drives 'like Fangio' until eventually,

> *Somewhere near Cleeve Hill*
> *he took the lid off the urn*
> *and threw the ashes into the wind.*
> *They blew back on us*
> *as I tried to take a photograph*
> *to send to his grieving brother.*
>
> *The ashes disappeared on the wind*
> *and were dust on our clothes.*
> *We shook it off, and I took*
> *a photo of the urn in the grass.*
> *As we say on these occasions,*
> *it was what she would have wanted.*

Jean wonders if, in some way, John is watching . . . are these ashes the end of the story, the absolute end? I say Harri P.J. is convinced they are not, although I can't share that conviction. What lives on, though, is the writing, the continuing movement through our lives of his poetry. As we descend down a different route, scuffing through brown, dead leaves at the edge of the lane, I carry the empty plastic bag in my right hand, and feel the fingers of both hands a little dusty from contact with the ashes. Back in the house Jean passes me a bottle of champagne to open: we drink a toast to John's memory, miss him, and get stuck into a roast chicken, cooked with lemon and ginger, roast spuds and a green salad; dessert, in homage to his fine story, is an apricot sponge, splashed liberally with curaçao, to moisten it a little.

Mary Lloyd Jones:
A Portrait of the Artist[1]

When they asked her in school what she wanted to be when she grew up, the little girl from Pontarfynach had no doubt about the answer: an artist. But she dared not voice it. Mary Lloyd Jones knew, even at the age of seven, that hers was a laughably outlandish ambition, so, to avoid the guffaws of her classmates, she offered up some suitably demure alternative, and kept her dreams to herself.

Inevitably, she found herself performing a range of life's more conventional roles, not least those of housewife, mother and teacher, but she remained doggedly true to that first desire. Mary Lloyd Jones is today one of Wales's most adventurous and provocative landscape artists, a passionate symphonist in colour, whose works in a wide variety of media – luminous water colours, battlesome oils, calico wall hangings of formidable scale and beauty – are in demand through the countries of Britain, mainland Europe and the USA.

So many of 'our' painters either fled the nest early, seldom to return (the Richard Wilson trajectory) or, like Graham Sutherland, flew in, already well plumaged, from the big nest next door. Of the hundreds of artists at work in Wales today, a minority, I'd guess, are native born, and many, finding Wales too hard to handle, have exiled themselves internally from their cultural context. Mary Lloyd Jones is a comparative rarity – a Welsh-born artist, a woman of *y fro Gymraeg* (Welsh-speaking Wales), who has stood her ground in Wales, engaging the more profoundly with the topography, history, folk life and languages of her country as her art has matured.

Welsh artists are sometimes warned off landscape painting. It is said to be an alien form, an English import; there were never the patrons in poverty-stricken Wales to foster the growth of an indigenous landscape tradition; Welsh artists would make more patriotic use of their time and talent reconfecting the *gwerin* or carving lovespoons. The trouble

---

[1] Published in *The Colour of Saying*, ed. Eve Ropek (Gomer Press, 2001). An earlier version appeared in *Planet* 88 (1991).

with this argument is that it neglects a centuries-old landscape tradition that is undeniably indigenous: that of the poets. The spirit of place has moved consistently through Welsh poetry, from the *cynfeirdd* down to modern poets such as Waldo Williams eulogising the Presely Hills or, in English, Chris Torrance, remembrancer of Cwm Nedd. It is a tradition not simply of surfaces, as in photographic views, but of depths and contested meanings. If permission is sought by the contemporary visual artist, here, surely, it is to be found. Mary Lloyd Jones, who often uses words or lines of poetry in her paintings, draws evident strength from her country's literary treasure hoard, although she, like many other visual artists, must wish sometimes that a modest fraction of the adulation heaped upon Wales's poets might tiptoe now and then in the direction of Wales's relatively neglected painters.

Most neatly representational landscapes seem to issue from a world that is anchored in the solidities of classical Newtonian mechanics: what the eye sees is what the hand attempts to paint. The modern artist, alert to the consequences of quantum mechanics, relativity and chaos theory, and conscious of the findings of archaeologists and anthropologists, knows that there is more to all this than meets the eye. The old strategies for pinning down visual images – perspective, due proportion, colour decorum – are incapable of articulating the complex phenomena with which an artist such as Mary Lloyd Jones might wish to engage. She has had to find new means of expression, although her main subject, upland mid and west Wales, is at least 440 million years old. It is between these poles that Mary Lloyd Jones's art moves, celebrating all the energies – geological, vegetable, animal, human – that have made her landscape what it is, and warning, long before environmentalism became fashionable, of the dangers of human alienation from the Earth. 'My aim,' she says, 'is not to reproduce outward appearances but to attempt to convey the spirit of a particular place. Through my work I try to create links with the past, with the lives of previous generations, with folk memory and with the myths and legends, all of which contribute to the atmosphere of a landscape. I would like to bring about a heightened awareness of the land and the multi-faceted nature of our understanding of it.'

She may have known from an early age that she wanted to be an artist, but it took Mary Lloyd Jones several decades to realise that her most rewarding subject would be the hills and valleys of her native *bro*, a rugged swathe of Ceredigion which might look today like the epitome of 'rural Wales' but which is one of the earliest sites of industrial despoliation in Britain, thanks to the lead and silver mining that was pursued here from the time of the Romans. Pontarfynach (Devil's Bridge), twelve miles east of Aberystwyth, gave her a warm and encouraging childhood, but artists were unheard-of creatures there, and Mary felt, as she grew up, that she would have to get away in order to become one. It's only since the 1980s that she has managed to 'come home', mining in the Ystwyth and Rheidol valleys an apparently inexhaustible seam of inspiration, and finding in herself the confidence to paint not as she 'ought' to but as she needs.

She was born in 1934 into a family of farmers and wool workers rooted, for as long as they remember, in the region of Pumlumon; she is sure she is of pre-Celtic stock. Theirs, she says, was a traditional peasant way of life, though there were books, newspapers and fiery discussions; her father was a wonderful storyteller.

'I was forever drawing,' she told me, 'and my parents gave me every encouragement. My brother was born when I was three, but there were no other kids around at all. I had to amuse myself. Drawing was my great entertainment.' Although steeped in all the nuances of twentieth-century Modernism, she seems never to have lost sight of the spontaneity and magic of childhood creativity. 'In a world dominated by Cartesian rationality and masculine logic, where only that which is measurable is given value, I wish to demonstrate through creative endeavour the importance of intuition, of lateral and irrational thought processes. Logic is not enough, and in our imbalanced culture to seek out that which is immeasurable is important.' Tapping such forces, she works powerful transformations.

On the daily trip to Ardwyn Grammar School in Aberystwyth, Mary would pass by the landscape which, to the mature artist, would become something of an obsession; to her, then, it meant nothing – just so much wind-blown grass. She had heard the jazz on the radio, and was eager to escape to the alluringly alien planet from which that tantalising music appeared to come.

Cardiff, where she entered art school in 1951, seemed indeed a galaxy away from the rural solitudes of Ceredigion. Lodging at Tonpentre, Mary would travel down to the city on the Rhondda train: 'I was shocked. Everything was so bleak, so black and filthy and awful, and I couldn't understand why nobody else seemed to be shocked. Cardiff was a terrific culture shock initially, but I was chuffed to be in the city and absorbed everything madly.'

The college course fell somewhat short of expectations: it was in the company of fellow students, headed by the stellar Ernest Zobole (1927-99), that Mary gained most of her education. 'Every day we'd take over a compartment on the Rhondda train and have intense discussions going down to Cardiff. If anyone was foolish enough to come into our compartment it was arranged that someone would throw a fit, and the intruder would soon absent himself from our manic seminar.' There would be sandwiches in the park at lunchtime, then a session with the art books in the Central Library or a visit to the National Museum's Gwendoline Davies Collection; the Impressionists exerted an irresistible pull.

So too did Rhondda-born John Jones, a student in the same year as Mary. They married towards the end of the course, and, after John's national service, left Wales for him to take a teaching job in Romford. There had been little discussion, in the ferment of the Cardiff years, of what it might mean to be a 'Welsh artist'; indeed, the words seemed to cancel each other out. 'In order to be a painter I had not to be Welsh, I thought. We felt we had been missing out by not being near London. That, we thought, was the place to be, so we were keen to make the move.' Their first daughter, Gudrun, was eleven months old; their second, Sianed, was born the following year, in 1959. They stayed three years altogether, but it was hardly the promised land of their imaginings, and they came back home every holiday, 'to keep sane'.

In 1961 they managed to return to Wales for good, settling in the Aberaeron area initially, and making a living as teachers in various schools and art colleges. In 1975 they bought an old school in Aberbanc near Llandysul, and converted it into a comfortable home with spacious studios and residential facilities for small groups of students. They were for many years a mystery tour destination for the WI and Merched y Wawr. Fifty at a time would troop into Mary's studio for perhaps their first confrontation with modern art.

To the fan of chocolate box scenes, Mary Lloyd Jones's work must look as if someone has gone crazy with a paint palette. She likes to help the sceptical viewer to a deeper understanding of her art by pointing to connections between her uncompromisingly contemporary works, with their abstracting tendencies, and the often entirely abstract design of something as cosily familiar as the traditional patchwork quilt. It was a revelation for her when, in the early '70s, her aunt dug out an old quilt made by Mary's great grandmother. 'Here was a woman artist using colour and form in an abstract, confident and emotional way, producing a large-scale and public piece of art.' The quilt, hung proudly in Mary's living room, was the permission for which her imagination had been waiting.

On the wall opposite is a deeply affecting portrait of her father which, painted in 1973, represents another significant advance, moving her on from experiments in geometrical abstraction towards an art that, still formally daring, concerns itself more centrally with the artist's own people, places and preoccupations. It was much praised in the 1974 National Eisteddfod. 'I like to have it around,' she jokes, 'because it shows people who are baffled by my squiggles that I *can* do "the real thing".'

Like Iolo Morganwg, that mercurial genius of the eighteenth century, she is a remembrancer, a praise-poet in oils and watercolours of the layered history and numinous forces of the land of Wales. 'The real thing', surface reality imitated in pseudo-photographic terms, is of no interest to Mary Lloyd Jones. Hers is a spirited, intuitive art in rebellion against stodgy academicism and the Sunday painter's fussing over authenticating detail. Like much Welsh poetry, her paintings have that rare ability to function both abstractly – as 'objects in themselves' – and as interpretations of specific and recognisable places. She talks of her attempt to honour the spirit of place as 'singing the landscape'. Hers is a considerable responsibility; for, having encountered the work of Mary Lloyd Jones, we are unlikely ever again to see the Welsh landscape as we did before: she broadens and deepens our under-standing.

'A painting *starts* with what I see, but what happens on the canvas or on the cloth is something else. At Ponterwyd, for instance, I found some quartz scattered in a certain shape on the hillside, and this suggested markings of a more human kind. When I worked up the painting from a number of small sketches I made on the spot, I deliberately emphasised and simplified those shapes. To give another example, the felling of the forestry is noisy and brutal, and the ground is left looking much like a battlefield. In my paintings I choose to use colour expressively. Red is the colour of blood, and my paintings show a land hacked and bruised, exposing raw and scarred tissue. Dancing lines echo the pattern of felled trees but also suggest that underlying life continues. I *have* seen in the landscape the colours I use, but I exaggerate them, make them more dramatic, bring them into collision with each other. I like using pure colour, without mixing it.'

She talks of getting herself psyched up for work in the studio, and her surfaces, with their urgent sweeps and Steadman-like splatterings, are alive with the excitement and energy of creative labour. There is no attempt to disguise her procedures or to feign completion. All too aware of humanity's frequently disastrous 'mastery' of nature, she refuses to submit the music of her complexly resonant landscapes to the impoverishing discipline of perspective. She can grow impatient with the rigidities of the rectangle, and explode her tableaux in irregular, tatty-edged shapes along the length of a wall. These apparent 'liberties' of form work in creative tension with carefully executed lines of stitching or gracefully delineated coils, dogs-teeth, bones, human and animal figures. Art that purports to be simply representational or imagist offers to do most of the work for its spectators: what you see is what you get. Her paintings are not for the collector of 'framed views'. Mary Lloyd Jones wants to involve her audiences, to make them participators in, rather than merely consumers of, her landscapes. Is that long reddish line a distant road, a watercourse, the head of a hawk? What are we to make of these visitations from aboriginal or Beaker art that our 'educated' eyes are pleased to read as an 'N' or a 'Y' or a stylised breast? And if that ancient quotation really is a vagina with eyes, does that begin to undermine certain assumptions about the predominantly male nature of the language of art? We share in her playful sense of ambiguity, her delight in interconnections and the relatedness of forms.

It is only since 1989, when she gave up her job as visual arts officer for Dyfed, that Mary Lloyd Jones has been working as a full-time artist. Visits to America and Ireland, where she found cultures that value their artists, encouraged her to take that important step. 'In those two countries, if you're serious about your art, you do it full-time. You know that it's okay to do it, you are not a freak, it's not some kind of hole-in-the-corner activity. Everywhere is not like Wales or England'.

In Philadelphia her friend Kathy Quigley, who participated in the Wales/Philadelphia Visual Arts Exchange some years ago, works in a building which is five storeys high and has twenty artists' studios on each. 'Trucks were pulling into this building and paintings were going out: there was a market there. Lots of young professional people in

America are buying art before they've bought their furniture.' It was frustrating to have to return to a country with an underdeveloped visual arts tradition, where few people visit art galleries and even fewer consider buying an original painting. 'There are now young Welsh artists, many of them women, who have gone to art school and want work in Wales. People should be buying this work and looking after these artists instead of concentrating solely on the mortgage and the Volvo. What we know about the earliest people, we know through art. And we are part of that continuity. If Wales can't be bothered about its art then it will disappear.'

The year 2000 finds Mary Lloyd Jones busier and more productive than ever. Travel – not only to Ireland and America, but Brittany, the Scottish Highlands and, in recent years, Rajasthan – has always refreshed her palate and proposed new ways of orchestrating colour. She manages, in spite of her foreign adventures and work for television and radio, to mount several exhibitions a year, and estimates that from the twelve or fifteen sketches that result from a day in the field she will produce annually about a hundred finished works.

Though rooted in *y fro Gymraeg*, Mary Lloyd Jones is neither land-locked nor history-fixed: the past for her, as for Iolo Morganwg, whose bardic alphabet inscribes transmuting messages across her landscapes, is an activist in the present. She is as intrigued by theories of relativity and chaos as by the desert light and sugared colours of a destination as new and strange to her as Rajasthan.

An exuberant celebrator of the diversity that feeds the very root of life, Mary Lloyd Jones invites us to enter into detail with the spirit of her chosen places, reconnecting our jaded, techno-conditioned sensibilities with those subterranean energies and the 'hen bethau anghofiedig dynol ryw' (Old forgotten things of humankind), to quote Waldo Williams, which in our frenzied pursuit of novelty we ignore at our, and the planet's, peril.

The Writing on the Wall

Land of Bards and Songbirds[1]

'The poet has a peculiar relation to the public,' the American Randall Jarrell said once. 'It is unaware of his existence.'

Now, in the 'gwlad beirdd a chantorion' this is not a thought that is ever supposed to cross the Welsh mind, least of all in Eisteddfodic August, when a nation of under three million people stages the largest cultural festival of its kind in the world, the twin peaks of which comprise the crowning and chairing of poets. Wales, our national anthem boasts, is above all a land of bards and songbirds (no mention of rugby players); here, for over 1500 years, the poet has been a man or woman of the people, active on the community's behalf in a way that is unimaginable in England or the United States. You'd have to go as far west as Nicaragua, as far east as Russia, it's said, to find societies where the poet is held in equivalently high regard.

But this rosy view of the unique social contract that exists between people and poet is conditional on the Welsh language, whose heartland erosion is a threat to the Welsh being of us all, whether or not we speak the language. There are writers bundling into Wales who have no idea where they are, and no intention of finding out. Anybody, it seems, can become a 'Welsh writer' – a 'Welsh writer' who, in the case of one such who has lived here since the 1960s, can write a review of the poems of Iolo Goch and confess cheerfully that until this moment she had never even heard of him. I estimate that about a third of the 158 writers of English in the Arts Council's latest *Writers on Tour* book are writers who have come to live in Wales since the 1970s. Many of these people have indeed taken pains to discover where they are, and have made important contributions to the culture; others have not. Once again the fate of the language has been the subject of the winning *awdl* at the National; chaired poet Idris Reynolds envisioned the Welsh language in the terminal grip of winter. 'Of course, spring will come again but not for the Welsh language,' he said. 'I fear I see

[1] First published in *Wales on Sunday*, August 20.8.89.

the death of the language in the Welsh-speaking areas of the countryside, and I am worried about that.'

Without the language, Wales would surely become in a short time as indistinguishably a part of England as has the once Celtic land of Dumnonia (Devon), and no amount of patriotic good works on the part of the English-speaking remnant could hold back from the brink of oblivion most of the other things we prize as elements of our distinctiveness. An early casualty would be our native understanding that poetry is as necessary to the wellbeing of a community as fresh bread or a decent pub.

It is sometimes assumed by those who write in *yr hen iaith* that the Welsh who write in English enjoy the prospect of a huge potential readership, but that is not how Welsh writers of English perceive the situation. They are only too aware that in English-speaking Wales the sense of a native 'reading public' is nearly non-existent; in the supposed 'gwlad beirdd a chantorion' where, as John Tripp has written, poets dissolve naturally into the people, those who write 'in the wrong language' are for the most part invisible and ineffectual, not because their work is 'no good' but because, thanks to the culturally deracinating effects of anglicisation, they lack a sustaining literary culture.

To many who have now been buffeted for generations by those anglicising winds, poetry has become an irrelevance, a debased bit of nonsense on a birthday card, an advertising jingle, some rhyme-a-minute Dai's sycophantic effusions in the local rag; or perhaps it's perceived as a product of the university, an academic's meal ticket. Those who find themselves alienated from 'literature' and educated into contempt for poetry rarely, if ever, happen upon the real thing. But when ambushed by it – at a poems and pints session, for instance – they often find themselves agreeably surprised that poetry is not, after all, the meaningless sideshow they'd taken it to be, but, with its unique and varied means of articulating experience, a power in their lives, something that speaks affectingly of and for them.

Where Welsh is spoken this is old news. In the strongholds of the language people are familiar enough with the many jobs a poet has to do: people's remembrancer, whistle-blower, consolidator, elegist, eulogist, satirist, entertainer, 'carpenter of song'. In an echo of those times when the poet was a centrally significant voice of polity, he or she will sometimes take a public stand, as in the cases of Waldo Williams or R.S. Thomas, on issues of national importance. It would be difficult to imagine *The Daily Express*, say, sounding out Poet Laureate Hughes on nuclear defence or toxic waste.

Too often in Wales, we don't know what we've got 'til it's gone, to borrow a line from Joni Mitchell. In the 'gwlad beirdd a chantorion' we should make much more, in both languages, of poetry's presence in the public domain. Many places in Britain have their 'city artist': Newcastle upon Tyne, for example, pays homage to native musical traditions by appointing a Lord Mayor's Northumbrian piper. As the princes of old had their court poets, why not a 'Bard to the Council' in Swansea, Bangor, Aberystwyth, Merthyr, and so on – or, developing the idea, bards to NUPE, the Wales TUC, hospitals, Women's Institutes, the Welsh Council of Churches? They could be usefully employed penning verses – not too mindlessly flattering, one would hope – for inscription on walls, or public proclamation or the pages of publications. Whether the highest 'court' in the land, the Welsh Office, should have its own bard under the present English incumbent might present problems: imagine R.S. Thomas as Peter Walker's bardic right-hand man . . . But he might be persuaded to settle for a fellow imported talent – Kingsley Amis, perhaps, or Attila the Stockbroker.

The Tradition that Might Be:
the Folk Poets of English-speaking Wales[1]

It becomes increasingly difficult, in this hyperactive TV age of invaded communities and crumbling traditions, for poetry of any kind to function. That Wales is still, just, more accommodating of the literary arts than most other countries in Western Europe, owes much to the manner in which Welsh poetry is intricately grounded in the popular base of its *bardd gwlad*, or folk poet, tradition. The comparative invisibility and inffectuality of English-language writing in Wales is surely attributable, in large measure, to the absence of such a tradition in her younger tongue. One glimpses fleeting shadows of it from time to time, but loose wires and lost connections are as defining of 'Anglo-Welsh literature' today as ever they were, and these odds and ends rarely come together for long enough to make up much of a coherent whole. As Chris O'Neill has said,

> . . . *every new Anglo-Welsh writer begins the tradition afresh. Or rather, with an imperative behind him and the vacuum in front, he selects a lineage from the more or less inchoate elements available and hopes that an audience will appear. There is a Past to his writing, but it is so jumbled that it can neither weigh him down nor carry him; he is uncomfortably free to make his own discoveries about where Wales is, and whether it is necessary, and whether he is necessary, and those other awkward questions.*[2]

The pathetic unpopularity of 'Welsh writing in English' should worry us. All that effort . . . Who's it for? Who bothers with it, outside the tiny coterie of magazine readers? Is it, after all, nothing much more than a cottage industry perpetuated to keep a few academics afloat? The historians of our 'tradition' point to its provenance in musty

---

[1] First published in *Planet* 72 (1988–9).
[2] 'Where We Are Now: A Note on the Most Contemporary Anglo-Welsh Poetry', *The Contemporary Literary Scene in Wales* (Yr Academi Gymreig, 1980).

parsonages and polite society, inferring, it seems, that we shouldn't trouble our heads too much that the majority of the population are hardly aware of its existence. It's an utterly arse-about-front literature, with school and college courses on it and the academic respectability of critical volumes written about it (by sometimes excellent and most necessary critics) – but hardly any readers. The few who do read Anglo-Welsh literature, the researchers continue to find, tend to be the Welsh-speakers; the English-speaking majority are reading Jeffrey Archer and Jackie Collins. A fetish of 'good taste' seem to have held us back from the vulgarity of wanting to connect with the people of Wales – which we could do much more of, perhaps, if we had some kind of parallel to the *bardd gwlad* networks and practices. Welsh writing in English has often paid respectful obeisance to the 'senior tradition', but it has generally gone its own haphazard way, paying insufficient attention to what in the Welsh tradition could help it to a stronger sense of form, purpose and appeal. The aspiring Anglo-Welsh writer peeks out onto what seems a pretty barren landscape devoid of the sense of a literary community enjoyed by a writer in *y fro Gymraeg*.

Saunders Lewis provides us with a succinct definition of the *bardd gwlad*:

> *The folk poet was a craftsman or farmer who followed his occupation in the area where he was born, who knew all the people in the neighbourhood and could trace their family connections; who also knew the dialect of his native heath, and every story, event and omen, who used the traditional gift of poetry to console a bereaved family, to contribute to the jollifications at a wedding feast, or to record a contretemps with lightly malicious satire. His talent was a normal part of the propriety and entertainment of the Welsh rural society, chronicling its happenings, adorning its walls and its tombstones, recording its characters, its events, its sadness and its joy. It was a craft; the metres, the vocabulary, the praise and the words of courtesy were traditional. It was not expected that it should be different from its kind. It was sufficient that it appropriately followed the pattern.*[3]

---

[3] Quoted in W. Rhys Nicholas, *The Folk Poets* (University of Wales Press, 1978).

Here is a description, in spite of its past tense, of a tradition that in *y fro Gymraeg* is still in reasonably good heart, and has transferred effortlessly to radio and television as among the most popular entertainment on Welsh-language airwaves. It has ancient antecedents, being, as Tony Conran has observed,

> . . . *the last decadence of the tradition of Taliesin, the magic craft that had once made kings by praising them in verse, now shrunk to chaffing fellow farmers about adjudicating a ploughing competition. However, it is still the central feature of the work of the true* bardd gwlad *or folk poet, the really functional art of community, celebrating with verse anything that happens that is noteworthy or memorable . . . There can be no doubt that this vast poetical output, from all kinds and conditions of men, but chiefly from rural localities, constitutes the greatest body of creative folk art in the British Isles and probably in Western Europe.*
>
> The Cost of Strangeness (Gomer, 1982)

To what extent is it possible for an English-writing poet to participate in this bedrock Welsh tradition? It certainly *has* been possible, albeit in rather exceptional circumstances: Cyril Gwynn, 'The Bard of Gower', who died in Australia in 1988 at the age of ninety, was probably as near as the Englishry of Wales have come to producing a typical *bardd gwlad*; the unusual disposition of pre-war Gower as a self-contained organic community being, of course, a pre-condition – as Harri Webb's recollection of him suggests:

> *Welsh speakers would recognize in him a mixture of Pontshaen and Wil Parsel, and might marvel that an Englishry could produce such a 'deryn'. But this was the special magic of old Gower. It was as Welsh as anywhere in Wales, yet used English naturally, without strain or shame or awkwardness or guilt or apology.*
>
> 'Webb's Progress', Planet 30 (1976)

For four decades, from the early years of the century until the mid 1950s when he left Gower for good, Cyril Gwynn was the chronicler of a way of life that is gone now forever. Ploughing match dinners, weddings, wakes, Christmas parties, Courts Leet and harvest suppers: no Gower function was felt to be complete without a 'yarn' or two from Cyril Gwynn. At the height of his powers he would go out two or three nights a week to fulfil his obligations as his people's poet:

> *From somewhere in the back of the village hall a lean, sunburnt, sandy-haired, unsmiling farmer makes his way half reluctantly to the stage. After the friendly expectant applause has died down he stands there for a moment or two, as if ill at ease and at a loss for his opening words . . . a moment later we are being slowly put under the spell of a new 'Gower Yarn – told in rhyme by Cyril Gwynn' – Bard of Gower. The style of the man and Cyril Gwynn's verses are Cyril Gwynn himself – quietly reflective, unspectacular, filled with a warm humanity and a gentle humour, moving slowly but firmly to the climax, which he usually reserves for the last line.*[4]

This could be a scene in any of those districts – Ffair Rhos, Mynytho, Penllyn – where the *bardd gwlad* has been an important part of community life, the only obvious difference being the linguistic one. Cyril Gwynn was in his day a Gower celebrity, while remaining entirely unknown outside the area; any notion of Swansea or Cardiff 'recognition' would have struck him as meaningless. As the 'laureate' of Gower, he wrote – 'with no pretension to literary excellence or grammatical perfection,' as he'd say – almost nothing that was not concerned with the peninsula and its people: the opening of a new road, the passing of a well-loved member of the community, the financial difficulties of farming, the beauties of nature, the arrival of a new vicar, the skills of miller and blacksmith – such, in true *bardd gwlad* style, were his subjects.

His was basically an oral craft. Like Dic Jones, the best known contemporary exponent of the art of the *bardd gwlad*, Cyril would do most of his composition, quite literally, in the field – ploughing or hoeing or turning hay; by the end of the day's work the poem would be there, in his head, committed for life to his prodigious memory. The speed and noise of modern farming, imposing mechanical rhythms and divorcing the senses from the stimulation of one's surroundings, must make it considerably harder to compose in this way.

His vision, expressed in the form of the narrative folk ballad, is informed by an awareness of rapid technological and demographic

[4] J. Mansel Thomas, 'Cyril Gwynn – Bard of Gower', *Gower* 4 (1951).

change in the wider world, and is basically conservationist. The town
(Swansea) is a place of 'noise and riot' where 'belching stacks obscure
the sky'. It threatens, in one of his prophetic dreams, to spill over into
rural Gower, resulting in the despoliation of the countryside and the
corrosion of social relationships. Life in his Gower is harmonious and,
apparently, classless:

> *We have no daily war to fight*
> *'Twixt capital and labour.*
> *Here each must work and do aright*
> *His duty to his neighbour.*

The suggestion is that the fragmentation of a class-divided society is
something alien that threatens from without. There is in fact ample
evidence of social hierarchy in Cyril Gwynn's arcadia, but conflict
between classes is merely a distant possibility held in check by a
collaborative ideology born of acceptance of the idea of Gower as an
independent, united community.

The real conflict in his verse is between Gower people and outsiders,
such as the Home Counties-type major or flashy snobs from town,
forerunners of today's yuppies. Their ostentatious authority, mediated
primarily through pompous language, is shown in opposition to the
down-to-earth and apparently 'backward' ways of the natives; the
outsider threatens to undermine local control of the situation, but it is
always local genius that wins through, and the intruder is finally
exposed as a foolish upstart.

Cyril Gwynn had a profound influence on a young contender from
Swansea who was to emerge in the 1960s with a rather wider
constituency to defend with his pen. Harri Webb, whose Gower family
enjoyed close ties with the Gwynns, has written of Cyril that he was

> *. . . I do not know how much of an example and a stimulus to my*
> *young imagination. I used to have many of his cheerful, simple*
> *rhymes, tales and musings by heart . . . I retained a fondness for*
> *them throughout the years of Ronsard and Baudelaire and all the*
> *other giants . . . And he established in my mind an image of the poet*
> *as essentially a social rather than a solitary character, one moreover,*
> *fortunate in his gifts, however humble, and under something of an*
> *obligation to spread them around for the pleasure of the people he*

belongs to, rather than to hoard them in the dank private cellars of introspection and incomprehension.

This, he concludes, was 'a priceless attitude to have inherited at this juncture'. For most aspiring English-writing poets such an inheritance is unlikely, unless they receive it by hearing or reading of such things in the Welsh-speaking parts. There has been no one like Cyril Gwynn operating in the English-speaking regions for decades, although certain individuals, like the late Mogg Williams in the Ogmore Valley and the doggerelising landlady Jan Smith of Caegarw, may have seemed intermittently to have been performing a few of the tasks of a folk poet.

Where Cyril Gwynn and others differ most from their Welsh-language counterparts is in their lack of cultural context. Although Cyril competed in one or two local *eisteddfodau*, he worked for the most part in isolation from the tradition, lacking the sense of a 'community of bards' that is the inheritance of a folk poet in *y fro Gymraeg* with its bardic contests, *athrawon beirdd* (poets' teachers), *nosweithiau llawen* and general atmosphere of informed critical debate. He would certainly have been nourished by something stronger than mere cultural 'seepage', because of exposure, in his youth, to the more eisteddfodic society of Briton Ferry and Morriston, as well as, later on, the Welsh-language culture of north Gower, but he would not have been drawn to his bardic role through any self-conscious assimilation to the tradition.

You can hardly have a folk poetry, of course, without a folk, a collection of people living within a defined territory, holding in common a sense of things done together in that particular place. There can be no community in Wales today as clearly defined as was Cyril Gwynn's Gower – itself broken up, now, into struggling mini-communities or strings of moneyed 'properties' where nobody knows anyone else and the sense of 'community' is as dead as poor old Phil Tanner. Given a locality which manages to retain some sense of community, the aspiring *bardd gwlad* has fertile ground in which to plant his or her seeds. Whether or not the would-be community poet's seeds germinate and take root may depend to some extent on applying lessons learned from knowledge of the *bardd gwlad* tradition.

A few years ago, a roadshow of local poets organised a tour of Gower pubs, drawing gratifyingly large audiences of fifty or seventy people at a time. Some of Cyril Gwynn's recently republished 'Gower Yarns' were read on these occasions, and they caught the ear, and the imagination, of a young Rhosili farmer, John Beynon, who shortly afterwards began to do something of a Cyril himself, treating audiences at the Young Farmers Club or Sports Club dinner to his own contemporary verse narratives, based on happenings in the locality. Reciting them, like Cyril, without reference to text, he was taken aback by their enthusiastic reception. 'In spite of television, or perhaps because of it,' he told me, 'there seems to be a terrific hunger in people for something that reflects their own community and way of life.' A sustaining reciprocation between poet and community is threatened, he seemed to acknowledge, by the influx of outsiders. 'Half the people in Rhosili are newcomers,' he said. 'Things are changing fast.'

Valleys communities might be thought to be more promising territory for the development of *bardd gwlad* practices. Here, indeed, we find a number of 'local poets' who manage, shakily, to carry on something of the *bardd gwlad*'s calling – by accident, usually, and without realizing it, which explains some of their weaknesses. Some of this material rarely rises above the level of that broken-backed doggerel beloved of the local press, or sub-Dylan baroque word-coils trying hard to be modern – what Kim Howells, formerly of the NUM, once called 'a dismal hash of sympathetic dirges about working in the bowels of the earth . . . tame, tensionless agit-prop . . . mawkish sentimentality'. Isolation is again the problem with many of these poets: they can drift through life as blithely unaware of the work of their compatriots – like Idris Davies, Gwenallt, Tripp, Webb – as of poets elsewhere – Mayakovsky, Brecht, Cardenal – who have made it new. The occasional grotesque patronising of their efforts by the media, always game for 'human interest', tricks some into thinking that they have somehow 'arrived'; they are perplexed, then, at their 'lack of success' on a larger stage which, self-protectively, they put down to the 'closed shop' exclusiveness of a largely unexamined (but not entirely imaginary) 'literary establishment'. It is a pity to see the raw talent of some of these writers frittered away into various dead ends through a lack of connectedness.

One of the more successful *beirdd gwlad* of the Valleys is Irene Thomas of Ebbw Vale, a witty and celebratory poet of the locality who has built up in a short time an eager following of 'non-literary' readers and above all, listeners – for this 'Artist, Ballroom Dance Teacher and

Spiritual Healer', with a glimmer of sequins about her, is quite a performer. She knows her people and their history thoroughly; she names them copiously in her poems; she has an unerring ear for their speech; she has an artist's eye for detail and a woman's way of seeing beyond the exhausted imagery of tip and pit wheel to more neglected signifiers of her people's way of life.

While the notion of an *athro beirdd* might be foreign to most of those who write in English, the writers' workshop, which has grown in popularity in the 1980s, can replicate the function of the poets' teacher, and has been in some cases influential in transforming the literary climate of an area. In one Glamorgan town a group of two or three unusually talented beginners, who were soon writing fully achieved poems, succeeded in conjuring up a keenly receptive public for their rootedly native work. Unfortunately, their manifest success caught the envious eye of some artsy shiners from outside who muscled in and hijacked this promising little scene; the rampant self-indulgence of these dabblers soon scattered a carefully nurtured audience, and the originators have been working patiently ever since to rebuild their bridges.

These various stops and starts may not be thought to add up to very much, but such activities, and the invariably positive responses to them, demonstrate, at least, a live enthusiasm for some kind of continuity of cultural traditions that are still, in the heartland, widespread and effective. Perhaps the biggest brake on the further development of a 'community poetry' in English, apart from the lack of the manifold support network afforded to the *beirdd gwlad* by their linguistic culture, is the current attenuation throughout the nation of both Welsh- and English-speaking communities. The relationship between poetry and people is, however, a two-way process, and the Welsh poet, in either language, can be part of the resistance. That this happens comparatively rarely in the English language is partly because too many of us – writers as well as readers and listeners – still don't sufficiently realize who we have been, and who we might become.

The Haiku: Some Observations

1. *Singing the dance of the atoms*[1]

Although I had been a reader of haiku for many years and sometime expounder on the form in writing workshops, it was not until two challenges lurched at me about a decade ago that I began to be a haiku writer. Since then hardly a day passes without me jotting down in the bum-pocket notebook some phrases towards the expression of a 'haiku moment' – 'a choir sways downwind from the pub, tied and suited, in a cloud of aftershave', from yesterday evening – which I might hope, later, to knock into shape as a functioning haiku or senryu.

The first of these challenges was to judge, with David Kerrigan, the Cardiff International Haiku Competition. Faced with a haiku mountain of over a thousand entries, we whittled them down to about a hundred which were worth serious consideration. En route we consigned to the reject pile efforts that read like alliterative newspaper headlines, sloganistic messages about drugs, dogs, religion and the fall of communism, whimsical generalised 'wisdoms', poetical Japanesey things full of 'myriad flowers' and 'russet foliage', and scores of five-seven-fivers whose authors seemed to be as bereft of notions about the function and feel of a true haiku as the competitor who hit us with an offering that was all of thirty-eight lines long. Bludgeoned by so many non-haiku, it was hard but necessary for us to stay alert to those delicate and subtle constructions whose quieter voices were in danger of being lost in the general hubbub. Not particularly fussed about syllable counts, we were looking for resonance and transformation, rather than simple imagistic description. Of the many excellent haiku that made it difficult to decide on the winners, we found a mixture of the traditional, owing much to classical Japanese practices, and those which refracted the haiku form through the sensibilities of their authors' own, occidental literary cultures. Although I had been reading Bashō and the Japanese masters (in translation) for years, I had read only a scattering of contemporary

[1] First published in *Blithe Spirit* (Summer 1999), the magazine of the British Haiku Society, as a contribution to a series of articles in which 'mainstream' poets are invited to expound on their enthusiam for the haiku.

haiku: it was a pleasure, in judging this competition, to encounter the work of haikuists such as David Cobb, Jackie Hardy and Dee Evetts, whose collections I later sought out and derived, perhaps, certain permissions from.

The other challenge arrived one morning in the form of an official chit from Swansea City Council ordering 'six short poems on the cosmos' (no less) for the walls of the new Tower of the Ecliptic astronomical observatory. My knowledge of cosmology being shamefully inadequate, I embarked on a self-devised crash course, hoping that some formal ideas might develop as my understanding grew. Voyaging outwards to learn about the mighty forces of the cosmos – the stars and galaxies, black holes and quasars – will propel you sooner or later on a voyage inwards, to investigate inner space and the realm of the atom. Among the books I read was Fritjof Capra's intriguing *The Tao of Physics*, which dovetails the findings of Einsteinian physics with similar insights, reached much earlier and along very different paths, from oriental koans and poetry. Faced with the abolition of the concept of absolute space and time, and the unification of all matter in the cosmic dance of energy, the Cartesian dualities of my atheist's world view gave way, gratefully, to an appreciation of the universe not as a series of objects but as a complicated web of profound interconnections. All that once seemed solid – this table, that rock – melted into processes and dynamic patterns, the ceaseless transformation of all things and all situations. For twenty-odd years I had felt the truth of, and tried to live my life by, William Blake's famous lines:

> *He who binds to himself a joy*
> *Does the wingèd life destroy.*
> *He who kisses joy as it flies*
> *Lives in eternity's sunrise.*

That guiding intuition was now reinforced by both western scientific enquiry and a philosophy discoverable in the art and wisdom of the east.

If to cling to fixed forms is to suffer and to kill, what are the consequences of this insight for the poet's, or the scientist's, observational practices? If the observer is as much a part of nature as the thing he or she is observing, there can be no such entity as an objective, immutable reality capable of encapsulation and definition by a detached outsider. Fritjof Capra quotes John Wheeler on this:

Nothing is more important about the quantum principle than this, that it destroys the concept of the world as 'sitting out there', with the observer safely separated from it by a twenty-centimetre slab of plate glass. Even to observe so minuscule an object as an electron, he must shatter the glass. He must reach in. He must install his chosen measuring equipment. It is up to him to decide whether he shall measure position or momentum. To install the equipment to measure the one prevents and excludes his installing the equipment to measure the other. Moreover, the measurement changes the state of the electron. The universe will never afterwards be the same. To describe what has happened, one has to cross out the old word 'observer' and put in its place the new word 'participator'.

In this participatory universe the familiar, absolute distinction between subject and object must yield to a fusion of identities and interchange of energies, as Bashō acknowledged when he advised his disciple Hattori Toho to go to the pine if he wanted to learn about the pine, and abandon his subjective preoccupation with himself: 'Your poetry issues of its own accord when you and the object become one . . .' The haiku's famous avoidance of literary embellishment, its disinclination to foreground the writer and his or her writerly skills, ensures that there is no distraction from the 'spiderness' of the spider or the 'treeness' of the tree. The haiku maker wants us not to look *at* a thing but to look *as* it.

The haiku, I thought for a while, could be the vehicle for my six short poems about the cosmos, but it didn't quite answer my requirements, and I chose eventually to adapt an older Welsh three-line form known as the *englyn penfyr*. Although the haiku and the Welsh nature gnome have in common such features as concision, observational accuracy and a strict syllable count, they differ in important respects. The haiku is concerned with particular times and places and has no truck with proverbial utterances, whereas the gnome is a sententious statement about universals. I wanted to mix some general observations about cosmological matters with comment on the human condition. The early Welsh nature gnome, representing perhaps the beginnings of science, combines the classification of natural phenomena, usually in the first two lines, with an aphoristic wisdom in the third; the form seemed ideal for my purposes.

My flirtation with the haiku was suspended for a while, but the form had acquired a fresh congeniality and importance for me. I continued to read and be inspired by haiku, to research the haiku's nature and history, and never to let a haiku moment pass without taking rough note. Soon after completing the cosmic gnomes this reader of haiku started to become a writer of them.

For all its apparent simplicity, the haiku, it seems to me, is a much more subtle, if not more complex, form than is often allowed, and it is widely misunderstood. In spite of its brevity, it is at revolutionary odds with our superficial soundbite culture, insisting on patient attention to the mystery, minutiae and essence of life, finding in the little things that we ruthlessly edit from our hurried existences the very savour of our being. The pared-down suggestiveness of its language makes it a wonderfully collaborative form in which the current between the haikuist's words and the reader is charged only by the reader's imagination – or, as Bill Wyatt said in an article I read many years ago, the haiku provides the fire with its wood, the reader brings the match.

I think a good haiku can be enjoyed by any reader, even without benefit of background knowledge, but there's no doubt, as with any art, that some understanding of the haiku's purpose and ways of working will greatly enrich one's experience of the form. Too often, when visiting schools, I am shown whole walls full of what the head-teacher has been pleased to call haiku, and when I doubt that any of these obedient five-seven-fivers are haiku in anything other than the straitjacket they're wearing, I am met with puzzlement and raised eyebrows. This simple yet demanding form is not the easy introduction to poetry-writing that many syllable-counting teachers seem to think it it is, and few leave school knowing the first thing about it. When we took David Cobb to the BBC studios in Cardiff after he'd won the Cardiff International Haiku Competition, there was a moment's awkward silence after he'd read his winning entry, broken only when the interviewer asked 'Is that all?' We seem to need lashings of salt and monosodium glutamate with everything, and are ill prepared for the subtle flavours of this delicate dish from the East. Give it time, give it space, I'm inclined to advise on such occasions; feel the atoms dancing and the universe altering around you.

2. And the 5-7-5 debate?[2]

Our decision to award prizes in the Cardiff International Haiku Competition to several poems which happened not to 'conform' to the

[2] Based on an item which appeared in *New Welsh Review* 17, Summer 1992.

'rule' that a haiku should have five syllables in the first line, seven in the second and five in the third sparked a lively debate in *The New Welsh Review*, with Tony Curtis and Rodney Aitchtey decrying our choice of winners. The conservative and simplistic assertion that unless haiku come dressed up in dapper little suits of seventeen syllables they cannot be considered haiku amounts to something of a Ped's-eye view of literary form that invited refutation.

The haiku, like the sonnet and villanelle to which Tony Curtis referred in his complaint, did not spring suddenly into fixed and immutable shape; it evolved from an antecedent form, and continues to evolve. What, I wonder, might have been the fate of the sonnet if Tony Curtis had been policing the literary streets of Sicily in the thirteenth century when the native *strambotto*, a single-stanza composition of six or eight hendecasyllabic lines, embarked on an unruly sprouting of extra and slightly shorter lines? Doubtless this miscreant concoction would have been arrested on the spot, charged with perverse poetic practices likely to cause a breach of the literary peace, and locked away for the rest of time in a cell with six bars in the window. The decasyllabic fourteen-liner known to us today as the sonnet might never have come into being; nor might George Meredith's sixteen-line sonnet or Gerard Manley Hopkins's sonnet of the twelve-syllable line – or are we to deny these experiments the title of 'sonnet', and charge their authors with wilful sonnet abuse?

Had such conservative attitudes prevailed in the East, the haiku, no doubt, would have been truncheoned into oblivion by the sixteenth-century poetry police when Japanese innovators started to detach the *hokku* or 'starting verse' from the *renga*, which could be anything from 36 to 1000 stanzas long, and tender it as an 'unfinished' but sufficient poem in itself. The Weights and Measures department would have been called in, and the offenders, charged with passing off as a fully fledged poem what was merely an intro, sentenced to seventeen years' hard labour counting the syllables in the *Yokohama Companion to Japanese Literature*.

There is always a rearguard resistance to change in the arts, but fortunately the haiku, once a controversial new form, survived its early detractors to establish itself as a respected entity and to gather around itself, in due course, the usual army of curators, part of whose job it is to ensure that it doesn't get up to any new and unpredictable tricks.

There has long been creative contention between the innovators and curators in Japan. The critic who insists on a three-line haiku seems to ignore the fact that in Japan the haiku is as likely as not to appear as a single vertical line, but not always. Presumably such critics would rule out of order Issa's (1762-1826) six-liner about the baby and the butterfly? They seem, invariably, not to require the *kireji* ('cutting word'), seasonal reference and Zen underpinning that are indispensable to traditionalists, but they must have their 5-7-5 syllables. This is a common prescription found perhaps most frequently in classrooms where little else is known about the haiku, and one which seems to be based on misconceptions about the haiku and the Japanese language. For the Japanese do not count syllables, they count *onji*, which, somewhere between the phoneme and syllable in terms of duration of sound, are not quite the same thing. A traditional 17-*onji* haiku when read aloud takes about half the time required to recite a 17-syllable haiku in English. It has been suggested, therefore, that a haiku of approximately 12 English syllables best duplicates the length of a 17-*onji* Japanese haiku. Most of the 'non-traditional' haiku favoured by David Kerrigan and I in the Cardiff competition were closer to the brevity of Japanese haiku than the presumed 'traditional' 5-7-5ers – although, speaking for myself, I valued successful 5-7-5ers no less than haiku with fewer syllables, and I would certainly not anathematise a haiku that strayed a syllable or two beyond the holy 17, as long as every syllable, as in William Carlos Williams's little word machine, had an indispensable role to play.

Lest the championing of 'non-traditional' haiku be thought to be some dastardly American plot, as suggested by Rodney Aitchtey, it should be noted that the first to advance the haiku from its established form were the Japanese themselves. Kawahigashi Hekigoto (1873-1937), Ogiwara Seisensui (1884-1976) and Nakatsuka Ippekiro (1887-1946) are just three of a generation born in the nineteenth century who, impatient with the fetishisation of conventional form at the expense of vision and vitality, formed such movements as the New Trend Haiku and the Free Metre Haiku. The free verse exponents proposed, broadly speaking, that the haiku should retain, in the spirit of Bashō, its Zen ambience and commitment to brevity; but it need not adhere slavishly to 5-7-5 *onji*. The curators, of course, voiced their objections, and continue to do so.

Beer, Bread and Ovaries:
On the Road with Iwan Llwyd and Menna Elfyn[1]

It would be, the Arts Council's Tony Bianchi told *The Western Mail*, the most extensive Welsh tour of America since Dylan Thomas's days. How much of a good thing that might prove was a question that darkened many a *bon voyage*: would *this* Swansea poet also come home in an elm suit? It seemed an ominous portent that just before leaving I was working for the BBC on a film about Dylan Thomas and Vernon Watkins, both of whom returned from their glory days in the States cold, silent and horizontal.

From a distance, November 1995, when the idea of this tour came to our agent in Philadelphia, Beth Phillips Brown, it looked irresistible. But as the moment approached, April Fool's Day 1997, we began to have doubts. Would there be enough money in it to justify this jaunt to our families? We had worked together before in various combinations, and were good pals, but would we still be friends after the intensities of a month's campus-hopping in the States? Irish friends who'd blazed the American trail before us had warned of disorientating airport fatigue, and the perplexities of too much hospitality or, conversely, the frustrations, in the homes of teetotal academics, of nothing like enough (shades of the Irish harper Turlough Carolan's famous curse on 'the ugly, undersized glass, and worse than that, the hand that doesn't half fill it'). Were we signing ourselves up for yet another overworked, underpaid stint of national service?

But we of little faith should have known that in the storyteller and poet, Beth Phillips Brown, and her co-manager, the publisher Thomas Rain Crowe, who arranged the southern leg of the tour, we'd found brilliant organisers. They ensured that we had the kind of wild and subversively wonderful time that is as rare in a person's life as the world-altering comet Hale-Bopp that we looked out for every night in Turtle Island's unclouded skies.

We also, of course, had a job to do. We were jetted or, in the Carolinas,

[1] First published in *Poetry Wales*, October 1997.

limo-ed from campus to campus, and did about fifteen formal
readings, attended by an average of about a hundred people a time
(there were also unscheduled readings in bars, people's houses and a
school or two). At most venues we were asked to run workshops or
take part in colloquiums (three a day sometimes) on a wide range of
subjects: Wales, Welsh literary forms and traditions, socio-linguistics,
class, the education system. Our college audiences didn't know much
about Wales but, in the way of American students, and with nothing
about them of the anti-intellectual 'cool' of too many British students,
they were questioning, open to what we had to say, and eager to learn.
Then there were the interviews with organs of the media as varied as
university TV stations and big city newspapers like *The Philadelphia
Inquirer* whose reporter, though she'd barely heard of Wales, decided
we were 'the Maya Angelous and Robert Frosts of a land that heralds
its plentiful poets' and found the Welsh language 'a harmonious cross
between throat-clearing and lisping'. She was also intrigued by what
we had to say about other aspects of the culture, such as the burgeoning
rock scene and bands like, er, Psychotic Monkeys and Catatonic.

Philadelphia, or more precisely the pretty town of Media on its
outskirts, where the magnolias and cherries were doing battle with late
snow, is the *bro* of Beth Phillips Brown and her husband, Will. Their
welcoming home in the wooded side streets became the tour's pit stop
where we'd break our journeys between gigs in order to pick up mail
and instructions, some clean clothes, a roast dinner (no 'mad cow' in
the US, or so they say) and fresh supplies of the handsome broadsheets
that Will prepared especially for the tour. Beth, one of many
Philadelphians of Welsh descent and a near-fluent speaker of the
language (Pennsylvania, colonised by Welsh Quakers and peppered
with names like Bryn Mawr, Berwyn, Gwynedd, Bala Cynwyd, was
originally to have been called 'New Wales'), used her extensive
contacts among the Welsh Americans to secure us both bookings and
financial support. In addition to major grants from the British Council
and the Arts Council of Wales, she obtained sponsorship from the
Twm Siôn Catti Legal Aid Defence Fund, Philadelphia Welsh Society
and various individuals who contributed in kind. The biggest donation
of all came from Beth herself who put eighteen months of her busy life
into the unglamorous chore of piecing the tour together, bit by
painstaking bit, and then, much to our discomfort, refused to accept a
cent in payment: she was doing it, she insisted, for love of Wales, and

that, please, was to be an end to the matter. Disbursers of insufficient (as usual) official largesse might note for future reference that had Beth Phillips Brown not made this generous personal sacrifice there would not have been enough money in the kitty for the tour to take place at all. Not that Beth herself, as large of heart as she is wicked of cachinnation, was complaining, other than remarking wearily on some sponsor's tardy subvention: 'The cheque, I suppose, is 'in the post', one of the three great lies of our time.' What, I wondered, were the other two? 'It's all down to computer error,' she replied, 'And 'I promise I won't come in your mouth'.' Beth Phillips Brown should be America's first ambassador to the Socialist Republic of Wales.

It was a triadic few weeks. The 'Three for Wales/Tri am Gymru' or the 'Three Welsh Poets', as we found ourselves billed on doors, noticeboards, windows and walls (it was well advertised everywhere), prompted an alternative three-part name for the tour from a mishearing of American idiom as we ordered breakfast in a diner on our first day. Both Iwan and I had been to the States before – Iwan made a memorable documentary series for S4C a couple of years ago – and we were more familiar with the mysteries of the American language than was Menna, a first-timer. 'How do you want your eggs?' the waitress asked the *prifardd* in his cowboy boots. 'Over easy,' replied Iwan. 'What?' exclaimed an incredulous Menna, 'You want bacon and *ovaries*?' And in due course Menna put that word together with certain other hedonistic priorities and rechristened us the 'Beer, Bread and Ovaries' tour.

Our first readings were in upper New York State, thanks to the hospitality of the poet David Lloyd (editor of the recent American anthology of Welsh writing in English, *The Urgency of Identity*) and his wife, the sculptor Kim Waale, who put us up in their Syracuse home and treated us to a night of sizzling blues in that city's renowned Dinosaur Bar. There were also memorable excursions to solitary Welsh chapels in the snowy farmlands around Utica. Like much of neighbouring Pennsylvania, this had been a strongly Welsh area; Utica, where we read to a notably Welsh audience, was once a centre for Welsh publishing. *Y Ddraig Goch* continues to flutter outside the occasional farmstead, and there are one-bar towns in the back of beyond whose Welsh beginnings are by no means forgotten.

'This, you bet, is a Welsh town,' said the barmaid with a voice like Bette Midler's in Stinger's bar, Remsen. She, like most of her customers that afternoon, wasn't Welsh herself, but they were all as proud of their town's Welsh provenance. Word filtered rapidly down the counter that here in Stinger's were real, authentic Welsh people from Wales, actually speaking, in Remsen itself at this very moment, that extraordinary language. A portly gentleman at the other end of the bar reached for his mobile phone. 'Get me the mayor,' he barked, 'Where the fuck's the fuckin' mayor? We got people from Wales here. I want flags and I want the mayor, get 'em here quick – so's we can give these guys a proper welcome.' That the mayor and the flags could not be located mattered no more to us than a missed bird in a turkey shoot (a popular pastime hereabouts), for the welcome lavished on us by Stinger's clientele that wintry afternoon could not have been warmer. As Iwan fed the jukebox with quarters, for country classics like 'Why don't we get drunk and screw?' and 'I wish hard livin' didn't come so easy to me' (which could have been the motto of our tour), those good ole Remsen boys 'n' girls kept lining up the beers, and would take nothing in return save a set of broadsides.

On the way back to Syracuse we passed near the controversial new Mohawk gambling centre at Turning Stone. The biggest Indian casino in the States, it has divided the Mohawks locally and caused bitter dissent among Native Americans everywhere. The 'modernisers' maintain that running casinos may be difficult to square with native traditions but, where unemployment is destroying the Native American soul, it's an activity that brings in big bucks and the possibility of survival. What's the use of such 'survival', argue their opponents, if the price that's paid for it is the abandonment of the tribe's fundamental customs and beliefs? A pathetic dilemma with disturbing echoes in the culture of one's own lottery-obsessed tribe.

At LeMoyne College, Syracuse, David Lloyd's university, we read to a full house of keen and responsive staff and students who seemed to have come to hear us out of a need for poetry rather than, as we had felt in Utica, for largely patriotic reasons.

Our usual procedure was to take it in turns to go first, middle and last, and to read about twenty-five minutes' worth of poetry each. I would read in English; Iwan would read his original Welsh first, followed by a translation; and Menna would do her usual graceful 'topping and tailing', delivering the first half dozen lines of a poem in Welsh, then giving the whole thing in English, and concluding with the last three or four lines of the Welsh original. Not everything was translated, especially where the music of the words was sufficient to convey most of the presence, if not meaning, of a poem, as was the case with Iwan's 'Far Rockaway' about a seedy Long Island town with a lovely name (Delmore Schwartz once wrote a sunny eulogy of Far Rockaway, but the decline into which the town has since fallen called for Iwan's poem to somewhat fabricate its praise). Audiences also had no trouble 'getting' Iwan's Welsh-only rendition of 'Muddy Waters', on which I joined him on blues harmonica. In fact they enjoyed the Welsh language hugely, and were fascinated to hear, and hear about a language of the 'UK' that is twice the age of English and as capable as their own of talking about cars and rock'n'roll, cosmology, prisons, hairdressers and sex.

Indeed, our poems of love and sex seemed to go down particularly well with our more vernal listeners, several of whom asked for copies of certain poems which they hoped would work a little magic on the girlfriend or boyfriend. A favourite with all ages was Menna's new poem about someone she'd seen on the *Sex Guide Late* show; this woman wondered whether she should go along with her partner's desire to shave her pubes in the shape of a heart, and dye the creation red. It gave Menna a long-awaited opportunity to use an ancient Welsh word for vagina, *'camfflabats'*, and make play with the more familiar modern expression, *'y llawes goch'* ('the red sleeve'), giving a whole new meaning to 'wearing one's heart on one's sleeve'. It was fun after the readings to see students breezing down the corridors of academe rolling the splendid *'camfflabats'* triumphantly round their mouths.

From straight sex to kinky, cymric S&M: Welsh Strict Metre. Back in Philadelphia, at the Poetry Centre in the Jewish YM/YWHA, Iwan and Menna led an absorbing 'masterclass' on the tortuous intricacies of traditional Welsh wordcraft. By the end of an intense two hours they had cantered their students through the bardic tradition, introduced them to the *cywydd*, *cynghanedd* and various forms of *englyn*, and drawn from the group a fully-fledged English-language *englyn unodl union* on 'flight' (a subject of concern to Menna who, whenever we boarded a plane, would fear, thanks to memories of rickety aircraft in Vietnam, that she was about to become the Buddy Holly of Welsh poetry).

It was in Philadelphia that we heard that Allen Ginsberg, whom we had met when he came to Wales in 1995, was dying of cancer. Iwan went to our 'local', John's Bar in Media, and returned a couple of hours later with an *englyn*:

Mae'n oer, a mi yn aros – rhyw awen
o foreau'r cyfnos;
mae'r cerbyd gwag yn agos
a Duw yn hwyr, daw y nos.

The next day Ginsberg was dead, and at a party given for us by the Philadelphia literati, some of whom, like the poet Gerald Sterne, had been Ginsberg's friends, the *englyn* was received in electrified silence.

Our next big hop was to Rio Grande, a sleepy campus town in southern Ohio, where Megan Lloyd has established a Centre for Welsh Studies. The town came by its name because a family of early settlers liked reading about the faraway American-Mexican war, fancied the name 'Rio Grande' and decided it would do nicely for their place. The county as a whole is called Gallia, a mark of the significant influence of Welsh settlers. In the nearby town of Jackson the police force, which had once been mostly Welsh-speaking, still sport the red dragon on their uniforms. Rio Grande is strictly dry, so we sought refreshment in the attractive riverside town of Gallipolis, a few miles down the road. In Mogie's Bar we caroused with the local judge, in baseball cap and shorts, and with an unrequited roving eye for Welsh women poets. He, like us, had enjoyed the '60s, but, like his President, had inhaled – 'you don't write for the papers, do you?' – absolutely nothing.

'You won't want to spend much time there,' a Swansea friend had said of Youngstown, Ohio. 'It's like a cross between Port Talbot and Blaenymaes. Desperate.' Youngstown, once at the heart of the American steel industry, is now the bleak epicentre of the 'rust belt', rife with murder, the mafia and the social disaster of 25% unemployment. But thanks to the generous and imaginative hospitality of the poets William and Betty Greenway, close friends who'd recently returned from a year's sabbatical in Gower, we were delighted to spend time there. Betty, who's from New Orleans, came to poetry later in life than William, but she's the real thing, particularly good on sex. William, born in Georgia, is acutely conscious of his Welsh ancestry, his grandfather having been a Methodist preacher from Crickhowell. His warm, wry, sometimes deeply sad poems about people, relationships, places are miles away from the pseudo-Celtic half-cockery of too many Americans of Welsh descent or obsession, and have won him admiring readers on both sides of the Atlantic. William was nominated for a Grammy this year, but Hilary Clinton, guess what, beat him to it.

Identity is an abiding concern in America today. What new identity is a de-industrialised Youngstown to invent for itself? How might an identity be restored to city centres when all the people have been sucked away from them by the out-of-town shopping malls? What is a feminist or post-feminist identity? (In one of our audiences was a self-declared 'Nazi feminist' – a Jewish one at that – who was distinctly pissed off that post-feminist Menna was happy to write for women *and* men of all ages and kinds.) What, if you're not 'Irish' or Cajun or Cherokee or 'Welsh', *is* your identity? We heard somewhere of a black female Cornish poet. Now it is just possible that there is such a being in the world as 'a black female Cornish poet', but that was not really what was being described: we were talking here of a black American poet who somewhere down the dimmering line of origin had had a great-great-grandsomething-or-other from Cornwall, and was probably no more Cornish in any meaningful sense than some of our so-called 'Welsh' writers are Welsh. Why don't the Americans get on with being American, in all its complex, enviable variety?

Suddenly, in North Carolina, it was Appalachian springtime. Thomas Rain Crowe met us at midnight at Asheville airport and drove us in a hired 'van limo' (with bar) to Cullowhee, an hour to the west. We awoke to mountains, blue jays and dizzying clouds of dogwood blossom. Thus began the busiest, most riotous week of the tour, 'doing' one or two leafy colleges a day, partying half the night, then driving on, to the music of Bonny Raitt, Pat Metheny and local country stations, to the next venue. Lots of sometimes intense, always enjoyable discussions with students and staff (some of the students are still sending me poems). And some richly rewarding encounters with fine poets such as Kay Byer, Janice Moore Fuller, Patricia Smith and Michael Brown, the last two being superb, flying-without-text performers. We talked sometimes of the difficulties of getting hold of each others' books. 'Why don't we see Welsh books in American bookshops?' a student asked. Almost as good a question as 'Why don't we see Welsh books in Welsh bookshops?'

Our last readings as a threesome were at Grinnell, a university town in the corn prairies of Iowa. The local organiser, Saadi Simawe, was an Iraqi exile who'd spent years in jail for his left-wing politics before seeking refuge in America (odd as that seemed to us). He and his wife Iman live the half-life endured by political refugees the world over: yearning for political changes that might enable them to return, finding next to no one in the host community who knows much or cares about where they're from, and raising their kids as more-or-less Americans who probably wouldn't want to go 'back' even if they could. 'How did you feel during the Gulf War?' I asked Saadi. 'This is the first time,' he said, close to tears, 'that anyone has ever asked me that important question.' It had been a period of torturous isolation and stress, and he was still bruised by the pain of it. We warmed to Saadi and he to us; he found a 'subversiveness' in our poetry that put a twinkle in his eye and reminded him, he said, of the poetry of his homeland.

According to Thomas Rain Crowe, recent research in America suggests that there are only 16,000 'poetry readers' in the entire country – and most of them are poets and/or academics. If this is the case, poetry would seem as futile a minority pursuit as, say, plumbing for the sake of playing with pipes, and fully deserving of a lack of public interest. But that's not, I think, how America seemed to us. There's plenty of poetry in America, and lots of interest in it, although, in both cases, probably not always where the researchers are looking for it. True, our audiences were largely college students and staff, but we weren't on anybody's syllabus, they'd neither heard of us nor (hardly) of Wales. Yet they came, they engaged with us, they bought our books. If we represented in a sense 'recognisable' poetry, what about the colossal appeal of the 'unofficial' poetry of pop music, blues, country and jazz? And the rappers and the cowboys poets and the poetry slammers? There can be fool's gold, of course, in all departments, but even in our limited experience of the culture we found plentiful nuggets of the genuine article, from Patricia Smith's lament for self-damaging urban youth to the Syracuse bluesman Roosevelt Dean's raunchy new song about 'The Milkman'.

It was a privilege and addictive pleasure to have been, on Wales's behalf, a fleeting part of America's richly varied poetic landscape. Apparently there's vague, rash talk of inviting us back. Wild horses . . .

The Writing on the Wall[1]

Possibly the best-known contemporary poem in Wales is David Hughes's message on the pavement at the entrance to Swansea's High Street Station, 'Ambition is critical'. A riposte to the notorious deadhand about Swansea being the graveyard of ambition, it confronts travellers, crucially, not as they leave the city but as they arrive, inviting a reconsideration of Thatcherist notions of ambition, and proposing an adventurous and generous interpretation of the word 'critical'.

Unlike the extracts of poetry which accompany the Cader Idris sculpture outside Cardiff station, which you have to choose to go and read, there's no avoiding David Hughes's message: you have to walk over his poem to get in or out of the station. His words, composed specifically for that spot, have intrigued, raised smiles and no doubt sometimes irritated hundreds of thousands of travellers, in addition to the tens of thousands who will have seen them sneered at in the early moments of the (ambition-free) 'Swansea' movie *Twin Town*.

Too little thought has been given to the notion of 'public art' in Wales, so that some pretty tacky and irrelevant follies get foisted on us from time to time. Without wanting to stray down a definitional cul-de-sac (what worthwhile art is *not* 'public'?), I'd like to suggest that we have at least one art form in Wales, poetry, which has been making itself socially useful for hundreds of years, and whose potential, in our ill-considered frenzy to plonk Vikings on hilltops (a recent Sweynseye whimsy), and prettify forest trails with pseudo-Celtic carvings, is too often overlooked by 'public art' and commissioning authorities.

With the Welsh Academy campaigning for the Assembly to have its own 'Official Poets', as did the ruling houses of Wales centuries ago, it is perhaps timely to consider the ways in which poets at a more 'grass roots' level might make themselves useful. Where the Welsh language remains strong, there is invariably a rooted understanding of the many roles performed by the poet, together with an awareness of the rudiments

---

[1] This essay is a conflation of two articles, 'The Art of Ambush', *The New Welsh Review* 17 (1992) and 'The Writing on the Wall', *A470*, April/May 1999.

of his or her craft. *Englynion* are still written for commemorative plaques and gravestones (the most obvious and widespread manifestation of 'poetry in public places'); *cywyddau,* as well as light, unpretentious verses are still crafted for weddings and other communal rites of passage. Sometimes a resonant few lines, such as the opener to Waldo Williams's 'Preseli' –

> *Mur fy mebyd, Foel Drigarn, Carn Gyfrwy, Tal Mynydd,*
> *Wrth fy nghefn ym mhob annibyniaeth barn.*

– will be translated to stone, as on the commemorative monolith at Mynachlog-ddu. Such things can happen in English too – the 'Fern Hill' quotation on a boulder in Cwmdonkin Park is an example.

Many poems in public places are extracts from pre-existing texts, and highly appropriate they often are. What interests me, as a 'municipal graffitist', is what can be done in 'site-specific' terms, where the poet, usually in collaboration with a visual artist, is called upon to respond to a certain brief with regard to theme and/or location. The experience of my first such commission, Swansea City Council's desire for a poem 'about the sea', confirmed what I feared from the outset might be a recurring problem with composing poetry for public places. In our pluralistic and fractured societies, deprived of a unifying ideology such as that provided by the Roman state or pre-Enlightenment Christianity, how is one to use evocative or emotive language to formulate a message for inscription in a public place which may command the assent of the majority? Although my first such effort, censored because of its reference to sewage pollution, was, I now think, less than successful, the council commissioned me again, requesting a text for the side of a new building near the Grand Theatre, incorporating references to 'sleep, dreams, memory, re-awakening and messengers (cherubs)' – in not more than twelve words. Then came the request for what would become the 'cosmic gnomes' which I produced for Swansea's Tower of the Ecliptic. With these and subsequent commissions I have invariably found myself facing alarming but exciting challenges in terms of both content and form.

Various site-specific commissions – for the Garden Festival at Ebbw Vale in 1992, a hospital at Bridgend, a housing project in Swansea – have followed on from the gnomes. My latest project is a bilingual collaboration with the poet Emyr Lewis and the artist Andrew Rowe

154 Footsore on the Frontier

for a site on the seafront at Porthcawl. It is a playful work, a huge sundial with an outsize icecream cone as its gnomen and a circular array of deck chairs, on which our poems are 'written', representing the stations of the clock.

Millions of words are written *about* buildings, but our civilisation has lost its nerve almost entirely for writing *on* buildings. Meaning, it is frequently asserted, is coming back to architecture, and arts of all kinds are being called upon to assist in the fugitive's return – all, that is, except the arts of language. At certain times and in certain places, however, words have been accorded pride of architectural place. The ancient Romans, the first to use lettering in a truly architectural way, glorified their rule with buildings, such as the triumphal arch, which seem sometimes to have been constructed primarily as frames for imposing inscriptions. Architects of the Renaissance and Baroque periods revived and developed the classical tradition, using lettering with great verve on anything from palace to church to country home. And the Victorians, on their pubs, chapels, hotels and grandiloquent civic buildings, were unabashed in their employment of words to extol the advantages of 'improvement' – 'REVERENCE IN MAN THAT WHICH IS SUPREME' – and to proclaim the vaunting scale of their geographic and cultural appropriations. In the twentieth century, there were experiments with words on Russian, German and Dutch buildings in the early modern period, and the Italian Fascists used imaginative lettering to bring poise and grace to their austere facades. But the tradition seems latterly to have died one of its periodic deaths. To ignore the once vital relationship beteween words and buildings, which can be traced back to the very beginnings of writing itself over five thousand years ago, is to deprive architecture of a unique means of articulating the sense of history, personality, wit and warmth that is so disastrously absent from many contemporary edifices.

'Never use black,' my old art teacher used to warn, 'and never use words.' He laboured hard to impress upon his benighted students the notion that the literary arts and the visual arts inhabit different universes; to mix the two was to court disaster – which translated, in immediate terms, as a clip around the ear. In art classes far and wide, I later found, this hostility towards words seems to have been rammed clumsily home; it was, perhaps, a lesson from which some of today's word-leery architects never fully recovered.

There are other reasons, no doubt, for the absence of purposeful words from contemporary architecture: the short life expectancy and constantly-evolving functions of many buildings; the paucity, in most countries, of significant examples of architectural lettering; the discouraging association of indifferent lettering with crass piles of breeze block and concrete; ignorance of the tradition of architectural lettering. There is also the problem that in a world of partial or partisan utterances, universal statements are not easily coined: the bland, the commonplace, the windily rhetorical or the clumsily divisive are obvious pitfalls.We are more accustomed to words on walls – 'Eat the rich' – as menacingly powerful fomenters of enmity. It seems that words in the public domain appear in the eyes of many architects as too volatile and shifty to be offered permanent space on the walls of the forum. To a page-bound poet, however, such a prospect is irresistible.

Ambush: that's the attraction for me in attempting to take poetry beyond its 'normal' ambit and offering it in the street, the pub, the club to the fleetingly curious or, more often, the indifferent and downright hostile. Arguments against using words on buildings are in my view either ill-founded or surmountable; writers, architects, sculptors and calligraphers should work together to re-appropriate and advance a tradition of considerable versatility and power.

In confronting the challenge of composing 'messages' for various architectural sites – and it has been among the most rewarding yet most difficult work I have undertaken in my career as a writer – I have had to address myself to the disastrous separation that has long existed between radical culture and stylised experimental language on the one hand, and popular culture and everyday speech on the other. How am I, as a poet, to use and extend all the techniques at my disposal while continuing to engage the sensibilities of a non-specialist public with little obvious 'art education'? I hope, yes, to beguile and persuade as many people as possible – I am not averse to the word 'entertainment' – but my poems normally invite their audience to make an effort: indeed, they are 'completed' only when they meet with the creative intelligence of a listener or a reader. Then there is the ever-present question of language: what register should I use in order to address the thousands, if not, over the years, the millions of passers-by who might encounter my wall messages?

New words are minted daily, but the basic popular vocabulary (of tired old English, at any rate) is diminishing. Sociolinguists say that the average vocabulary of English-speakers is only about 3,000 words, which is an eighth of Shakespeare's; journalists working for the tabloids, which average a vocabulary of 500 words, are instructed to write for an audience with a reading age of twelve. Some of the most important 'public' words – 'glory', 'honour', 'victory', 'rejoice' (thank you, Mrs Thatcher) – no longer seem to ring true. The outlook would seem to be bleak for the worker in words. But paradoxically, certain forms of address, such as poetry or rhetoric (in the Ciceronian rather than windbag sense), may offer an extraordinary opportunity to re-charge language, to make speech stand out from the glut of random images that surround it.

The competition posed by advertising for any kind of non-commercial or 'subversive' message is formidable. It is estimated that urban man or woman receives daily no fewer than 6,000 advertising messages; only the startlingly unusual stand out and have much chance of 'influencing' us. Although advertising has stolen the fire of poetry and art, the techniques thus filched have sensitised large numbers of people to a range of aesthetic possibilities which might not otherwise have been available to them. Certain townscape word-artists such as the Canadian Vera Frenkel and the Americans Bruce Nauman and Jenny Holzer have sought, with their spectacolour board and neon messages, to work within and against the advertising media. Holzer's 'Protect me from what I want' over Piccadilly Circus is, in the age of AIDS, haunting and memorable. Bruce Nauman makes creative play of contradiction: in one piece, he alternates 'Silence is Golden' with 'Talk or Die'; in another, the come-and-go of just two letters sets 'Eat' alternating with 'Death'. But many, like Frenkel's 'There's no rush', lack tension and resonance. Partaking all too readily of the gimmickry and disposability of advertising, they may catch the eye but rarely detain the imagination.

The dross ratio is even higher, of course, in Anon.'s efforts with a spraycan. Most graffiti are banal and repetitive, sad lunges at humour by unfunny drunks or whimsical stabs at 'profundity' by self-pitying space cadets. But others, in their raw boldness or baroque wit, leap out at you and lodge in the mind, with none of the p.r. hype that attends a Holzer or a Frenkel. A couple of local favourites include the legend, on a lone stretch of wall that was all that remained of Llanelli's Duport steelworks, 'Maggi been ere', and the republican observation daubed on Briton Ferry bridge, 'Caesar hasn't a clue what's going on'. It was snuffed within hours by Caesar's secret police.

Most graffiti – 'Don't drink and drive/Take speed and fly' – are of a random, top-of-the-head variety, their siting in drab places invariably implying a riposte to the concrete slabwork on which they appear, a limited yet heartfelt form of architectural criticism. There is sometimes about these messages – 'Tony woz ere' – a simple need, given the speed and confusion of life, to slow things down by making a mark, putting your stamp, however insubstantial, on a bit of the world. Graffiti – even when signed in this way: Tony who? – are usually anonymous and spontaneous, amounting to a collaborative kind of folk art rather than a painstaking and individualist act of creativity.

Like Tony – and Lord Byron, indeed, whose vandalistic autograph on a classical Greek column is now a tourist attraction – I have long been fascinated by writing on walls, as both reader and writer. My words, however, fulfil only some of the requirements of full-blown graffiti. They are, yes, unsigned; they speak, I hope, with a 'public' voice; they may amuse; I hope they stimulate and provoke. But I don't even 'write' them myself – the inscription is done by a professional artist; my creations – in metal, slate, portland stone, glass, neon – are meant to last; months of research and crafting may go into their composition. The biggest disqualifier of all from the Worshipful Company of True Graffitists is the fact that my wall writings are commissioned, actually asked for and paid for by precisely those authorities who spend thousands of pounds a year rubbing out the works of the moccasin-wearing true graffitist: they are, in short, legal and 'respectable', though I may imbue them with subversive intent. While graffiti and advertising are useful points of reference, I am bound to acknowledge, as someone who 'writes' three-dimensionally on specific structures, that my endeavours belong primarily to the exciting yet absurdly under-exploited tradition of architectural lettering.

These municipal commissions have usually obliged me to relate my compositions and their execution as closely as possible to their intended sites. The artist, with the painter and decorator, is invariably the last to be engaged on a project – someone who is implored, at the final, desperate minute, to 'tweak the architecture up a bit'. 'Enhancement' is the coy expression normally deployed for this eleventh-hour struggle to dignify inadequate architecture by endowing it with meaning. Happily, the Tower of the Ecliptic job was not like this. Here, for once, all those involved – architect, stained glass artist, sculptor, wordsmith – were in creative contact throughout. The

158   *Footsore on the Frontier*

rehabilitation of this ideal, and the frequent collaboration on single projects of many kinds of artist, refers us back usefully to times when the arts (an anachronistic term) were indivisible, and incorporated what today we think of as 'science'.

A most rewarding commission lately has been for a series of poems on the theme of the human body for a glass artwork, designed by David Pearl, in the foyer of the Princess of Wales Hospital, Bridgend. These poems, all in the form of a question, are seen by hundreds of people every day. Not everyone will think of them as poems, and reactions to them vary considerably, from fascinated engagement to voluble contempt. It is good, whatever, to have some readers – many more than would read a poetry collection – and to hope that one's efforts might occasionally make themselves useful in people's lives.

Lipstick on the Gorilla?
A Note on Public Art

A wavy line drawn by a child in the sand, an *englyn* on a gravestone, a brick through a window, a signature in ghostly aerosol pastels in some dingy underpass: we like to make a mark, to leave a trace that asserts an existence if not an identity – 'Dai woz ere' – against the clamour and disintegration of dizzying times.

Invariably obliterated by the incoming tide, such 'evidences', endless in their variety, represent an attempt, however fleeting and irresolute, to share with others a sense of self in a certain place at a certain time. Most of these things are little more than doodles, but they are born of the much suppressed instinct to 'make' that dwells within us all. Few of us, at least in western societies, expect to move much beyond the doodle stage: the division of creative labour has ordained that only specialists will make, while the rest partake – or refuse to partake, which is the more likely consequence of the long-standing and deep-rooted alienation of the creative impulse.

The artist in most western countries is perceived as a lone crank on the irrelevant fringe, a figure of fun or contempt whose occasional 'rebellious outbursts' are little more than the yelps of a frustrated ego. This caricature, particularly of the visual artist, swills into Wales with *The Sun* and other organs of enlightenment; but we are fortunate in this country that at least one line of cultural defence, that of language and literature, remains relatively intact, so that (to turn the infamous dictum on its head) when we in Wales hear the word 'gun' it is still possible for us to reach for our culture. As the language dies back in its heartlands, so it drags into forgetfulness our people's awareness of how poetry was once central to the national polity. Any recollection of a natural participation in and acceptance of poetry and the arts as a fundamental part of one's social and spiritual being is very faint in the anglicised areas of Wales. The *cerdd* (poem), at least where the Welsh language survives, still manages to perform the inestimably valuable balancing act of being both ordinary and, at the same time, magical. If this culturally sustaining consciousness has sunk to a residue elsewhere, it is nevertheless a residue begging to be used, not only by literary artists but makers of all kinds.

'Art in public places' and 'public art' are loose and imperfect shorthand terms, interchangeable but not strictly speaking synonymous, which signify artworks sited in public spaces, be they mountain tops or city streets. All art, as a form of social communion, is public, whether encountered in a gallery or a town centre. 'Art in public places' differs from art intended for galleries in that its conception and execution invariably take into account the architectural, social and cultural contexts of chosen sites – although this is not to argue that 'art in public places' is necessarily superior to or more desirable than art in galleries. No doubt people who want to experience sculptures and paintings like to see art in galleries as they like to see bread in breadshops. If they want to buy bread, they don't want to have to go scouring public places in the hope of finding the occasional loaf.

Although the incidence of 'art in public places' probably pre-dates the Stone Age, it is often considered a (frequently unruly) child of contemporary civilisation, partly because of the comparatively high level of funding and organisation brought to the practice, and partly because of the media attention it attracts. In recent decades, most public art projects in Wales have been overseen by Cywaith Cymru/ Artworks Wales. Cywaith Cymru grew out of the Welsh Sculpture Trust which, formed in 1981, was committed, in a spirit of benevolent paternalism, to making art more accessible to the people. The Trust celebrated its tenth birthday by changing its name to Cywaith Cymru/Artworks Wales and taking on a broader responsibility for encouraging the placing of art in public places. In 1991 Cywaith Cymru took over from the Welsh Arts Council as commissions agency not only for sculpture but for all the visual arts. It has been a catalystic and innovative organisation, initiating and supporting a wide range of projects in both rural and urban Wales. Thatcherist 'market forces' ideology, still damagingly with us long after the departure of its begetter, changed the climate in which Cywaith Cymru had to operate. Towards the end of the '80s it became apparent that commercial and political interests, many of them not Welsh in origin, were increasingly attempting to bend the work of Cywaith Cymru to their own ends. Garden Festival Wales, for instance, held in Ebbw Vale in 1992, started by being design-led, but its development was quickly hijacked by marketing operatives. Cywaith Cymru's artistic vision and directorial authority were undermined by the agendas of local politicians and financial conglomerates who were stridently opinionated about what they felt public art to be. In the world of public art, as elsewhere in society, there has been a growing disinclination to listen; assertion and inflexibility are frequently the norm.

If, as it sometimes seems, even the makers of art for public places are vague about what it is, where it is, who does it and for whom it is created, it is not surprising that a wider public, which includes of course those with the money and power to patronise artists, is moved sometimes to express bemusement and bafflement, if not outrage and contempt, when confronted by art. Too often the 'providers' of art are inclined to shy away from the challenge of laying the foundations for a broader understanding of art's intentions, and simply hope 'to get away with it'.

One of the most public of arts, whose contemporary practitioners invariably find themselves engaging with the conservative and timid expectations of their clients, is stained glass, an artform in which Wales is an under-appreciated world leader. Stained glass, as an architectural medium, is not an art for egotists awash with emotion and world-excluding 'personal vision': it is framed by the window which in turn is framed by the building, whose form and function the designer is constrained to acknowledge. A further and frequently damaging limitation is offered by the client, who may have rigid views about content and style, born of prevailing suspicions about 'modern art', and the widespread expectations of this particular art that it should be some vague imitation of Victorian reproductions of medieval glass. The customer here is not always right, and pandering to his or her wrong-headedness does the art – and its practitioners in the long run – no favours at all. Amber Hiscott and David Pearl, who trained at the world-famous school of architectural glass in Swansea, and are internationally renowned for their innovative work, have always refused to provide the roses, curlicues and 'lifelike scenes' that have sometimes been asked of them. They often find themselves in a lengthy process of negotiation with a client in order to 'turn the commission around' rather than accept unquestioningly the customer's initial brief. They both work according to the firm principle that they never accept commissions which are mere money-spinners. If they ultimately reject or are rejected by conservative patrons, then so be it: art comes before business. 'Clients, as it happens, often respond well to this kind of negotiation,' David Pearl told me. 'It's like you or I setting a brief for an engineer: we may have a starting point for what we want, but it would be folly to expect our engineer to execute in full our initial layman's brief.'

The often uneasy relationship between the artist and his/her public nurtures a debilitating lack of confidence between artists and those who commission their work. One squeak of ill-informed 'criticism' from a voter writing to the local press may be enough to frighten the city fathers off an innovative and challenging scheme of public art. Rather than confront and attempt to dispel the general benightedness – no easy task, it must be admitted – the artist is inclined to maintain an apologetically low profile. In this climate, the financial argument that is invariably invoked against anything controversial will meet with little resistance in its summary dispatching of the scheme to oblivion. Art, to most municipal authorities, is an optional extra, and the first thing to be dumped in hard times. The argument has yet to be won that what constitutes the culture of a city should be accepted by its citizens as being no less important to its wellbeing than sewage and refuse disposal.

Because of its usefulness in recent years to urban regenerators in both North America and Europe, 'art in public places' has become fashionable, 'the latest thing'. There is suddenly a lot of it about which, when it fails, simply adds to the fog and static through which more successful work has to struggle for attention. It is, however, nothing new. At a conference a few years ago the artist and critic Peter Lord, pointing to the Carew Cross, offered us a public artwork that was a thousand years old; it had been made and erected at about the same time that Hywel Dda called the tribal leaders together at nearby Whitland to codify Welsh law. He articulated perhaps the most potent and challenging definition of public art of the weekend: 'I believe that art in public places should always be public art. Public art is an art that addresses a people collectively rather than as individuals and that expresses the identity of the culture. In Wales, therefore, the question "Which culture?" is an inescapable context in which public art is made and one about which the moral sculptor must come to a view. The indigenous culture offers a model of public art in the form of a tradition of praise poetry which is over one thousand years old.' Although no longer abused as a 'Fascist' for his advocacy of the principle of differentiation and particularity, as he was on one occasion in the mid '80s, Peter Lord's analysis came as disturbing news to those who had not engaged with the matter of Wales as he had done, and it can still ruffle feathers.

Goscombe John's Hedd Wyn memorial at Trawsfynydd or his monument to Evan and James James at Ynysangharad Park, Pontypridd are two of the relatively few Welsh public artworks of the earlier twentieth century that are grounded in their cultural context. Probably neither of these has entered public consciousness as fully as the clenched-fist Llywelyn ap Gruffydd which has managed to battle free of the institution, City Hall, Cardiff, in which it is confined, to strike out defiantly across the imagined nation. When art moves physically as well as psychically beyond the portals of its authorised sancta and seeks a role in the everyday world, the results can be unpredictable and explosive. Art has certain 'ghettoes', most obviously the gallery, in which it can get up to more or less what it likes; the public will take or, more likely, leave it. But when art confronts people in the places where they live and work, some viewers may react with discomfort to the statements it makes or the questions it poses. There was a huge furore in Whitland in the early '80s over the Cofeb Hywel Dda: a vociferous minority was vehemently opposed to the memorial, and did their utmost to prevent the project going ahead. This reaction was typified by an employee at the Whitland creamery who, on his way each morning to the factory, would drive up close to Peter Lord, hard at work on the memorial's paving, and mutter from his car window, 'Why don't you fuck off back to where you came from?' This response, Peter believes, arose not because the man was baffled by the demands of this large-scale work, but because, on the contrary, he understood it only too well.

Similarly, in Swansea, recent attempts to extend the council's public art programme from the newly-created maritime quarter into the city centre met with an unprecedentedly hostile media campaign which resulted in the abandonment of the scheme in its entirety. It is all very well peppering a maritime quarter playground with numerous and varied works of art which prove popular with visitors, residents and, because of the international plaudits they scoop, even sceptical councillors. But it is quite another matter to bring art right into the architecturally banal heart of the city and require it to meditate there, in Welsh, English and Swansea dialect, on 'the magic of place'. The three poets commissioned to undertake this work (Menna Elfyn, David

Hughes and myself) intended that their words – in the paving, up lampposts, over benches, and associated with sculptures – should amount to a celebration of Swansea and its place in Wales and the universe. We worked for about a year and a half with Robin Campbell and Brenda Oakes of Swansea City Council to bring our ideas to fruition, but it took only a few days for an inaccurate leak about one component of the scheme to result in the project being abandoned. *The Swansea Herald*, an advertising freesheet owned by *The Daily Mail*, informed its captive readership that the use of Swansea dialect in the scheme was 'taking the mickey out of the local patois' and was 'in extremely bad taste'. The following day, council workers were sent out with hacksaws and screwdrivers – in Swansea the UK City of Literature 1995 – to remove all poems from street furniture and fittings waiting to be installed. A couple of weeks later, *The Herald*, preening itself on its victory against public art at the eastern end of Oxford Street, set its sights on Will Alsop's innovative design for Tŷ Llên, the proposed national literature centre, at the western end. It was, declared *The Herald*, parroting Prince Charles, 'a capricious carbuncle on the face of Swansea', and the people at the Guildhall were a 'bunch of civic comedians'. The council, far from robust in their defence of public art at the best of times, caved in without a murmur in the face of this philistine front-page onslaught, and Alsop's superb design, which would have been to Swansea what the Guggenheim is to Bilbao, was cast out. Arts and planning policy in Swansea, which in the 1980s was a leader in this field, seemed suddenly to be dictated by the advertising industry. The mounting on a plinth of a redundant ack-ack gun at the gateway to the city a few years ago announced the death, for the time being, of public art in Swansea.

The Swansea debacle shows how fragile are the structures on which the advocacy and practice of public art in Wales are founded. The vision and commitment of individuals have been crucial to some of the major achievements of the past ten years: the late Ioan Bowen Rees, the former chief executive of Gwynedd County Council, invited Cywaith Cymru to collaborate with him on Parc Glynllifon; landowner Peter Wilson commissioned sculpture to 'landmark' his stretch of south Pembrokeshire coast; Robin Campbell worked, on behalf of the council, in Swansea's maritime quarter, pioneering Wales's first 'Per Cent for Art' scheme. However, too great a reliance on the energies and influence of inspired individuals such as these is, all too clearly, not without its dangers, particularly if there is insufficient knowledge of and commitment to public art on the part of the authorities within the parameters of which such benevolent individuals operate. There are also within such bodies suspicious or even malevolent people whose negative influences are becoming increasingly pervasive. Given the prevailing weakness of official commitment to schemes such as 'Per Cent for Art', these new puritans don't have to wield much guile or power in a society whose members have little or no art education, to retard or indeed close down an entire programme of public art. They may well be in a position then to advance an alternative agenda. As the curtain came down on Swansea's Oxford Street artworks, out from the wings leaped a County Council graphic designer with plans for a massive sculpture of Sweyn, the supposed Viking founder of Swansea, as large as the Statue of Liberty, which he wanted sited at the top of Kilvey Hill. These plans for a gigantic, horn-helmeted, wind-blown Sweyn were the source of much amusement among the Swansea arts community – until it was realised that this remarkable pile of Nordic socialist realism seemed to be just what leading councillors and planners wanted: the feasibility of Sweyn, they declared, would be investigated.

While it was, in Swansea, as if the previous ten years had never been, and the process of persuasion and education looked as if it would have to start again from scratch, the situation appeared altogether happier in Newport, whose programme of public artworks was inspired, at least in the early stages, by the example of Swansea. Thanks largely to Newport's cultural services officer Peter Cole, the principle of the indivisibility of art and the town centre seems now to be accepted. Some of the artworks, notably Peter Fink's 'Steel Wave' on the west bank of the Usk, were initially controversial, but, with the support of a sympathetic local press and the enthusiastic involvement of councillors on public art working parties, challenging works have won acceptance and even popularity. Fink's bold red structure, which makes a statement on the centrality of seafaring and steel to Newport's evolution, features prominently in the council's promotional literature, and is perceived, along with more figurative commemorative works elsewhere, as an important component of the town's identity.

Although serious practitioners of public art tend to disdain the 'Fly 'em in, bolt 'em on and bugger off' school of sculpture – 'crash art' or 'plop art', as it is also known – it is evident that the level of commitment to cultural and historical contexts varies considerably among artists working in this field. Most would agree that the exhibition-circuit syndrome – 'people plonking their stuff around the country without any consideration of what a given space is about', as I once heard it described – should be discouraged, and pains taken by facilitators and makers of art to attune themselves to a culture's multiple frequencies. It is a matter of 'learning the language', not necessarily *yr iaith* but the diverse and complex language of the culture as a whole, and its particular dialect; the question then is not so much 'Is this good art or bad?', but 'Who needs it?'. When, in this context, art is successful, there need be no contradiction between the local, the national and the international.

It is entirely expected, no doubt, to pay lip service to the principle embodied in the public art buzz word 'site-specific', if for no other reason than that disregard for the *genius loci* might prompt some local genie to start rattling the England's Glory. An apparent commitment to 'site specificity' on the part of some urban regeneration specialists seems sometimes only skin-deep, merely an articulation of the requisite 'politically correct' noises to 'facilitate' what might in practice amount to the actual destruction of what is specific to a place. A minority of those involved in public art in Wales are Welsh-born, but many have worked with enthusiasm and sensitivity to graft themselves onto the culture, learning the language of the place and speaking it with their own dialect. But there is no shortage of those who have breezed in from 'the international arts world' who have little or no understanding of where they are, and who proceed to bestow upon the natives grotesquely inappropriate projects (see at Corwen, for example, Wales's most laughable blob of public art, the statue of our great national lump of toffee, Owain Glyndŵr). I remember Ned Thomas, when he was director of the University of Wales Press, being phoned by a bright young thing at Garden Festival Wales looking for ideas, and generously exposing the extent of her ignorance when, towards the end of her interview, she said to him 'Now . . . writers: there must be writers?' Apprehensive that Garden Festival Wales, instigated by Tory government policy and managed largely by marketing people, would not speak the language of its place, some artists declined to participate; there was a comparable reserve in the same quarters towards involvement in the Cardiff Bay scheme.

From artists who have taken the trouble to learn the languages of the places they live and work in, we often hear words such as 'love' and 'care'. Landscape artists who are responsive listeners to the dialects and meanings of their chosen places can often draw people's attention to aspects of their locality of which they may not be aware: Robert Camlin, for instance, working on a project in Newport, rediscovered the way in which the now culverted Pill had determined much of the lay-out of the older town – reappropriated knowledge which has consequences for the development of Newport's public art programme.

This ability to decipher languages and read landmarks is essential to the devising of art appropriate to given communities, for some sites are not in the control of any one community but, possibly, several. Most practitioners acknowledge in theory the importance of community involvement in public art schemes, while admitting shortcomings in practice. Some, such as Nick Clements of the Pioneers group, are relatively easy with the idea: 'We can involve the whole community in these projects, which can be spiritually uplifting,' he said. 'We often start with nothing in mind, not predetermining the end result. We turn up and gradually make things happen.' At Blaena, for instance, where the Pioneers were to enjoy a long-term involvement, they spent their first few sessions sitting down and drinking tea with old miners, listening to their stories. Various specific projects evolved, and continue to evolve, from this open-ended approach. 'Unlike others, the Pioneers have never had a public outrage because we communicate,' he said. Sometimes, however, mention of 'community involvement' can draw groans of frustration from those planners and architects who, observing that elegant cities are not built by part-timers and amateurs at the weekend, tend to argue that community involvement, politically correct as it may be, does not necessarily determine that the art is good, and is no automatic check on the proliferation of banality.

This remains, however, one unresolved, problematic area of public art. There are three main sets of players to contend with here: those who commission artworks (enablers), those who create them (makers), and those who have to look at and live with them (audiences). Because their interests and expectations will not always be synonymous, there is often the temptation to avoid controversy by playing safe and calling in Messrs Caution and Bland to oversee the installation of works that, being invisible and ineffectual, will give offence to no one.

The chief enablers of modern times are the planning departments – of south rather than north Wales these days, because of the relative

168 Footsore on the Frontier

impoverishment of local authorities in the north. They are more frequently formulating public art spaces but they often fail to engage with the role of the imagination in the initial decision-making process. The tendency is to plan a large-scale environment and then, when it's all but complete, call in the artist to 'improve' it. Forgotten, all too often, is the third of Vitruvius's triad of conditions for a good building: commodity, firmness and delight. Artists are required, usually at the last frantic moment, to do a variety of things that planners cannot, from healing society's wounds to bestowing 'meaning' on indifferent architecture: they call such acts of desperation 'lipstick on the gorilla'.

The motives of the new Medicis, be they planning departments, ephemeral leviathans like Garden Festival Wales, or the Cardiff Bay Arts Trust, are invariably associated with urban regeneration and the need to attract inward investment. There is bound to be conflict at times between the ways in which an indigenous community, including that community's artists, perceives and desires to symbolise itself, and the signals which the often non-indigenous Medicis want to give out to the potential inward investor. Artworks celebrating the distinctive political identity of the industrial south, for instance – liberal initially, then socialist and anti-capital, always anti-Tory, with nationalism emerging lately at the local council and Assembly levels – might be deemed perturbing to the eyes of Japanese or American investors. As the international businessman looks forward to the predictable decor and comforts of a Marriott or a Hilton, hotels which can be relied upon to be more or less the same in Cardiff as in Dubai, so, it might be felt, he will be looking for reassuringly familiar 'international' art in the converted foreign slums into which he is being asked to sink his loot. I have attended a number of conferences over recent years in which businesspeople have been assured by academic specialists in urban regeneration that art, far from being a zanily erratic subversive force, could be, if carefully managed, profoundly investor-friendly.

Armies of well-paid buffer-folk exist to 'manage' art and to act as intermediaries between the three main groups involved. If they are insensitive to the intentions of art and insufficiently attuned to cultural specificities, the results of their mediation may well be 'safe' or irrelevant art. But the best of such people, committed to effective art and conscious of the culture within which they operate, play an invaluable role: it is no coincidence, perhaps, that many are themselves practising artists. They are well placed to open up the lines of communication and to develop the various structures for interaction that, given current levels of ignorance and suspicion, may have to exist before most public artworks can come into being.

There is rarely sufficient money and time allocated to the processes of interaction. Organising a competition for a public artwork design is time-consuming and expensive; it is easier and cheaper – it may of course be more appropriate in many cases – to opt for a commission at the outset. There is a danger that if enablers feel excluded from a scheme they will be reluctant to defend it if it runs into difficulties, such as falling behind schedule or meeting with press hostility. In Newport, a 'working parties' system evolved as a result of disappointingly conservative proposals for a commemorative sculpture to mark the 150th anniversary of the Chartist uprising: a statue of John Frost in top hat rousing the people to action, and so forth. The council set up a working party, comprising fifty per cent artists, fifty per cent council representation, in order to pursue more imaginative possibilities. There was an open competition, and briefs were sent out to 500 prospective artists. The seventy preliminary proposals that were received were whittled down to four, and eventually Chris Kelly won the commission to undertake the work. With council members actively engaged in the briefing and selection process, and a sympathetic press, there was no negative reaction when this innovative piece turned up several months late and well over budget. The members of Newport's working parties change, but the fifty-fifty balance remains the same, and the system continues to be effective.

The significance of the role of the press, whether one is effecting an 'art transplant' or attempting to produce artworks with community participation, cannot be overstated. The degree of damage done to the arts, and the visual arts above all, by an ill-informed if not actively hostile press is truly shocking. The inadequacies of the education system are, of course, part of the problem. There is little that artists can do to alter the general situation in education, but there is much on a local scale that can be achieved. For example, the artist Mick Petts' use of hazel wood in one of his projects resulted in the re-introduction of the practice of coppicing, and groups such as the Pioneers can affect remarkable transformations in schools, hospitals and communities by working with people on specific projects and passing on a variety of skills. An artist can often be more effective as a catalyst than as a maker, a maverick licensed, like Shakespeare's wise fools, to talk to anyone – members of a council, say – on equal terms. Although figurative work often results from community projects, participants invariably derive from such projects a much greater appreciation of abstract work.

The future presents public artworks practitioners with various challenges. One is the continuing prevalence of numerous mini-Platos, in the media and local authorities, who want, at best, neutralised art in their municipal republics. It will be necessary to struggle for opportunities for artworks that are innovative and take risks, and to resist the confection of art that is bland and servile, decorative and rootless. The aftercare of existing work is a serious matter that has not yet been adequately addressed; some of that work could be relocated from time to time, or even shunted into redundancy compounds if subjected to a periodic 'relevance review' and found wanting. And it should never be forgotten that that there could be times and there are certainly many locations where the spirit of place should be left to itself, with no intervention by art at all.

Mrs Gerard Manley Hopkins:
The Media and the Arts[1]

The Welsh visitor to Ireland or Scotland who picks up one of their national newspapers, *The Scotsman*, say, or *The Irish Times*, will find any pleasure taken in the cultural maturity of those pages somewhat soured by pained recollection of the media Noddy Land we seem to inhabit back home. The last time I was in Cork, *The Irish Times* offered me, in the same issue, half a page on the John Hewitt summer school, together with half a page on the 'point of view' technique of James Joyce's *Ulysses* – and this was just a fraction of the paper's generous and challenging coverage of the arts. Imagine *The Western Mail* devoting half a column, let alone half a page, to a serious interrogation of the Welsh Academy's annual conference or an analysis of Shelley's influence on the poetry of Idris Davies. The national fifteen might sooner don miniskirts and take up lacrosse (not, perhaps, such a bad idea).

As far as television, radio and the popular print media are concerned – and the situation is worse in English than in Welsh – the artistic products of the nation are normally treated with the superficiality of the press release and the soundbite, or overlooked entirely. It is only in a couple of literary magazines read by a few hundred people that consistently serious discussion of the arts takes place, but their coverage cannot pretend to be comprehensive, and the quality and pertinence of their commentary is erratic, varying from the kind of criticism that is enriching of not only the arts but of life itself, to the impenetrable contortions of the scientising jargoneers, and the mundanely incompetent. The majority of the population have no access to such debate, and remain in almost complete ignorance of their writers, painters, composers, dramatists and sculptors.

'I don't know much about art, but I know what I like, and I like what I know' would seem to be the tail-in-mouth 'philosophy' of most

[1] This essay is based on a talk delivered at the 1989 annual conference of the Association of Artists and Designers in Wales, held in the Davies Memorial Gallery, Newtown.

of those who purport to review the arts in the mass media – or, more often these days, *pre*view the arts, which boils down to regurgitating press releases. Content with their own ignorance, they do little to broaden their intellectual horizons, and make no demands on art or artists, thereby encouraging comparably low expectations in the 'consumers' who read them. 'The poet must know everything,' Hugh MacDiarmid used to growl. So too, no doubt, should the critic. It's an impossible ideal but a useful goad: surely he or she who ventures to deliver an opinion on the arts to tens of thousands of readers or viewers should feel uncomfortable with anything less than making a major effort to learn everything they can about the arts (and science and politics and . . .). This is not so that they can flaunt their knowledge in the manner of certain hyper-educated pontificators who may prove as philistine as the demolition gangs of the 'I know what I like' school, but rather that they may cleave to such knowledge and experience as an essential part of their equipment, without which a critic is unlikely to appreciate a work's context and intentions. Before he can draw a reader's attention to a work of art in a suitably informed and informative way, the critic himself must first have *attended* to the work, giving it time and consideration as a made object in its own right, and not as some representative of a school, trend, fashion or type: humility before the created object, in a spirit of openness and enquiry, rather than the parading of critical dogma mediated through (undefined) terms such as 'artistic merit' (who says?), 'values' (whose?), 'quality' and 'standards'. In addition to attending to the work, the critic needs also to attend to the reader, the critical relationship being a tripartite one. Who is the art for? Who is the criticism for? Her job is to offer an appreciation of the uniqueness and value of an artwork, an exhibition, an *oeuvre*, saying, in effect, 'Look, dear reader, at this new thing that has been brought into your world, listen to what it has to say, the questions it asks . . . We have been given this good work, let's notice it, let's carry it through: it should be seen, known, valued.' As Gerard Manley Hopkins suggested, worthwhile criticism is, at the very least, an act of acknowledgement:

> *What I do regret is the loss of recognition belonging to the work itself. For as to every moral act, being right or wrong, there belongs, of the nature of things, reward or punishment, so to every form perceived by the mind belongs, of the nature of things, admiration*

or the reverse. And the world is full of things, phenomena of all sort,
that go without notice, go unwitnessed.

One of Wales's most sensitive and culturally alert of literary critics is
the English poet Jeremy Hooker who made a similar point no less
memorably when he wrote of the desire 'that nothing, least of all a
work of the human heart and mind, should go unnoticed.'

The criticism that knows exactly what has to be said, even before
the artefact has been examined, is usually the palsied fruit of the kind
of critical mind which has suppressed its own creativity and wants
power over others; in its buried resentments, it has a terrible capacity
for destruction. There are, indeed, plenty of critics who seem to hate
art: if they can't make it, they'll break it. And there are breakers, of
course, in the seemingly opposite camp, whose weakness is too
unquestioningly reverential a regard for the creative act, and a consequent
inclination to praise everything, no matter how inadequate it may be in
part or in whole. For just praise to ring true, there needs be a critical
climate in which the careless, the incompetent, the pretentious, the
phoney are fearlessly identified and sent on their way. Being 'kind' to
poor work does neither art nor artist any favours.

While one expects a critical article to intimate something of the
principles on which its judgements are based, one welcomes in addition
a flavour of the personality of the critic as a whole man or woman, 'a
perplexed and feeling human being,' in Jeremy Hooker's words, who
brings 'our full humanity to the act of understanding'. This sense of
self, invariably present in a good literary essay or journalistic feature,
is likely to have positive consequences for the writing, which should
be the lively and engaging medium through which the critic's
relationship with the reader can be pursued rather than her ego
imposed on that reader. A writer's response to an artwork will be
embodied to a considerable extent in the *manner* in which that response
is couched in literary terms. How refreshing it is, when ploughing
through one of the 'quality' London papers such as *The Guardian* or
The Observer, to happen upon an old friend like John Berger (not that
I have ever met him, but such is the passion and clarity with which he
writes about art and relates to his readers, that I *feel* as if I have been
enjoying his stimulating company for years). The contrast in tone
between Berger's engaged, exploratory writings and the haughty,
amused, disparaging heehaws of many of his fellow columnists throws

into grotesque relief 'that touch of iconoclastic arrogance' which Emyr Humphreys has identified as 'the hallmark of readability in English criticism'. It is neatly exemplified by a single, notorious sentence by the poet Anthony Thwaite in an essay on contemporary British poetry; having written off the English-language poets of Wales, Thwaite goes on to say, 'The difficulty of the Welsh language *may* be hiding from non-Welsh readers the best poetry being written in Wales, but one rather doubts it.'

Anyone trying to write readable criticism for the popular media is likely to find themselves at odds with the muddled linguistic codes of the newspaper world, with its readiness to simplify and foreshorten, and its gusto for 'bonking', 'quizzes', 'probes' and 'Red Robbos'. In this climate, a word such as 'disinterested', for example, meaning 'objective' or 'free from bias', *not* 'uninterested', hasn't a chance. Aware that one has little control over the ways in which copy may be cut or rewritten, one adapts to circumstances and attempts to anticipate and therefore sidestep interference, a kind of self-censorship. As a junior reporter in the English Midlands, I was threatened with the sack for using the word 'penis' in a review of a film called *Percy*: never, I was told, was that word to be used in a family newspaper – although 'male member', with the editor's permission, might be permitted.

One of the unlikeliest jobs I have had was 'literary editor' of *Wales on Sunday*, its first and last. In the months leading up to its launch, during which I was part of a team employed in producing weekly dummies of the paper (which, bizarrely, hardly any of us were allowed to see), I was not alone in believing that we were labouring to bring forth a 'quality' weekend paper for Wales, like *Scotland on Sunday*, a kind of Welsh *Observer*. To those with such expectations, the first edition was a disappointment, but we consoled ourselves with the naïve hope that things could only get better. For a few months I was allowed to edit a weekly books page, but there was a coup at the palace when my immediate (and supportive) superior was away on holiday: I picked up the paper one Sunday to discover that 'my' page was full of book puffs – about footballers, war, popstars and spies – written by 'reviewers' of whom I had never heard. This was Thomson House's way of saying 'Jenkins, you're fired'.

In its downmarket lurch towards bigger profits, *Wales on Sunday* demonstrated many of the practices and attitudes that frustrate a serious approach to writing about the arts. The drive to sensationalise, personalise and dramatise everything encouraged me to be protective of my material – by, for example, withholding certain information that the subs could be relied upon to milk for a juicy headline. When, for instance, I somehow persuaded 'them' to let me write a whole page about Gerard Manley Hopkins, to mark the centenary of his death, I deliberately avoided any mention of the poet's sexuality, for fear of some ludicrous and irrelevant headline – 'Gay God Boy in No-Holds-Bard Welsh Monastery Romp' – towering above a sober consideration of his literary career. That may not, in retrospect, have been such a wise move: I had ordered a sketch of the poet by his sister, Anne, to accompany the article, to which my sub-editor appended the caption, 'Gerard Manley Hopkins, as sketched by his wife', thereby committing to treasurably implausible wedlock our homosexual Jesuit priest.

In spite of the huge importance of the arts in people's lives and to the economy, it is extraordinary how little attention, in comparison to sport, they are accorded by the media. Compare, for example, *The Western Mail's* half an arts page, with the four pages devoted to sport every day, and the frequent additional sports supplements – an imbalance common to most newspapers, both tabloid and broadsheet. In the relatively parsimonious allocation of space to the arts, some artforms, notably books, films and pop music, fare much better than others, although all suffer from the media's obsession with 'the human interest' angle and 'rows' about finance.

When I worked for *Wales on Sunday* I asked one of the deputy editors why the visual arts in particular were given such poor coverage. Art, he replied, was perceived as a minority interest; photographically, works of art tended to reproduce somewhat flatly in newspapers, so the predictable but unsatisfactory solution was to stick a human being in front of them; most newspapers were interested primarily in personalities, and many artists were 'funny coves' who were reluctant to talk, and didn't, like film stars, run off with women. He admitted that often enough the art that 'made the most noise', rather than that which was most 'deserving', would be likeliest to attract media attention, especially if it was perceived to be 'shocking' or could be 'shown up' as a sham. So, a picture of Prince Charles throwing up his hands in dismay when he unveils a new sculpture in Swansea's maritime quarter, is manna to *The Evening Post*: the paper does not consider it needs to make the effort to enquire whether or not the sculpture is any good. For years, the only consistent reference to the visual arts in the *Post*, apart from re-hashed press releases, was a regular cartoon strip about an artist called 'ap Hazard', whose drip-feed message, week after week, was that artists were moustachioed aliens in French berets and striped burglar-shirts, who were 'abstractionist' con men using the public's 'gullibility' and ignorance about art (and who, in part, might be responsible for that?) to 'get away with it'.

Occasionally, of course, worthwhile criticism of the visual arts will appear in the national and local press, but this seems to depend either on a newspaper buying in the necessary expertise or on the fortunate accident of a reporter who just happens to enjoy art and who knows enough about the subject to hazard a supportable opinion. The likelier situation is that the job of profiling an artist or 'covering an exhibition' will go to the lowliest cub reporter who is too inexperienced to be entrusted with anything else. Eighteen-year-old trainee reporter Nigel Jenkins is fairly typical of the local 'art correspondent': one of my first assignments was to review an art exhibition at the local gallery; when I protested that I didn't know the first thing about painting, I was told to 'just do it, make it up, nobody'll know'; it was an hour out of the office, if nothing else.

Many reporters being, like most people, consumers of popular culture, there is normally a sufficient supply of hacks willing and able to turn in reasonably well-informed copy on entertainers and entertainment – the 'light', unthreatening end of the arts spectrum. Rock music, film and television, forms awash with fantasy and 'human interest', are front-line forest-fellers and paper-sellers, and no editor would tolerate a situation in which they were inadequately covered. If, to some reporters, drama is considered film's poor cousin, it is nevertheless an art with which journalists are inclined to feel at home: its apparent kinship with the excitements of film and television, and its engagement with personalities, conflict, action, ideas, politics, used to ensure that in most newspaper offices there were two or three young recruits who would be keen to give their A-level adjudications of Shakespeare and Shaw a more practical application. The reviewer's apprenticeship in wintry village halls, with endless permutations of *The Wilmslow Boy* and *Blithe Spirit*, might lead eventually to more demanding and rewarding assignments. Within a year or so of joining a group of papers in Leamington Spa, I found myself reviewing companies such as the RSC at Stratford and the Belgrade, Coventry; I remember the heady, sweaty tensions of having to produce, during intervals and in the darkness of auditoriums, 300-word reviews for *The Birmingham Mail*, ready to be phoned over as soon as the curtain fell, or working through the night to deliver, by 9 a.m. sharp, a verdict on the latest John Arden play. There was nothing exceptional, in the 1960s and '70s, about that kind of commitment towards the craft and responsibilities of the reviewer. Most 'regional' or 'provincial' newspapers had several youngsters on the payroll eager to extend themselves in more creative ways than 'straight' reporting allowed, together with older members of staff ready to offer them supportive criticism. There was never an 'arts desk' in the same way that there was a sports desk, where you wrote exclusively about sport, but there was the sense of an arts team, who, like everyone else, did courts and councils and cats up trees, but who gave the best of themselves, they liked to think, to writing arts reviews and features. Although this kind of apprenticeship system has broken down to some extent, and the bland superficialities of the preview are favoured (by whom?) over the salty discriminations of the review, a degree of responsibility towards drama does survive fitfully on certain newspapers. If *The Western Mail* can find no member of staff to review a production, it will still pay (peanuts, admittedly) for one of Wales's two professional drama reviewers to do the job.

Music, apart from pop, fares worse. It used to be the case on most newspapers that if there was nobody on the staff capable of writing about jazz, folk and 'classical' music, an expert from outside would be engaged to advise and write on those genres. The best of such writers – Keith Hudson, for instance, the editor of *Taplas*, who used to write on folk music for *Wales on Sunday*, or Aldon Rees, of the music department at Trinity College, Carmarthen, who used to write on art music for *The Western Mail* – were able both to address the expectations of the cognoscenti and to offer much to readers who had perhaps only a passing interest in such music. Informed attention to what is perceived within journalism as the 'less popular' arts (dance is another form that suffers badly), is now rarely sought, so that for many of the arts there is virtually no forum in which successes and failures can be analysed – or even acknowledged.

Literature would seem to enjoy a higher profile in the media than some other artforms. Readers of *The Western Mail* are fortunate that at least one staffer and a regular freelance columnist, Meic Stephens, are passionately committed champions of the book, but their advocacy of literature is limited by the amount of space they are allowed and by an apparent lack of coherent vision 'at the top' as to the role of literature not only in the newspaper but in the culture as a whole. There is no books page, only a books column, in which there is room to do little more than mention half a dozen Welsh titles in passing; four or five international titles are given soundbite reviews; and perhaps once or twice a week an author is profiled or a book reviewed at greater length. The paper's somewhat leisurely books coverage tends to be retrospective and overly reliant on handouts. Months after the London broadsheets hailed Niall Griffiths's novel *Sheepshagger* as a triumph, readers of *The Western Mail* were still waiting to see it reviewed; and Menna Elfyn's comparably eventful new collection, *Cusan Dyn Dall/Blind Man's Kiss*, was welcomed on the arts page of *The Western Mail* by a 'review' which was no more than an unattributed reprint of the book's blurb. A fully empowered literary editor would want to anticipate such milestone publications as these, and encourage readers to feel that their newspaper was thinking critically for itself. S/he would also be sufficiently acquainted with Welsh literature, in both languages, to be able to liberate poetry from the back-page ghetto where it was briefly allowed an emaciated inch or two, into a vibrant engagement with current affairs. Occasional poems could be commissioned, as a cartoon is commissioned, to cast a unique light on contemporary events; or an existing poem could be re-published, such as, for example, Peter Read's humorous poem about 'Firkin Pubs' might have been, in response to Culture Secretary Chris Smith's recent censure of the trendy re-naming of public houses. Most editors are afraid of poetry; they simply do not appreciate that, if it were imaginatively deployed in the main body of the paper, it could bring something truly distinctive to their pages.

The treatment of literature is even more haphazard and reactive on regional papers where there is next to no sense of responsibility towards a local or national literary context. 'Is poetry dead?' asked the freesheet *Swansea Advertiser* a few years ago, over a photograph of Dylan Thomas's grave, proceeding to answer in the affirmative by publishing half a dozen doggerelish ditties by 'local poets' of whom no one, for good reason, had ever heard. Bereft of any sense of literary discrimination, papers such as *The Evening Post* will regularly publish the gallumphing eulogies of some 'local bard' who knows no more about poetry than how to rhyme 'life' with 'strife', while largely ignoring the output of Swansea's genuine poets. Local newspapers and greetings cards give poetry a terminally bad name.

There are no easy answers to most of the problems that beset the crucial relationship between the arts and the media, although solutions may begin to emerge from such actions as monitoring and lobbying the media, instituting press awards for arts coverage (a job for the Arts Council?), developing a specifically Welsh education system, and encouraging indigenous journalistic talent to stay and work in Wales. Until we have an informed and critical media, Mrs Gerard Manley Hopkins, the gay priest's wife, will continue to mock our newspapers' artistic pretensions.

Land of Re-invention

A Snowball's Chance[1]

*We will fight with conventional weapons until we are losing, then
we will fight with tactical nuclear weapons until we are losing,
and then we will blow up the world.*

Morton Halperin, Pentagon official

'The court finds you guilty of criminal damage for cutting the fence at
the US Naval Facility, Brawdy.[2] You are fined £40.'

After the case, my partner in crime Dot Clancy and I, and four or
five friends, sat round in a caff mulling things over – love, terror,
nukes, madness, the usual cheery small talk of the war-obsessed. Dot
told us of some Greenham women who'd 'gone a bit over the top' after
their arrests; they were promptly 'sectioned' and stowed away in a

[1] First published in *Radical Wales* 17 (Spring 1988).
[2] The euphemistically entitled United States Naval Facility, Brawdy opened in 1973 as
'The US Oceanographic Research Centre', an innocuous sounding name suggesting to
the casual observer that nothing more dubious went on there than a touch of marine
biology. Information as to its true purpose was not available in Britain; researchers had
to go to the United States to find out, in publicly available documentation, what those
sheds in the Pembrokeshire fields were up to. They discovered that the 'NavFac', as
the Americans called it, existed to track down ships of the Soviet Strategic Submarine
fleet, enabling the US, as or before war broke out, to destroy the Russian submarine-
borne deterrent aimed at America. It gave the US the ability to launch a first-strike
annihilation of the opposition's nuclear weapons while retaining intact and ready for
deployment its own nuclear arsenal. This represented a destabilisation of the MAD
'deterrence' doctrine, an *un*balancing of the 'balance of terror' whereby, in theory,
each side is deterred from attacking the other by equally dreadful consequences for
both. This non-NATO 'facility', concerned solely with the defence of America, not
Britain, was therefore the top nuclear strike target in 'nuclear free Wales', and rated
alongside the main American nuclear bases in Britain on the Soviet Union target list.
Construction of the base began in 1971, without Parliamentary approval or even
discussion. Without anyone noticing, it seems, seven large subterranean levels were
excavated under the cliffs, and a conduit tunnel was driven to a junction unit on the
bottom of St Bride's Bay. From that point cables ran hundreds of miles southwest into
the Atlantic to terminate in a series of hydrophone chain-arrays. The base, a focus of
anti-nuclear protests throughout the 1980s, was closed in 1995 following the
disintegration of the Soviet Union and the supposed end of the Cold War. It is now a
business park.

mental hospital instead of being called to account for their actions in court, a practice eerily reminiscent of our supposed enemy's treatment of dissident mavericks.

We have become used to being derided by opponents of the peace movement (the war movement, should we call *them*?) as dangerous cranks or, more charitably, sainted fools with our idealistic heads in the clouds. Those with theirs locked comfortably in the sand call on us constantly to justify, explain, make apologies for our perverse beliefs and actions. The reasonable humanity of the masters of war and their fans is rarely put to such tests: they are commonsensical realists with right and wisdom (not to mention God) demonstrably on their side, while we are written off as a bunch of soft-hearted, woolly-headed nutters. In the matter of nuttiness, indeed, one is bound to concede a point, for who, in brooding on these things, has not felt, at the very least, a little dizzy at the prospects? I remember spending the best part of a summer trying to write something about 'it all', reading about and thinking on it several hours a day, seven days a week, surprising my staid self by responding to a sudden urge to rush outside and hug, hug tight the trunk of a tree, to keep some kind of hold on the world. Reports come in of others feeling the mental pinch. A friend in the Guildhall described how a colleague in his department, a 'job-house-and-family-type' with no particular interest in politics or the bomb, had suddenly had the whole obliterative vileness of the nuclear 'thing' come piling in on her brain, and had suffered a nervous breakdown at her desk. In less traumatic, perhaps unnoticed ways, it lays a finger upon us all, we're each of us 'touched' by it, the 'don't-cares' and 'it'll-never-happen' ostriches as much as the rest.

Few of us, fortunately, are as demented as the institutions, procedures and language of the author of our nightmare, the warfare state. Take, for instance, officialdom's nuke-speak: words don't connect with the values they purport to name when we have a government publication describing as 'disagreeable' or 'regrettable' the 40,000,000 deaths they expect in Britain in a nuclear war – deaths, by the way, which our Eagle 'protector' would sanitise as 'collateral damage'. Or take our illuminating experiences at Haverfordwest Magistrates' Court. Neither Dot nor I was willing to plead guilty to the charge of criminal damage, because we both believe that participants in the 'Operation Snowball' fence-cutting campaign are acting in order to prevent the biggest crime that has ever been planned by the

deformed human mind. Those entrusted with administering the law
rarely share this view, seeming generally impervious to arguments
based on the Genocide Act and various instruments of international
law which proscribe nuclear weapons, quite unequivocally, as illegal.
British law, it appears, is not particularly moved by high moral
principle founded on a belief in the sanctity of life; mere life cuts little
judicial ice. But demonstrate concern for the wellbeing of property,
fence-cutter, and you might just be on to a winner, for the only
possible defence against a charge of criminal damage is that you did
what you did 'with lawful excuse', i.e. 'in order to protect property'.
This endearing legal nicety was tried on recently by two Llanishen
fence-cutters who were found not guilty, somewhat to the consternation
of the Crown Prosecution service.

The Llanishen cutters' appeal to the wayward good sense of Cardiff
magistrates encouraged me to mount a purposeful similar defence
before the Haverfordwest bench. Dot, a part-time nurse from Cei
Newydd (New Quay), was on first, but farting about with legalistic
quibbles and hair-splits was beyond her sorely stretched patience.
She's still got her sense of humour, though. On the day of the demo
she had turned up at the submarine spy post dressed appropriately as a
yellow submarine, complete with periscope, a joke much enjoyed by
most of those in court as she showed the magistrates some
photographs of herself in full submarine splendour. Then, to sum up,
she fired straight from the heart in a short, emotional statement electric
with her love of the world and the life that's on it, and her profound
fears for its future. But they didn't go for it. She got the usual £40 and,
for her refusal to pay an earlier fine, the bailiffs were ordered in. Ah,
Dot, I thought to myself, not enough about property, property's what
they want to hear . . .

I kick off with a little verbal football about the ownership of
perimeter fence and contents. Everyone, including until recently the
Crown Prosecution, has taken the US NavFac to be the property of the
USA Department of Defence, but now, it seems, it was in MoD
ownership all along (this, no doubt, makes the 'alien' fence less alien
to the natives, more abuser-friendly). Then we go on to a consideration
of the name: Brawdy, Breudeth, St Bride's Bay – the bay of Brigid, or
Ffraid in Welsh, Christianised Irish goddess and later Celtic saint,
patron of the soil, fertility, healing, learning, poetry and the crafts; a
maker, in other words, a life-sustainer, the very model of Celtic

hospitality, and the polar opposite of the destructive potential embodied in the American first-strike dream factory perched on the shores of her bay. But she too knew war: her son Ruidán was killed in one, and her lamentations were the first wailings of woe ever heard in Ireland.

The bench, I can see, are already growing restless. I explain this apparent diversion by restating the foundation of my defence against the charge – my concern to protect property, and therefore my tenderness towards this particular *bro* and all the property in it: its farms and fields, its houses, churches, pubs and, I suppose, its cars and videos, washing machines and caravans – everything, in short, that is held in individual or common ownership (although any concern for the lives of the owners themselves is, in the terms of the Criminal Damage Act 1971, an irrelevance).

How is all this property threatened? I suggest that the Soviet Union, in seeking to wipe out a base that gives a first-strike advantage to the US, would need to hurl something a little more volatile than a hand-grenade at the NavFac. The smallest nuclear device in their armoury, a one-megaton airburst missile, would probably do the trick – perhaps two or three of them, just to be on the safe side. Because a one-megaton bomb packs a punch equivalent to one million tons of TNT, it is reasonable to assume that the property of southwest Dyfed would suffer a certain amount of damage. Indeed, all property within a radius of five miles would cease to be recognisable as such: farewell the villages of Solva, Hayscastle, Broadhaven, Newgale, Roch, all farms, all scattered cottages and homesteads. At ground zero all quadrupedal and bipedal agricultural property would be vapourised, and six miles away the hair and feathers of such property would vanish in a puff of smoke, and the skins of all property be burnt to shreds. Up to thirteen miles away, the eyeballs of property would melt. Radiation to property growing in the fields would render that property inedible, and therefore valueless; those fields would be unproductive of further property for many years to come. The 'plume' from the explosion would spread damage to property much further afield. If, for instance, there were a 15 m.p.h. wind blowing in a south easterly direction, property between Brawdy and Swansea would soon be receiving a dose of about 1000 Rads which would induce in that property lethargy, convulsions, vomiting, bloody scouring and death within days.

I point out to the magistrates that in order to present a workable defence I am not obliged to claim that I cut the fence in order to protect my own property. This, I admit, is fortunate for my case because, living in a terraced house in Mumbles, I cannot pretend that damage to my own property would be in any way significant. True, those 1000 Rads breezing around the countryside could certainly find their way to Mumbles, in which case my baby daughter, her mother and I would be killed, but my property would be far enough away from the blast at Brawdy to escape virtually unscathed. About the only damage I can offer the court on the property front are two fatally irradiated goldfish and a crop of inedible rhubarb.

At the end of my twenty-five minutes or so, I hoped I had convinced the bench of the four requisite criteria of my defence: that I was motivated by a desire to protect property; that I felt the property to be in immediate need of protection; that the means of protection of property adopted by me were 'reasonable having regard to all the circumstances'; and that my beliefs in this matter are honestly held. But I had obviously fallen short somewhere because they found me guilty.

Perhaps they found me weak on the third point. Perhaps they felt that my vision of eyeball-popping, skin-frazzling, soil-sickening nuclear devastation to property was ill-matched by the action I took to try to prevent it. Cutting half way through a single strand of wire at the submarine spy base was, they may have felt, pathetically inadequate and not at all 'reasonable having regard to all the circumstances'. Perhaps they were hinting that next time I should put aside the ineffectual hacksaw blade and adopt more purposeful methods, such as taking a chainsaw to the fence or ploughing through it with a JCB.

Or perhaps they thought I was talking a load of rhubarb. Either way, INF tinkerings or not, the madness goes on.

The Diary of Prisoner WX 0674

9.ix.88

'For your refusal to pay a fine of forty pounds for the offence of criminal damage, the court sentences you to prison for seven days,' says the chairwoman of the bench, with half-moon bifocals and cut-glass Tory accent. They'd asked about the amount of cash on me, and I'd declined to tell them, anticipating that they'd have me taken down to the cells, like last time, and robbed by a policeman – of the single penny, on this occasion, that I had baited my pocket with. But I'm sent down straight away, and led along a row of transit cells, about half of which are occupied, mostly by youngsters, their heads at the rectangular openings in the metal doors, indulging in mild cheeking of the policemen passing to and fro. 'Hey man!' and ''Ippie!' they shout as I'm led past them and into a cell of my own. A solicitor I went to school with – who may or may not recognise me – walks up and down outside looking for a client; our eyes lock for a moment as he peers in. I sit down on the bench in this little cell for what turns out to be quite a long wait, listening to the youngsters ribbing the police and getting bawled out in turn, moaning for cigarettes and lights for cigarettes – the abiding obsession of this world of prison. Nothing to read but the graffiti, including 'Kill the poor' scratched in a join between bricks. I wonder how often, and for how long, these youthful habitués of these cells have been in before: they seem well known to the police and to each other. I have been here already in the imagination, and so far it's fairly predictable and unalarming. If I'm of 'good behaviour' I'll be out in less than a week, and anyway I could choose to cough up, if it proved to be too much of an ordeal, and be released forthwith. The totalitarian regime of boarding school has prepared me well enough for prison; my footling sentence of a few days is nothing much; all that's worrying me is the prospect of being banged up with Radio One twenty-four hours a day. Am led out after an hour by a policeman who, in contrast to his curt address to the youngsters, refers to me as 'Mr Jenkins'; he leads me to a dark 'garage' area where a police van is waiting; seats along the sides, frosted plastic windows through which, nevertheless, the outside world is roughly discernible, and metal grille-work all round. Inside are four youngsters, three of whom are loud with frightened bravado, and the fourth silent, clearly shaken by the experience, and straining to deliver a weak smile when cajoled by the others. And there's an older, bearded man, forty plus, sitting beside me, who says not a word, his only communication being his handing back of a cigarette to the lad on my other side. Learn later that he has grassed on them for some big deal involving £30,000, and that they are all going down for thirteen years. The drive takes us along the Kingsway, past the Guildhall and down Oystermouth Road to Swansea jail, or Cox's Farm as it used to be known. It's a lovely, sunny day. The doors of the prison are opened and the van drives through. There's a neat garden with a little fish pond, and some kitsch plaster ornaments on its edge; across the way are the hospital block and chapel. 'The Gang of Four' are called out first, motioned through a barred door by a severe-looking Englishman in a white cotton jacket and wearing half-moon, gold-rimmed glasses; reminds me of the sort that could have been one of Dr Mengele's experimenters in Nazi Germany. He calls me into a little anteroom, and tells me to put my handkerchief and belt in a plastic icecream carton. Am then locked in a tiny cell no bigger than a phonebox, and sit there for at least an hour waiting to be processed through 'reception'. Graffito scratched on the door: 'Dai Jones of Burry Port, unknown expert on burglar alarms' . . . Can't have been that expert to end up in this little kiosk. Young cons do the ushering. One shows me into an anteroom to be questioned by a medical officer about physical and mental health, suicide attempts, drugs. He asks if I have ever had an overnight stay in a hospital, presumably to see if I am used to being away from home in the care of an alien institution. I think my eight or nine years' 'educational' sentence should be ample qualification. Back then to the kiosk for another half hour or so, listening to the sounds coming from outside, and instructions being given to those before me to call the screws 'sir'. On then to another encounter with Mengele. Sun streaming through the windows, the leaves of a stunted prison-yard oak fluttering in the wind, just the other side of the glass. Mengele, humourless and severe, makes a list of my clothes, books, etc. It seems I am allowed to take neither my books nor my notebook to the cell. There is a debate about whether I should be allowed to take my contact lens case and soaking solution. Based on the rules in Bristol, it's decided I am not allowed to take them, and had better leave my contact lenses behind with the rest of my things. I explain that I can't see too well without the lenses, and they relent. I can keep them in, but still can't retain the equipment. Hope I can find some way of keeping them safe overnight. They obviously have no idea how contact lenses 'work', and no experience of prisoners wearing them. Can keep watch, pen and today's *Guardian*, but am denied paper (hence this diary kept in shorthand notes in the endpapers and margins of Gwyn Thomas's *Sorrow for thy Sons*, which I don't retrieve until later). Am told to strip off in a booth, under the eyes of Mengele, and then to take a brown dressing gown and have a shower. One of the young cons brings me some clothes, draping them over the half-door of the shower: dark grey socks, underpants marked 'PD' (Prison Department) above a representation of Mrs Windsor's tin hat, light blue T-shirt, vest, blue overall-material trousers, and a smart blue-striped shirt. The first pair of slip-on shoes that he slides under the door are too tight, and I ask for something bigger. Am moved on to a nearby room where a young smoker, in his own clothes, is sitting. He's a remand prisoner, free therefore to wear his own clothes until convicted, to smoke as much tobacco as he wants, and to drink a can of beer a day. He's been in before for many things, he tells me, but believes he can get off this latest charge and has high hopes of going straight. Often beaten up by the police: wet blanket treatment that leaves no bruises. 'What you in for?' he asks. 'Cutting a strand of wire during a CND demo at the American base at Brawdy,' I reply. 'Fuck,' he says, 'there'll be more than a strand of wire destroyed when they drop the bomb.' One of the young cons brings me a metal tray with cod, chips and peas, an inedible wodge of semolina, and two tasty bread rolls. Remember how Waldo enjoyed the bread during his stay here thirty-odd years ago: 'Swansea jail makes the best brown bread in the whole of Wales'. The quiet young lad from the bus is brought in – Crowe, I hear them calling him – and the three of us chat until a screw comes to take us to the cells, passing down a corridor where we pick up sets of kit: two blankets, two sheets, a pillowcase containing various odds and ends – shaving cream, shaving brush, toothbrush, soap, plastic beaker, plastic knife, fork and spoon, and change of underclothes. We are then led to the left, and left again through a door, and up a single flight of stairs, at the top of which we are told to sit on a bench. I turn my head and realise that here we are in the wing itself – 'A' Wing – with a huge window at the far end, two landings above us, and rows of metal doors. Have all the time been expecting the squalorous stench that I'd heard about – of piss, shit, dope and tobacco – but there's none of it. The screw leads us up two flights of spiral staircase, situated in the middle of the wing, to the top floor, the fourth. At first he makes to show me and Crowe into a cell on the town side of the building, but then changes his mind. 'Nicer view over here,' he says, leading us to cell no. 12 on the south side, with a view of the sea. A cloud of flies lifts up as he shows us into a scruffy cell that hasn't been cleaned since the last occupants: that, of course, is our job. He locks us in: we are prisoners. We introduce ourselves. He is Billy Crowe from Ton Mawr. He's only twenty, and should, in principle, be in the youth wing, for those aged between sixteen and twenty, but they seem to have overlooked this. Good view from the window, if you stand on the chair beside the bed. I choose that bed, Billy the one by the door. West Glam County Hall fills about two thirds of the view, but to the left there's a good slice of sea, the new hotel, the roofs of the light green sea-front houses in the maritime quarter. Below is Shop Four, another large building and some smaller ones. Don't know what goes on there. Can see the entrance to the prison, and the office alongside – watch the shifts come and go. The cell is about fourteen feet by eight, barrel vaulted, its fluorescent light smeared with blood; buff gloss painted brick walls, dirty grey lino tiles on the floor. The window is about two feet by two, with three horizontal bars on the outside and an open grille on the inside, through which it would be possible to stick an arm to wave, should some friends appear on the grassy twmp opposite. Old socks, shoes, fag ends, dead matches, torn-up letters litter the floor. On a noticeboard, and on either side of the door, are soft-porn pin-ups of women in various poses of fake allure. The door is of the classic prison type: metal, patterned with bolt-heads, with an oval inset at eye-level in which is situated the peep-hole, which is occasionally flipped open and peered through by a passing screw. I feel sorry for Billy. He's dazed, hadn't expected to be sent to prison today – for failing to pay a fine of about £80 for some petty vandalism or theft). He's been given fourteen days, and so can expect to get out on Friday, in a week's time, although he's due to appear in court again on Thursday to answer a smash-and-grab charge, and is afraid he'll be sent straight back here to do some more weeks or even months. Apparently he'd been on the piss with some mates and had taken a shine to a pair of trousers in a shop window – needed them to get into a club on the Kingsway. So they smashed and grabbed, with consequences he's now coming to terms with. Is worried what his 'missus' (girlfriend) will say when she finds out he's in jail – and what his parents will say. He had hoped to join the army, but this latest bout of trouble has wrecked that plan. He'll have to stay on the dole and do hobbles, such as plastering for his father. He's edgy and depressed: 'I don't know how I'm going to get through this, it's doin' my 'ead in, it's really doin' my 'ead in. I'm never coming back to this fuckin' place, never – I'm going straight from now on.' His main concern is smoking; makes a great fuss about cigarettes; only has a tiny amount of tobacco on him, no skins, just one or two matches. This is his biggest worry – and how to kill time. I'm glad of the *Guardian* I was allowed to bring in, and get stuck into that, even the business pages, although I balk, still, at the sports section. I offer him part of the paper, but it's beyond him. He's a *Sun* reader. Later he asks for the section with the crossword – he does the *Sun* crossword regularly. I wince for him because I know he's not going to be able to do it; tell him that I can't do it – which is true, I'm hopeless at crosswords – and wish him luck, offering my pen. He gives up after a minute or two. He's twitchy and bored, longing for a radio, just can't settle to anything. About 4.30 the cell doors are opened, there's a flurry of slopping out and replenishing of water from the recesses, and we are called down for tea, a tray of gristly stew, anaemic cabbage, real mashed spud, brown bread and more semolina. With our mugs, we go down to the kitchen on level one to collect our tea. Cons in aprons are doling out the grub, almost every one of them plastered with tattoos. Back in our cell, Billy says as we eat that he's recognised a friend of his who he didn't think was in here, which cheers him a little, but he's constantly anxious about his parents, who are supposed to be moving house this weekend, and about his 'missus': 'First thing I do when I get out of here is get out of my 'ead and shag the arse off her'. He's missing his usual Friday night routine of getting pissed on the Kingsway and rolling home about 4 a.m. After about an hour they open the cells and we wash our cutlery and mugs in the recess, and place the metal trays for collection on the landing outside our door. Then we're banged up again. Lovely sunset, turning the County Hall pink – warm evening, heavy traffic on Oystermouth road. I read the paper. Billy nods off, wakes, prowls, stands on the chair to gaze out of the window, longing for Radio One. It suits me fine that we don't have a radio, but I feel sorry for him that he hasn't got one to take his mind off his troubles and the prison noises of metal banging, keys clinking, footsteps passing on the landing, dropped plastic cups, wall-muffled voices, and an eerie yelping sound, every fifteen minutes or so, echoing from a nearby cell into the yard. At nine I hear the familiar toot of the *Celtic Pride* preparing to sail to Cork. Pee into slop bucket before bedding down; it stinks – full of previous inmates' piss. Fortunately they've left behind, also, a plastic mug, so I pour a little water into two mugs and drop my lenses in for the night. We switch out the light about half nine. 'It's like a church,' says Billy of the shadows cast across the barrel-vaulted room by the bars in the window. The bed, although short and narrow, is comfortable, and it's easy to fall asleep. During the night, when the traffic dies down, I can hear clearly the buoy in the harbour mouth, clanging continuously, and sounding at first like distant snatches of indistinct radio – organ music, perhaps.

10.ix.88
Saturday. Cell door unlocked about 8. Slop out, piss, quick wash, then down to kitchen to collect breakfast: one rasher of bacon, tomato, bread and butter, pint of tea; decline the porridge. An hour later we are called down to complete the reception procedure. As we're sat on a bench, waiting to see the Prison Officer, a towering, muscly con strides over and says 'Which one is Jenkins?' Then he holds out his hand to shake mine, and, as we shake, he presses a surreptitious stash of tobacco into my palm. 'CND,' he rumbles, 'I admire what you done.' Apparently he and many others heard about it on the radio last night. Throughout the day I get cons muttering 'CND', smiling, sticking up their thumbs in support. The Prison Officer asks if I have any complaints. I say we haven't anything to read. 'I don't like to see people without books,' he responds, instructing the screw at my side to see that I get a book. The screw asks me if any book will do, and I have trouble explaining to him that almost *any* book will *not* do: what would be best would be two or three of the books I'd brought with me. He doubts that this is possible – forms to fill in, it's the weekend, etc. – but he'll see what he can do. Waiting to see the doctor, I talk to a bloke with his hand in plaster. He's going out for the day on Tuesday for his son's funeral; the child had died a cot death, aged six weeks. He *seems* not to be too wound down by this, but in this grotesquely macho

environment where the only emotions freely expressed are aggressive
ones, there's no knowing what he's really feeling. Out for an hour's
worth of 'exercise' on the yard in the northwest corner, a sort of mini
soccer pitch. Circle the yard a few times, then sit down, back against a
wall, with the Vetch's huge lighting arm towering above, and black
Kilvey to the east. Everyone's smoking and gobbing spittle the length
of the lined-up boot-soles. A time for tall, macho, criminal tales, from
one chopsy skinhead in particular, who rabbits on about the cars he has
stolen, the drunken driving he's done, the times he's been done for
driving while disqualified. Try to draw the silent man on my right into
a conversation, but he remains silent. The garrulous are matched by the
isolated types: the tall man, toothless but for a pair of canines, who
rambles briskly round and round the yard talking busily to himself,
looking up to mutter curses at the screws as he passes, only ever
seeming to say 'Fucking cunts'; or the eyes-down, purposefully
strolling black man who does nothing but walk, and seems to have
nothing to do with anyone else. After dinner a screw comes to say I
have a visitor. Surprising, because I hadn't filled in a 'VO' (Visiting
Order) and left it at the gate – didn't even know, in time, about the
correct procedure. He leads me down to a wooden building at the back
of the hospital block, I am frisked, and then shown in – and there are
my two lovely girls. Delyth has brought some Toblerone and cartons
of orange juice. I am told to swap seats with her: my back must be to
the wall and I must be facing the table-on-a-dais at which are perched
two screws, making sure that nothing naughty goes on, like drug
passing. Angharad holds out her arms to me for hugs, which she has
never done before. Lovely to see them both. I can cope with this,
because I saw them yesterday and will be with them again in a few
days' time, but such visits, happening only once a month, must be
poignantly bittersweet occasions for men who are locked away from
their families for years. We have nearly an hour together. The
atmosphere is rather like that of a hospital visiting area, although there
are other tensions: men and women hugging and kissing, rather
ferociously in some cases; many mothers bring their children and
babies. Back in the wing, one of the screws appears at last with three
books, and I offer Billy *It Was Twenty Years Ago Today* thinking that,
having lots of pictures, it might be more appealing than either of the
others. He doesn't get far with it (neither, later, do I), but he tries the
Swedish book, which, indeed, does seem to hold his attention for some

of the time. I get stuck into *Sorrow for thy Sons*; a little difficult to concentrate because I sense that Billy wants more chat than I am used to giving out, and seems to be somewhat startled that I, for hours on end, can go on reading. Billy lives for Radio One – and for now, therefore, doesn't have much to live for. Not much graffiti in the cell: a few patches, here and there, of sentence-days etched like matchsticks, for the crossing off, in platoons of seven, the con's name followed by the length of sentence: 'Hughesy of Glynneath 3 yrs'; 'O'Brien July 87 – July 88 For Farting on a Bus'. Then there are the proverbial wisdoms: 'Happiness is a journey, not a destination' and 'A friend with weed is a friend indeed'. 'Joint' is nearly always spelled 'jiont'. Billy too got an unexpected visit today – from his parents, his mother in tears, his father taking the mickey. Both are afraid, he says, of him going the same way as his elder brother, who spent two years in jail. Then there's his cousin, Ioan, who is inside here for some buggery offence. 'Mad bastard,' says Billy, 'split her arse in two. The girl said it was rape, but she wanted it really.' Who wouldn't? As the sun goes down this warm Indian summer's night, I could murder a pint.

11.ix.88
Rain in the night, and the County Hall showing white against an endless grey sky. They open the cells at 8. The usual slop-out, down to collect breakfast, then settle down to write this, but am interrupted by the unwelcome call to go out for an hour's 'exercise'. Spent longer today walking round the yard. A team of three con joggers, running round the prison for charity, pass repeatedly through the yard; one shouts 'CND!', winks, smiles, thumbs up. The usual loners out there doing their reclusive shuffles. The black man is referred to by one group, within his hearing, as 'the fucking wog'. Billy very worried about running out of matches, although relieved that his dire tobacco shortage has been solved instantly by yesterday's sly gift to me of the quarter ounce of tobacco. He has traded a little of it for a packet of skins, but has only one match left. Back in the cell, we try to split this match into four. A pin is needed for this job, but we don't have one. I try splitting it with fingernails, but it's too clumsy a method. We take some staples out of the prison regulation booklet, but they prove too flimsy. No luck with hard flakes of paint either – too brittle. Later he manages to swap one roll-up fag for five matches. Billy is also very worried about taking a shit. Time is certainly short at slop-out breaks,

but there are usually one or two toilet bowls free, and a crap in relative comfort is possible. This is too public for Billy – yet he doesn't want to be reduced to having to crap in the slop bucket in the cell. He presses the bell by the door which calls the screws' attention by emitting a buzzing noise and lighting up, both inside and outside the cell, a red light. It can take ten or more minutes for a screw to respond – if there are any on hand at all. Billy's told by a con parading the landing outside that there are no screws around, and he'll have to wait a couple of hours. Hours later, still wanting this shit, he's told to wait until next slop-out time, in an hour and a half. Some farting relieves the pressure, and he manages, just, to hold out. We're supposed to have been supplied with many things we don't have: pillow, brush, comb, toothpaste. Billy, who prides himself on being a snappy dresser, is concerned to keep up his appearance, and tries to comb his hair with a plastic fork. We hear rumours about a man in another wing who's locked up all the time, and daily smears himself with shit, after which he is hosed down by the screws. Radio One-type songs from other cells, the hurting songs of men's memories, sparking others to join in the choruses. Billy spreads cake crumbs on the windowsill, and a starling comes down to peck at them: we admire the brilliant colours in its 'dark' and 'dull' plumage, the lovely sheen of the feathers. Every morning a screw comes in to test the window bars by tapping each one with a metal bar in the shape of a long, shallow 'S', making sure we haven't been up to any sawing in the night. Here the working class are jailers to the working class. Some people here have reached the end of their world – 'Life + 1 Day'; there was never much in life for them, and there's nothing now for them, and nothing in the future, except poverty, trouble, pain, anxiety. Why then should they be fussed about the threat of nuclear war? Just a grand suicide, taking the hateful world with it, and all the misery. Certainly some of the 'support' I've had comes from men who see CND actions as nothing more than an anarchistic swipe at 'the system'; there are others, no doubt, who regard me as some kind of irritating do-gooder. In the evening, Radio One blares out from next door, the prisoner in there singing out loud with the chorus, banging furniture and chucking plastic mugs. I stick my head out of the inner window and catch a flavoursome whiff of hash, maybe from next door. Billy and I get talking – about his girlfriend – 'We'll go for a steak when I get out, she can pay'; about his horse, a stallion he bought at Gowerton mart; about fishing with his father in the bay, from a 22-foot old lifeboat they keep in the marina. He describes stopping the boat way out in the middle of the bay and slipping into the sea for a swim – 'It's weird out there, really, really cold. Shit, I miss the missus.'

12.ix.88
Poor night's sleep, thanks partly to the blanket I have to use as a pillow. During slopping-out, I lean on the landing railing watching the men go to and from the recesses with their bowls, jugs and slop buckets, some hovering outside the recesses cleaning their teeth. There is a terrible greyness about most of them, accentuated by the lacklustre tattoos on the skins of nearly everyone. Many English prisoners here, mainly from London. Blokes with green stripes down their trousers are escapees; don't know what the yellow stripe down brown trousers signifies. After breakfast, stand at the window watching the workers file into County Hall; another worker is on the street with a plastic bucket, picking up rubbish. Prisoners everywhere, inside and outside Swansea jail. Four days in here is bearable; four weeks, certainly, would be a different matter, let alone four months or four years. But the 9 to 5 treadmill of the prisoners outside these walls is a sombre challenge I can do without. Billy's not a bad lad at all, and has probably learned to steer clear of this place in future. Nor is he thick. It's just that he hasn't been encouraged to make the best of himself, and, like many in here (and out there), doesn't seem able to tap his potential. The waste, the stunted growth – like the measly ash tree in the exercise yard, which can never get enough sun, although in a certain early and watery light it takes on a subtle greenish hue suggestive of what, in better circumstances, it could possibly be. 'I want to swim in the most ample lives,' said Neruda when asked why he was a socialist. Billy likes the sound of this, and scratches it on the windowsill where the paint has flaked away revealing plaster, which is easier to write on. The slop bucket, similar to a nappy bucket, has a smell of its own, irrespective of what Billy and I deposit in it, a foul, ammoniac stench which, as soon as the lid is lifted, leaps into and down the room, heading straight for the window. The rest of the wing go off to work at about 9.15, but for some reason I am not called, so I sit down to read *It Was Twenty Years Ago Today* by Derek Taylor, which turns out to be tediously self-indulgent. Within a few minutes a screw turns up with Billy: at last, the system has realised that, for his

age, he is in the wrong wing; so he has to pack up his things and head for the youth department. I tell him to keep the Knut Hansen book, which he's already a hundred pages into, and seems, to his surprise, to be enjoying; hope he finishes it, but he'll probably fall in with a radio, and that'll be the end of reading, for life maybe. I tell him not to come back. 'I won't,' he says. And somehow I think – I hope – he won't. The experience has been a considerable shock to him. Am left alone, now, with the pin-ups, the Lady Di lookalike sprawled on her back, showing off, with ice-instant smile, the pink folds of her vagina. Bright sun casts across the bottom of my bed the sharply defined shadow of the window grille; then the sun's obscured by cloud and the bars disappear: freedom. And what is freedom? The terrible, tedious treadmill of prison, of prisons of various kinds beyond these stone walls. Is Billy's smash and grab a lunge towards freedom? Are the girlie pics stuck with spunk or semolina to the walls of every cell a glimpse of freedom? 'Muffy was yu 22.6.88'. To make a statement, to get it heard; the fight for the freedom of articulacy. My trousers keep falling down. No belt allowed, and no loops around the waist through which to thread a piece of string, even if a piece of string could be found. Which it can't. No doubt against the regulations. Strangely disabling to have trousers constantly sliding towards the floor. Expect all morning a summons to see the governor, doctor, etc. to go through reverse reception procedure, as one of the screws last night told me would happen, but no one comes. I look out at noon for the demo on the twmp opposite which Delyth said CND were organising, but nothing (learn later they'd staged the demo on a different twmp, one overlooked by the youth wing). Stew for lunch, mash and cabbage, followed by stodgy sponge and custard. When in the early afternoon there's still no call, I begin resigning myself to not being released until Wednesday. Then a Welsh-speaking screw, who is by no means unsympathetic to the CND cause, rolls up with a huge pile of cards and letters from supporters – at least 40 of them. Wonder how on earth, in the middle of a postal strike, they'd managed to send them, but then see from a notice in *Sanity* (which Nick Guy sent) that there was a *Cyngor* and a Hinkley Point meeting on Saturday at which, obviously, these cards had been collected. I ask the screw, in my faltering *Cymraeg hanner byw*, when I'm to be released, and he goes to find out, confirming on his return that yes, I'm a late addition to the list and am to be released tomorrow. It's pizza, spaghetti and mash for tea. Decide to remove some of the sexy women from the walls and, using mash for glue, replace them with the cards I've been sent, rather than stash them unseen in an envelope at home. Also stick a cutting from *Sanity* on the wall about the spectacular efforts of the Jesuit priest Daniel Berrigan to oppose the war machine. So, tomorrow, Tuesday, I'll be out. Don't want, though, to be released a moment earlier: have heard that one of the first things they'll do in the event of a nuclear war is let out all the prisoners. Early release therefore a somewhat inauspicious sign. At about 8.30 hear the bolt being slid into place on the cell door. Restless night, watching the light changing, listening to a Yorkshireman on the twmp opposite shouting to the Englishman in the cell next to mine. As the street lights are extinguished slowly around 5.30, the shadows of the bars on the ceiling are gradually rubbed out, and the metal door takes on the blue metallic sheen of dawn. Homely coo of the pigeons in the eaves as the traffic noise builds up, the sirens begin their days' bee-barping, and the external prisoners, who need no walls or bars to lock them in, drag themselves to their labours. I fold the blankets and sheet, 'pack' my envelope, and sit waiting for the screw. He comes about 7.30, and leads me down to the reception area. 'Are we going to see you back here again?' he asks. 'There's always the possibility,' I reply, 'as long as there are nuclear weapons'. 'Thought you'd say that,' he says. A few days in jail for me risks nothing – it's just something that I, at this moment, am in a position to do, not being employed and therefore not being sackable. At the counter, he gives me back my own clothes and shoes, and then shows me to the discharge room, surely the happiest place in the entire establishment. I slip out of the prison uniform into my own clothes. Am led then to an office next door where I have to sign some forms, answer some questions, and show them my appendix scar, as proof of identity. Only then can I be released. They give me £2.06 – presumably the 1p I came in with, plus a travel allowance of £2.05. They lead me to the main gate and open it for me to walk through. I sit on the wall outside for ten minutes or so, waiting for Delyth and Angharad to pick me up, nodding good morning to the prisoners trotting into the jail to do their daily stint as screws.

The Language of Liberation[1]

Cymru, Wales, the Principality, the region, Englandandwales, the nation, the country, Britain, England: what and when do *you* call Wales?

Anyone who has been abroad will know that for the rest of the world Wales hardly exists. Ireland, sure. Scotland, OK. But Wales? Whales? It's in England? A town, perhaps? A river somewhere? If we are known at all it is thanks largely to a clutch of 'stars' – Burton, Bassey, Tom Jones, Dylan T. – and, once upon a time, our *équipe de rugby*.

It is hardly surprising that we have this identity problem with other people when we have it so badly ourselves as we dispatch our postcards home to 'Merthyr Tydfil, Inghilterra' or 'Dyfed, Angleterre', by no means confident that 'Cymru/Wales/Pays de Galles' will, on its own, deliver the goods. The confusing and contradictory terms we use to describe who we are and how we relate to the wider world must rule us out, in the eyes of many, as serious contenders.

The affliction of slithering nomenclature, a telling indicator of political morale, goes back a long way. Our forebears, the *Brythoniaid* (Ancient Britons), had the run of the whole island of *Prydein* (Britain) and thought of themselves as the true Britons for centuries after the arrival of the Saxons. These Germanic people corralled us behind Offa's Dyke and labelled us *welisc* or Welsh, 'strangers' in our own land; we began to talk of ourselves as the Cymry, or 'compatriots'. When empire-building England commandeered the term 'British' as a nifty official catch-all for everyone in these islands, we were distinguished by some, for a while, as the 'Cambro-Britons'.

Now, from a distance, things seem to have settled along fairly logical lines: we are a nation called Cymru or Wales, part of an island called Britain (which is also a state) which is in turn part of Europe. But come in closer, and such simplicities craze into a squabble of terms.

Take the word 'Britain' (sometimes with the prefix 'Great', to ditinguish it from the territorially smaller Brittany). The English have

---

[1] First published in *Radical Wales* 25 (Spring 1990).

never been happy with it, being dimly aware perhaps that 'British' originally referred to the Britons or Welsh and, strictly speaking, 'includes them out'. So with no sense of incongruity they cheerfully refer to these multinational islands as 'England' and rub out the identity of everyone else in the countries of Britain who is not English. On the other hand, when they are thinking politically their political state is Britain, never England. This gives them imperial sway over those lesser entities worldwide who have been fortunate enough to benefit from the imposition of 'British' civilisation. 'Britain is Empire, genius, destiny: a civilisation for export which includes a political culture,' wrote Neal Ascherson recently. 'To mouth the words "English Government" is to betray that dream in which Westminster institutions transcend mere nationality and become universal, a legacy to the world.'

Cutglass and cricket, the fox hunt, the bowler hat, the 'Mother of Parliaments': this is what the English 'Establishment' has offered the rest of the world as the image of 'Britain'. And, as Raymond Williams argued (in *Radical Wales* 23): 'The Welsh and the Scots, like the majority of the English, have had to put up with a version of who they are . . . in the interests of this unity called 'England' or, more artificially, the 'United Kingdom'. Not just the version abroad, but the more effective version at home.'

We lap up this dominant version and obligingly rub ourselves out every time we use 'the nation', 'national', 'the country' to refer to what are in fact three-and-a-bit – arguably five-and-a-bit – distinct nations. Every day in the news media are items that contrast events in Wales with the situation in 'the rest of the country', implying subtly, insistently that Wales is *not* a country, merely a part of one. The habit is deep-seated and may be found even in ideologically pure organs like *Radical Wales*! In falling for this – or the amorphous administrative hybrid 'Englandandwales' – we allow the British State masquerading as a nation to overrule our sense of Welsh nationhood, and end up feeling as lost and powerless as a 'nation' of North American Indians on a state-sanctioned reservation. So let us talk of 'the national team', but let us also talk, by logical extension, of 'the national press', and mean *Golwg, The Western Mail, Wales on Sunday* – not *The Sun* or *The Independent*, which might be more accurately referred to as the British press.

The term 'international' is hardly ever dared, in anything other than a British/world context, outside the realm of sport. This means, of course, that we are allowed, and allow ourselves, only to *play* at being a nation. The 'home team' in the 'international' against England will be Wales, yet our 'Papur Cenedlaethol Cymru' (National Newspaper of Wales), *The Western Mail*, can offer us pages of what it calls 'Home News' that are all about – England. Feeling dizzy? Or provincial? Wales is allowed 'international relations' only under the banner of Britain; but if we accept that Britain is composed of a (debatable) number of nations, then surely relations between those nations should be described as 'international'.

Those who are edgy about the idea of a Welsh nation avoid the word 'Welsh' at all costs and opt for 'region' or 'Principality', battening us securely under monarchical, Unonist hatches. So we end up with organisations with coyly non-committal titles like 'the Wales TUC' or 'the Wales CBI'. When the English-language authors unionised in 1982 they would have nothing to do with this pussyfooting 'Wales' tag, and chose to be known full-bloodedly as the Welsh Union of Writers.

Let's start the new millennium as we mean to go on, by getting straight in our heads and mouths our terms of self-reference. It's time we talked ourselves out of provincialism and into the dignity of mature nationhood.

Land of Invention[1]

While poets, singers and patriotic warriors are the heroes of our national anthem, the achievements of Welsh scientists and technologists, out of all proportion to the size of population, are unsung and all but invisible. Whole fifteens of 'patriotic warriors' may be confidently recalled in rugby clubs throughout the land, but ask anyone to name just one Welsh scientist and they'll bounce back, almost certainly, with the ignoramus's defence, 'a contradiction in terms, mate.'

What little science (literally, 'knowledge') we have of ourselves. Poets have been championed now and then as suitable candidates for a Nobel prize, but only one contender from Wales has actually won a Nobel, and he, Brian Josephson from Cardiff, is a scientist whose work in low temperature physics is on the threshold of revolutionising computer technology. Poetry and science might seem to inhabit mutually exclusive worlds but it is to poetry that we must look, the medieval 'nature gnomes' –

> Cold bed of fish in the gloom of ice;
> Stag lean, bearded reeds;
> Evening brief, slant of bent wood.
> (trans. Tony Conran)

– for the beginnings of what has become a remarkable if unacknowledged Welsh scientific tradition. These chains of frequently three-line verses amount to a methodical investigation of natural phenomena, classifying the effects of, say, winter in terms of physics, botany and zoology, with, often, an aphoristic observation in the last line proposing an elementary psychology.

'Of all the human activities where Wales has excelled it is in science that our contribution has been superlative,' says the Aberystwyth-based space scientist (and Assembly Member) Dr Phil Williams. He cites figures such as Robert Recorde (d. 1558) of Tenby who wrote the first

[1] First published in *Wales in Our Own Image* (In Books, 1999).

book on algebra in English and invented the 'equals' sign (=); Alfred Wallace (1823–1913), the naturalist from Usk who beat Darwin to the discovery of the principle of 'the survival of the fittest'; Corwen-born David Hughes, inventor of the microphone and the teleprinter; Evan Williams of Sychpant, 'the most outstanding Welsh scientist of all time', who discovered the meson particle. The most important Welshman alive, he argues, indeed 'possibly the most important person in the world', is Diserth-born John Houghton who, as chair of the scientific committee of the Intergovernmental Panel on Climate Change, is responsible for the scientific evidence for global warming. Houghton's reports led to the crucial Rio and Kyoto summits, and international agreements on the imperative of radically cutting carbon dioxide output.

If science, being an international pursuit, has drawn Welsh brains to institutions all over the world, it has also generated more than enough home-based activity to make a scientific career in Wales an attractive option. Wales ranks top in the United Kingdom in terms of both the amount of money spent on invention and the successes resulting from that investment. The University of Wales, the second largest in the UK, has £150m worth of equipment and a huge fund of pioneering expertise which is available to industrial and commercial concerns – who also, of course, have their own research scientists and innovation programmes.

We are moving through a period of dizzying change, in which all that once seemed solid melts into 'For Sale' signs. For most of humanity's brief time on Earth we haven't needed to agonise too much about the future, because what could have been perceived as 'present conditions' must have seemed to endure unchangingly for millennium after millennium. Now, suddenly, in the last few hundred years, the changes have been relentless, and who knows what tomorrow might bring? Our children might walk on Mars, but they might also be wiped out by plague, poverty, nuclear holocaust, global ecological collapse.

Some of the 'biggest' science of contemporary Wales, and to many the most disturbing, is in DNA research and the genetics revolution. At the Institute of Grassland and Environmental Research (IGER) near Aberystwyth they are genetically modifying grasses to breed hardier, higher-yielding, pest-resistant strains. At the Univeristy in Swansea they're breeding male-only tilapia fish to increase the yield of Third World fish farms. At the University's College of Medicine in Cardiff they're lighting up human cells with the bioluminscence of the firefly in order to investigate the behaviour of live cells in diseases like rheumatoid arthritis.

Wales is where the Industrial Age that shaped the modern world began, but that Age and the subsequent Petrochemical Age are in historic transition to the Biotech Century in which, as demonstrated by scores of projects throughout Wales, our country is playing a leading role. Genes are the raw resource of a new epoch in which the information and life sciences are fusing into a single powerful technological and economic force.

This transforming world presents us with great intellectual and practical problems, in addition to profound moral dilemmas. A society in which most people seem to believe in astrology and half the population think the sun goes round the earth is hardly fit to form an opinion on such vital matters as, say, the corporate ownership of life patents. To make the most of the possibilities and to confront the dangers, we need in Wales a new, non-acquisitive politics, an educated and informed populace, and the vision to create opportunities for ourselves, rather than hang about waiting for 'inward investors' to drop in and sort us out.

Ffiw!
Three Steps to Devolution

Before: 'Once more with feeling'[1]

I want a political orgasm (the editor did ask for a *personal* response . . .), I want us all, or most of us, to come together, for once, and say 'YES! c'mon, let's go for it NOW!' Or become a tribe of mere wankers in some eternally ignorable western county of England.

This, I feel in my bones, is Wales's last chance – a chance maybe too late, and possibly undeserved. I've been edgy about it for at least a year, not trusting Labour's shifty manoeuvres on devolution in the run-up to the general election, and seriously doubting until recently (late July) that the Welsh had enough self-respect and gumption to embrace even the milk-and-water powers that are on offer.

But I'm cheered by Labour's increasing resolution, the positive polls and the glorious battiness of the mini 'No' campaign. Wales may now be in with a more than reasonable chance, but amnesia and self-doubt – call it apathy, if you like – could still strangle the baby at birth. 'If only you knew,' the late John Tripp wrote in one of his poems, lamenting the disabling consequences of Welsh people's ignorance about their own country, and suggesting that, equipped with an understanding of who they are, the Welsh might really go places. There's no time to do much about that ignorance now, so I suppose that in addition to the routine political footwork of leafleting and persuading we are going to have to rely on an inordinate amount of glitzification – rolling out the Terfels, Giggses and Tony Blair's gnashers – to give a sexy shine to our rather dull-sounding D-word. A good 'Yes' vote in Scotland is also going to be a significant diminisher of Welsh wobble.

Would that we and Scotland had had the 'Doomsday Scenario' verve in 1992 to attempt a 'Velvet Revolution' against yet another Tory government foisted on us against our political will, by establishing defiant national parliaments in Cardiff and Edinburgh – but that, after

[1] This section first appeared as an article in *Red Kite*, Summer 1997.

hundreds of years of colonialist 'accommodation', is not how England's little butties are inclined to behave. We just go on taking the punishment.

Twice a year I take a party of American students on a mystery tour of Wales. The place that moves them most is the drowned valley of Tryweryn, especially if the water's low, exposing the road, the hump-back bridge and the outlines of fields and houses. The Americans are shocked that this entire community was wiped out – not in medieval times but as recently as the 1960s – so that Liverpool Corporation could build a profit-making reservoir. They find it difficult to believe that although the Welsh were united, for once, in their opposition to the plan (with the exception of George 'Viscounts Against Devolution' Thomas and one or two other quislings) they were powerless to stop it. 'Everyone in Wales should come and take a look at this sad place,' said a student on one of our visits. Yes, indeed. And they might like to take a look at other sites of our continuing powerlessness: Selar, Bryn Henllys, the land lost to roads and the military, the estates devasted by poverty and hopelessness. And they might, on 18 September, feel like doing a pitifully modest something about it.

It's going to be a long, tense summer, and 18 September, whatever the result, a birth or a death, is likely to be an emotional day.

I'll be spending that weekend at the annual conference of the Welsh Union of Writers in Rhayader where our topic will be 'Sex: the Great Welsh Not?' I remember the leaden disappointment of 1 March, 1979 only too well. Let's hope, for sanity and tomorrow's sake, we'll be spending that weekend toasting a Great Welsh 'Yes'. I'm tired of living in the land of cul-de-sac, the land of wasted opportunities, the land of treading water invisibly, the land of dim memories and no ambition for itself. I want a rebirth, a making: lights, sound, action . . .

And that slippery slope of ill repute? Pass me the Mazola, cariad . . .

During: a devolution diary

11.ix.97
Scotland's big day. Am certain they'll go for it, but they might waver on the tax-varying powers. I don't think so, though. After *Horizon*, about the dinosaurs and the comet that fell into the gulf of Mexico, probably finishing them off, settle down with some Speckled Hens to the results programme on BBC 1. Watch until about 1. Don't sleep

well. Come down at piss-breaks to catch ten minutes' worth gobbets of wonderful news from Scotland: they're doing it, they're going to pull it off. Me naked before the screen. Us. Naked beneath an acid rain. Still? Forever? We don't have forever at our disposal.

12.ix.97
Seven o'clock news: 'YES YES' for Scotland. Good turnout, absolutely unequivocal mandate for a Scottish Parliament. Pundits say this could add between five and fifteen per cent to the Yes vote in Wales. Pathetic that we have to rely on this slavish me-tooism, but that's how it is. Seven hundred years of colonisation take their toll. That Union Jack on the church tower has been there for weeks now, flying at half mast all last week, then raised back to the top of the pole after the funeral. They promised they'd put the *draig goch* up there during Devo week. Where is it? A branchy tree trunk which has been floating in the bay for the last few days finally attracts the council's attention. Men with tractor and chain saws come and chop it up, just before the tide comes in around midday. Put finishing touches to my translation of Menna's Asheville poem, all about the timidity of the Welsh. Train to Cardiff, for pro-Devo poems'n'pints bash. Arrive in time for a pint at the Vaults. Like all rush-hour pubs, crowded, so sit in shade at plastic table in the windy alleyway outside, watching people, the people of Wales – students, shoppers, tipplers, power-dressed city workers – walking down Queen Street in the sun. Which way will they vote in a week's time? What do they know? This time round the intellectuals, writers, journalists, local government reps and politicos seem informed and, generally, united. But I don't think most of the people have a clue what it's about. Café culture. Like London. Feeling cold, move on to the Cottage where I end up sitting, reading Ian Hamilton Finlay, in a nest of 'No' vipers who'd been in Cardiff to barrack Tony Blair. Their talk is idiotic. They nudge each other and point 'silently' to my 'Yes' ribbon. 'One of them.' They are wearing 'No' T-shirts. The Welsh love that word. Much easier to say 'No' than 'Yes'. At the Royal the build-up of an audience is depressingly slow. Will there *be* an audience, other than the media who are there in force, including John Humphreys? Raymond Garlick being interviewed. Côr Cochion singing for the cameras. No drinkable beer in Scott Room bar. Go down to press bar. None there either, but Alun Rees is there. Neither of us optimistic about Thursday's outcome, facing the agonising problem, then, of feeling

contempt for your own people. The place gradually fills; not a full house, but a respectable sixty or seventy people. Readings from Alun himself (more excellent Taffy doggerels), Robert Minhinnick does a brilliant rhymer on Carys Pugh. His and Alun's poems should be published straightaway – but, such is the poverty and timidity of our culture, where? [As I write, Sat morning, I hear *live bagpipe music* drifting up from Mumbles; the Union Jack still flies, it's sunny, windy, cooler, rain theatening. But live bagpipe music . . .; somebody releases his pigeons; they go round and round the roof tops, round and round; then back to the hutch.] John Osmond reads Webb's 'The Stone Face', Garlick reads some limericks, Rhodri Morgan reads a piece about the Gododdin, for the Scottish connection, and Abse's 'Return to Cardiff': this politician knows his literature and his writers. The 'No' campaign: where are their choirs, poets, culture? Neither they nor their few MPs could discuss Cardiff writers, or, probably, any writers anywhere. Readings by Mike Jenkins, Catherine Fisher, Iwan Llwyd (does two stints, somewhat to irritation of Janet Dubé who hadn't been called to do her one, and was leaving as Robert called her back to read 'The Bells of Rhymney' with a Carmarthen twist at the end). Have to use mike for my own reading: techno pop booming up from below. Chandelier overhead moving and tinkling, insistently tinkling in some breeze from somewhere. Basini reads Patrick Pearse. Menna reads a few. No great confidence at large that we're going to pull through on Thursday.

12.ix.97
Sunny, blustery day. Read papers, make bread, grab quick bowl of soup and fresh bread, then cycle into town to help with leafleting during the 'Yes' campaign's long afternoon of rock in Castle Square. Huge numbers of skateboarders and many other youngsters pulled in by the bands. At its height a reasonable, though not huge audience. Must have dished out many scores of leaflets and stickers, ribbons of which I wound scarf-like around my neck, for easy carrying. The sunny weather (only one short, sharp shower) and people's readiness at least to take the leaflets (comparatively few blatantly refused, some of whom said they'd be voting 'No') lent us an upbeat mood. Fellow campaigners talk of their mood swings – sometimes think it's going our way, other times doubting the situation. Apparently the 'No' campaigners have a stall in the market. See not a single 'No'-sticker or

activist all day. Where are *their* rock bands, folk singers, poets? They have none, no culture, want Wales to have no culture, to cease to be. Miss the Three Amigos, but catch the excellent Boys from the Hill. Then there are four more bands, all sounding much the same. Get into many discussions with people I give leaflets to, most of whom are keen supporters, if somewhat startled to find that this is all taking place on Thursday. Some bizarre responses, like a woman who'd been to London to take part in the Di wake, who had not voted for eighteen years on religious grounds, but thought she might possibly make an exception on this occasion: she believed that very soon there'd be no need to vote at world level, because all would be ordained by Jesus Christ. I asked her how, say, Hindus and Muslims fitted into this picture – she admitted this seemed a bit of a problem. No *Evening Post* or anyone else present. But we touched many hundreds of people today. Dave Hughes, Rex, John Ball and Debbie were supposed to meet me in the White Rose at 8.30, to go leafleting and arguing around the pubs, but no one showed up. Can't say I was sorry. Shouting politics to drunks in crowded pubs not an inviting prospect. Yowlers through the streets as I write. Tired.

14.ix.97

Take the girls to the Leisure Centre for swim, then home for chicken dinner. Out on bike later, to a 'divertissement' at Tŷ Llên devised by Jeni Williams to launch her book *Interpreting the Nightingale*, with Fern and Jan from Volcano reading with her. A bit like Regency or Victorian genteel parlour entertainment. Not much humour, but maybe there just aren't a lot of laughs in nightingales. Café Dev's blues fest in Wind Street car park. Bands on back of a lorry, not a bad crowd considering nippiness of the afternoon. Great, tight, electric blues. Love this music, want to play it. Rex there dishing out leaflets. I take over and wander round giving out stickers and talking to people about the campaign. Pretty positive responses, some very eager if not angrily in favour of the Assembly. 'About bloody time,' is something I often hear. As well as the quiet, sometimes slightly haughty '*I* am voting "No".' Fair bit of good-natured drunkenness, people coming and going across the road to replenish plastic glasses. Find myself speaking to a little guy who looks rather like a sinewy Khasi, who's in a great political rage, and very much in favour of voting 'Yes'. He is scheming to blow up the Severn Bridge – both of them, why not? – says he's determined to do it. He's got it in for Tony Blair too. Wants us to run our own show. Stop the pollution, which he believes is seriously undermining his health. 'It's the oil, the oil in the sea, it's killing us all . . .' He wants to give me a can of cider, lots of shaking of hands; an angry nationalist who's never joined Plaid but will be voting Yes on Thursday and blowing up the bridges, the pair of the fuckers. Sexy, slightly sozzled forty-five year old, swaying and dancing to the music, takes a leaflet and asks me to slap a sticker on her, peeling back her lapel, so I can stick it on her shirt, at which she gives me a wicked little smile. But then she wonders what it is she seems to be supporting. 'I don't want to vote for that, do I?' she says, boozily puzzled. 'Don't you want the Welsh to have a say in running their own affairs?' I ask her, 'Do you want to go on being run by Tory quangos? Do you want more John Redwoods and William Hagues running Wales?' 'Tony Blair,' she says, 'Tony Blair I want. I'm voting "No".' 'Well this is Tony Blair's baby, it's his idea,' I tell her. 'Honest?' 'Honest.' 'Well I'll vote cowin "Yes" then,' she cackles, and wobbles off to dance solo on the tarmac in front of the stage. Chat with Dick Ellis and Nigel, who runs the Chattery, an Adelphi original, who'd sung an entertaining *double-entendre* folk song at the nightingale do. Big grey clouds bundling in from the west, and rain starts to fall. Get on bike and cycle to Woodman for meeting with David about a project at the Princess of Wales Hospital, Bridgend. Some people now want to name *everything* after her. The Princess of Wales Memorial Referendum.

15.ix.97

A day at the desk, most phone calls getting round, inevitably, to the impending probable disaster. Chat with Siân Edwards who, lifelong pacifist, (half) jokingly refers to the armed struggle from now on. Imagine: the only 'nation' in the modernising world that opts for slave-status. A distinctive, utterly unique nation . . . of mindless self-damagers. Phone X to try and persuade her to vote 'Yes'. She knows nothing about it but says she'll vote 'No'. Even thinks William Hague is still the Secretary of State. Debate on HTV: latest poll gives the 'Yes' vote only about eight points ahead of the 'No', with a huge percentage of the population, about a third, undecided.

16.ix.97

Into town in car to cart some of Terry's books to Siop y Werin for the Books Council pick-up, and fifty to Waterstone's for the launch. Get a couple of anatomy books, for the hospital project. At John Penry's I bump into Guto ap Gwynfor who tells me his daughter was out canvassing yesterday. She met an old bird who thought she'd vote 'No' 'because we were invaded by the English 300 years ago, and if we vote "Yes" the English might do it again.' *Evg Post* offer £100 for me to write a short piece for their *Swanseas of the World* supplement. If its anti-Welsh Ed. does a 'No'-vote editorial I will refuse. Disgusted by their biased, inadequate coverage of the campaign. Warm, sunny day; blue sky, blue sea. Cycle into town for talk and reading at Tŷ Llên by Gillian Slovo. Have a strip of stickers hanging out of my shirt pocket, inviting people to help themselves. Many do. No sign of any 'Nos' in the bar of Tŷ Llên. Notice the Union Jack has been removed from the church flagpole, and nothing in its place. Church no doubt expressing 'neutrality' until after the vote. Around 7.15, last full eclipse of the moon of the twentieth century.

17.ix.97

Warm, sunny day. Spend the morning doing invitations for Terry's launch and dealing with various phone calls. Sneering piece about Wales in the *Guardian*. Typical English superciliousness. Proofs arrive for *Ambush*. Write an eight-page discussion paper on literature and arts policy for Plaid. Best get it done now; can't imagine having the *hwyl* for it after a 'No' vote on Friday – or for anything else either.

18.ix.97

The day. Summery, cloudless, orangey dawn glow plumping up the light, long after the sun is fully risen. The last day of living in hope for Wales? Spend morning preparing intros and chairman's report for Union conference. Paul Poplawski phones to report ten students for creative writing MA. Robin phones to ask for 1000 words for *New Welsh Review* by middle of next week on my response to the outcome. Smug Langlandish tones of an English 'No'-vote loudspeaker touring the streets, 'Vote "No", vote "No" to a waste of millions of pounds that could be spent on more nurses and doctors, more hospitals and schools. Vote "No" to this gravy train. Vote "No" to an expensive talking shop. Vote "No" to the breakup of the United Kingdom.' Two men on church tower roof fiddling with the flagpole. Fixing it? No flag. Hazing over by mid-afternoon. After tea and music practice the four of us go down to the hall to vote, an umbrella apiece as the rain pours down – though it's still quite warm. Sultry and wet. I'd like the girls to make the mark themselves, and the people at the desk says it's probably not allowed but they'll turn a blind eye. So Angharad comes into the booth with me and makes the mark in the top box, folds the slip and posts it. The black box by now – about 7.45 – is pretty full, though they expect the weather to have deterred some voters. Rain stops, but it remains hazy and gets dark. Foghorn sounding. High tide by 10.30. Polling stations closed at 10.00. The die is cast. Roger Dobson, freelancing for *Independent* and so on, phones to talk about the language of love and sex re. an article he's preparing on the Union conference. I feel utterly flat and deflated, in preparation for the worst. Channel Four had said a couple of weeks ago they wanted me in Cardiff as a panellist on their all-night Referendum Results show, but I'm glad they didn't get back to me. Don't fancy staying up all night making pithy pertinent remarks about the disaster that I'm sure will loom in on us as the night progresses. And back then by train in the thin dawn light, exhausted and bereft of my nation. It's like a teetering love affair – well, it *is* a love affair: is there, on Friday morning, when the anticipated *letter* arrives, still going to be the love there used to be – until, just lately, it all seemed threatened by what one had hoped was a stupid misunderstanding? Will we fall back into each other's arms in tearful, smiling relief? Or is it 'Dear John' time? And how the hell, then, to live a useful, hopeful life? At this point, of course, the metaphor breaks down: because you begin to accept, after a painful love affair, that there are indeed other possible lovers in this huge world – but there is only one Wales. Sit down at 11.15 to watch the Referendum coverage – and am there until gone 4.30 in the morning. It's on a knife edge until the very end, with the border areas – Wrexham to start with – declaring solidly for the Nos at the beginning of the evening, and the Nos leading the field, by a narrow margin, until the very last count. Ynys Môn only just scrapes in with a 'Yes'.

19.ix.97

It's looking bleak. When Cardiff goes down to the 'Nos' at 2 a.m. I switch off, and rise to go to bed – but I switch back on and continue watching. Peter Snow's swingometer team unable, until about three counts before the end, to hazard a prediction, it being, all the time, 'too close to call'. Alternating scenes of glee and despair in the respective campaign headquarters. Against expectations, the very last result, Carmarthen, delivers a decisive number of 'Yeses' that tips the whole thing suddenly in favour of an Assembly – by a majority of 7,000 votes, or 0.6 per cent. I feel euphoric, tears streaming down my face, hair standing on end. Wales, by the skin of her ignorant, confused, divided teeth (watch your metaphors, Jenkins), is on her way to a future. After a lie-in and late breakfast I write a letter of thanks and congratulations to Ron Davies and send him a copy of *Acts of Union*.

After: 'Ffiw!'[2]

And with one bound Wales was free – free of the masochistic habits of a colonised lifetime which encouraged others to walk all over her and which threatened to deliver, at long last, the *coup de grâce*. The mark Wales made on her ballot paper turned out not to be the signature on a suicide note, as many feared and some hoped, but a shaky declaration of existence and intent.

We have a future – unlike, I am delighted to say, certain of my poems. Never again will I have reason to perform 'Land of Song', the vulgar rant that was my white-heat response to the disaster of '79. History, in the run-up to this year's referendum, did seem grotesquely to be repeating itself, with Gangs of Six, 'talking shops', and the No-hopers trying to bribe us with as many hospitals and schools as we've sheep on the hills; there was even a re-run's touch or two of farce, as when the presumably 'socialist' Carys Pugh told Peter 'bad rubbish' Hain to shove off back to South Africa. But '97 is '79 back-to-front, and history did not after all do an inaction replay.

For months I'd been steeling myself for the worst, while doing my small bit to stave it off. The suspense, in that last week, was akin to having the suspicion of a serious illness and waiting for the result of a test that would either condemn you to death or propose a new lease of life. Few expected a repeat of '79's four-to-one wipe-out – Mrs. Thatcher and co. had seen to that. But could a mere eighteen years have worked enough of a revolution in the Welsh psyche to deliver even a modest 'Yes'?

The closeness of the race was exquisite torture. There was little

[2] This section first appeared as an article in *New Welsh Review* 38, Autumn 1997.

surprise in the border constituencies turning red with refusal one by one, but when at 2 a.m. Cardiff delivered its lumpen 'No' I felt sure we'd had it, switched off the TV in disgust, and started climbing the stairs, wondering where in Hodge's hell we go from here. If we couldn't pull off an Assembly at this uniquely propitious moment we'd never do it. We seemed to have blown the last of all our last chances. So what now? Suicide? Opium? The armed struggle? But before I reached the landing, I turned, retraced my steps, fortified myself with a Jameson's, and switched the telly back on – to witness in due course, with tears streaming and mouth agape, the most joyous political turn of tide I have ever known.

I thought of absent friends – John Tripp, Harri Webb, Gwyn Alf Williams – who'd have relished this truly historic occasion, although like many a 'Yes' campaigner they'd have been far from content with the pitifully inadequate powers we've been offered. And I raised the tumbler to some lesser televised heroes of the moment, people like Gwynfor Evans, John Osmond and the hundreds of unsung activists who for decades have struggled ceaselessly for Wales to get off her knees and declare herself 'Yma!' But most of all I cheered – silently, so as not to wake them – for my daughters, Angharad (10) and Branwen (8). We'd all gone down to the polling station together, and Angharad had drawn my cross for me, lightly sketched at first, to be sure she got it right, then bold, black, unequivocal. The youth of Wales seem much more confident and enthusiastic about an Assembly than those who fought for God, King, England and Empire in World War II. With a fair wind behind them, they should grow into a Wales that is theirs for the making, a resourceful, energetic, exciting country that is visible and useful in the wider world, and fully present to itself.

There is, of course, a long way to go. September's vote is but a timid beginning, and there is bound to be all kinds of trouble ahead. It's not true, though, as Viscounts Against Devolution claimed, that the Referendum 'divided Wales': Wales was already divided; the Referendum simply underlined the urgent need to address the problem of our complex internal divisions. In the spirit of the 'Yes' campaign, all parties should pledge to sink all sinkable differences, and work through – and beyond – the Assembly to break down barriers, allay fears, and, while celebrating regional distinctiveness, construct for the first time ever an inclusive sense of Welsh citizenship.

Tribalism, apathy, ignorance and a lack of self-respect have been our biggest enemies of late. The Yes vote hasn't conjured them out of existence, but the Assembly makes it both possible and necessary to take them on. The difficulties are formidable. You have only to look at *The Irish Times* or the newspapers of Scotland to appreciate how backward and inadequate are the Welsh press and media. As the Assembly campaign demonstrated, a purposeful debate about Wales is hamstrung when so few people read, watch and listen to Welsh news and current affairs. No doubt they'd care more, in due course, if we had a relevant and modern education system that addressed the younger generation as Welsh Europeans.

Jobs, housing and health will surely be high on the Assembly's priorities. It is shameful that thousands of our people, locked in poverty and despair, endure lives that are hardly worth living.

We will be told, of course, that there are limits to what an Assembly of this kind can do. Sooner or later, no doubt, having developed a taste for Welsh democracy, we'll feel a lack of Welsh muscle in the body politic, and will have the confidence to help ourselves to the powers we need to shape the Wales we desire. In the meantime, it is very heaven to be out in the light, breathing fresh Welsh air and savouring the prospect of a tango or two with a dancer called tomorrow.

Swonzee, iz it?[1]

It's a long way from the border with England, but Swansea, within whose magnetic field I was born and, after many absences, continue to dwell, has always seemed to revel in the invigorating contradictions of a frontier town.

Climb any of the seven hills on which Swansea, like Rome, has been built, and much of the city's changing story can be read from the landscape. Brooding Kilvey, shrouded throughout the nineteenth century in clouds of sulphur and arsenic, offers perhaps the most dramatic prospect.

Long gone, apart from some criminally neglected museum pieces, are the stacks and foundries that cluttered the valley below when Swansea was 'Copperopolis'. Where smoke once belched and furnaces roared, there is now a lake and, until recently, a somewhat implausible Hilton Hotel. The big buildings in this landscape – the sprawled shopping sheds, the DVLC at Morriston – declare that Kings Copper, Coal and Tinplate are dead; an economy which was dependent on heavy industry as recently as the mid-1960s has transformed itself, so that now a startling seventy-eight per cent of Swansea workers are employed in service industries.

The attempted sophistication towards which Swansea has lurched lately has tended to erase many of those features that made Swansea distinctively Swansea. Out-of-town retail parks have killed off much that was quirky and enjoyable in the city centre shops and caffs. Drinking haunts of character and risky unpredictability have been 'improved' out of existence, their individuality exchanged for period or theme 'environments' that can be purchased by the yard.

Swansea never fully recovered from the breaking of its urban heart in the bombing raids of World War II. Older people still yearn for the

---

[1] This was Swansea poet David Hughes's 'title' for a street map display box which, as part of the censored and abandoned city centre street poetry project, was 'printed' in metal but unscrewed before display and stashed in a padded envelope, as was every other word of the project's Swansea dialect items. This essay is based on a two-part series written for *The Western Mail*, published on 30 September 1990 and 1 October 1990.

pre-war town's idiosyncratic charm, and they resent the crass ranks of concrete shoeboxes that were thrown up in its place.

The thirty-year redevelopment of the blitzed zone seemed to provoke a general 'improving' zeal in areas untouched by the bombs. It is difficult to believe that a feature as distinctive as High Street Arcade could have been demolished to make room for Oldway House, surely one of the most ambitious essays in urban barbarity to be found anywhere in Europe.

At the gateway to the city the despised tin sheds of Parc Tawe advertise a seam of Philistinism embedded deep in Swansea's soul which, if it prevails, could yet blight the city's prospects.

In striking contrast, just a few hundred yards away, is the internationally acclaimed Maritime Quarter. There are people in neglected parts of Swansea, however, who have reason to take a sceptical view. David Hughes,[2] a poet with a keen ear for the local dialect, captures the mood:

> *Ayve done some fancy work round air, avenay?*
> *Sorl been tarted up like roun byer Lehja un South Dock*
> *Ew doan see flats like at up Blineymice.*
> *Meenmy brother ewsed t dive inner dock –*
> *Few tryed at now ewed crack ew ed onner yot.*

A key ambition, as Swansea reappropriates its maritime identity, is to use the sea and the river to unite a city that has long been divided between smug middle-class west and working-class east. A symbol of that division is the River Tawe itself, over which the spoils of freshly affluent Swansea have so far failed to find a way. The barrage across the river mouth, which when it was completed in the early 1990s was Wales's first, has yet to fulfil the role envisaged for it in this process. As the tidal mudflats disappeared from sight, it was expected that there would be set in train a programme of building and renovation on the eastside, with the Tawe, navigable now for several miles upstream, supporting a river-boat service, bringing the run-down waterside areas into new relationships with each other and with the city. This has yet to happen. A second Tawe crossing was opened, but only to cope with

[2] David Hughes's dialect poetry, and much else, is published in his collection *Tidy Boy* (Swansea Poetry Workshop, 1998).

increased volumes of traffic. An opportunity was lost when a pedestrian walkway across the barrage failed to materialise. This could have initiated the re-conquest by the people of Swansea of the commercial docks east of the river: housing, leisure and new commercial activities would be welcome additions to the traditional business of the port. Changing energy patterns will lead in the longer term to the demise of oil as a dominant fuel: huge acreages of eastern Swansea devoted at present to oil wharves and storage tanks could be released eventually for all manner of uses, from housing to energy generation.

There's a famously inadequate statue of Dylan Thomas in the maritime quarter which earned the redesignation, soon after it was installed, as a 'Portrait of the Artist as Somebody Else'. It features a chair facing west, towards deeper Wales, and a figure, neither quite seated nor quite standing, gazing hopefully in the direction of London. The statue bears little resemblance to Swansea's most exploited tourist icon, being closer to a cross between Harry Belafonte and Johnny Mathis (or should that be Mathias?). But it does perhaps offer an inadvertent comment on the uncertain direction and wavering identity of the poet's native city. Not for the first time in its thousand-year history, Swansea is suffering an identity crisis.

Swansea began as a frontier outpost from which, initially, the native Welsh were excluded, and it has persisted ever since in being something of a border town. Here the coal measures run into the millstone grit. Here east Wales ends, west Wales begins, and the rural rubs up against the urban – there are cows grazing on Kilvey Hill, within a mile of the city centre. Here many who thought they were only passing through have been beguiled into staying, finding Swansea, by and large, welcoming to the stranger – although the Irish once, and the gypsies today, have suffered slander and persecution. Here, most obvious and inescapable of borders, the land meets the sea, in a contest whose bias is told by the ancient tree stumps sticking through the sand at Brynmill. And here Beauty and the Beast cwtsh down together: if Swansea people are aware of extraordinary natural beauty in the nearby Gower coast, and the handmade charms of the maritime quarter, they have also had to endure pollution and ugliness on a scale to match Swansea's world-class role in the Industrial Revolution. With the demise of heavy industry, most of that squalor has vanished, but other kinds of ugliness persist. No doubt the concrete brutalism of certain post-war buildings will fall in due course to the demolition gangs; harder to remedy are the poverty and hopelessness of the outlying dole estates.

Convergence and contradiction are the spice of a border town. But when fundamentals such as purpose and even precise location are thrown into question, a shiftiness sets in, and confidence begins to slide. Once it was simple. Swansea was, roughly, an area contained within a four-mile radius of the centre, a collection of urban villages in which, by moving half a street, you could – and still can – cross from one suburb to another. But, in the '90s, businessmen and economic geographers urged us to embrace a creature called Swansea Bay City which gobbled up everything between Port Talbot and Burry Port, a concept about as enticing as week-old laver bread to many a downtown Swansea Jack still trying to catch up with Swansea's elevation to city status ('Yea I knowzits u city/burile olliz call it town,' says a character in one of David Hughes's dialect poems). Then Swansea Bay City, after local government re-organisation, gave way to the comparably amorphous City and County of Swansea.

Swansea now finds itself wondering, much as it did at the beginning of the nineteenth century, what is the reason for its existence: industry and commerce, trade and transportation, or leisure and tourism?

In a sense, the Swansea Jack in David Hughes's poem is right. Swansea is still a town and has yet to win its city spurs. More assertive now than at any time since the war, returning a proud 'Yes' to the Welsh Assembly in the 1997 referendum, and planning an Olympic-standard swimming pool together with a new home for the national Industrial and Maritime Museum, Swansea nevertheless lacks the conviction that drives a Cardiff or a Glasgow or its Irish 'twin' Cork – indeed it suffers from a paranoia verging on the pathological about Cardiff. In pursuit of the image rather than the substance, Swansea's strivings to be 'modern' and 'sophisticated' are inclined sometimes to backfire, the results of which are irrelevance and ugliness. How they do things in London or New Jersey or *Cardiff* may well have something to teach us in Swansea, but we should not automatically assume that what they do elsewhere is best for us, and that we need not waste too much native thought on native problems.

Kneeling mindlessly before the Golden Calf of inward investment while neglecting to support indigenous ventures; planning to dump an alien wodge of Torremolinos on the seafront at Mumbles; threatening to repeat Birmingham's Bullring error by building a car-intensive mega-mall in the very heart of the city; allowing some of Swansea's most venerable buildings to rot while dithering for years over new uses for them; lavishing millions on the kinds of junky tin sheds and glass pyramids that were the ruination of many small American towns twenty-five years ago; rejecting Will Alsop's revolutionary design for Tŷ Llên, the national literature centre, in favour of a twee and cack-handed 'Edwardian' rehab (Alsop later recycled the design at Peckham, winning a major architectural prize) . . . these are not the actions, or rather inactions, of a city that is confident of itself.

Swansea is rich in people, places and activities to celebrate, but too often we are unaware of them, or we take them for granted, and only when, like the Mumbles train, we notice that they have gone do we begin to realise what we have lost.

Most profiles of the city make reference to Swansea's production of chinaware in the eighteenth and nineteenth centuries, but how many people – in Swansea, let alone elsewhere – realise that the city is today of international importance in the field of architectural stained glass? Everyone's heard of Bonnie Tyler who, fair play, still lives in Swansea – but far fewer, I'd imagine, are familiar with the name of John Cale, a local lad, now resident in New York, who is Wales's one toweringly original contribution to contemporary music. And everybody's heard of the Grand Theatre, even if they go there only for the panto, the opera and the tribute bands, but a number of innovative drama companies, particularly Volcano Theatre and Theatr Tir na n-Og (formerly Theatr Gorllewin Morgannwg), widely acclaimed elsewhere, receive in Swansea nothing like the recognition and support that are their due.

A local asset beyond price is the Welsh language, spoken by ten per cent of the population. Those who have struggled so selflessly to defend and advance the language deserve monuments on each of Swansea's seven hills. Official indifference and obstructionism have been formidable, particularly in meeting the demand for a third Welsh-medium primary school. The dogs of amnesia, hungry to devour local particularity and distinctiveness, are ever at the gates. Swansea would do well to abandon recalcitrant attitudes towards its Welshness and embrace it as a pillar of its identity.

Swansea is where nearly half the people of western industrial, or 'formerly industrial', Wales now live – many of them in conditions of deprivation that have shocked commentators from developing countries. In the nineteenth century, some thought of Swansea as 'the metropolis of Wales', and in the twentieth it decided to declare itself a city. If it can shrug off what remains of its provincialism, and identify and trust in its varied indigenous strengths, it may yet arrive, in more than just name, at that desirable condition of urbanity. 'Ambition is critical', says an inscription outside the station. Quite. We need to celebrate what we have, and make the most of the unique wit, energy and creativity of Swansea people to forge a city that is both unashamedly Welsh and European. We may have a way to go, but there's still nowhere in the world I would rather live.